ABOUT THE AUTHOR

Mikiso Hane (1922-2003) was Szold Distinguished Professor Emeritus of History at Knox College in Illinois. He enjoyed an illustrious career in the field of Japanese history, publishing fourteen books and numerous articles.

JAPAN
A SHORT HISTORY

MIKISO HANE

ONEWORLD

To Rose, Laurie and Jennifer

JAPAN: A SHORT HISTORY

This edition published in 2013

First published in Great Britain and the Commonwealth by
Oneworld Publications 2000

Copyright © 2000 Mikiso Hane

The moral right of Mikiso Hane to be identified as the
Author of this work has been asserted by him in accordance
with the Copyright, Designs and Patents Act 1988

ISBN 978-1-78074-256-4
eISBN 978-1-78074-333-2

Printed and bound by Nørhaven A/S, Denmark

Oneworld Publications
10 Bloomsbury Street
London WC1B 3SR
England

Stay up to date with the latest books,
special offers, and exclusive content from
Oneworld with our monthly newsletter

Sign up on our website
www.oneworld-publications.com

Contents

Preface

In this survey of Japanese history I have sought to present a general account of the developments in Japan from past to present, surveying not only political and economic matters but more especially, social, cultural, and intellectual issues. Japanese names have been presented in the traditional style, that is, surname first and given name second. The Hepburn system has been used to transcribe Japanese names and terms. In the pre-modern era it was the common practice to refer to people by their given names. For example artists and poets are referred to as Hiroshige, Utamaro, Bashō and so on.

I wish to thank my friends and colleagues at Knox College for their kind support. I also wish to express my gratitude to members of Oneworld Publications for their valuable editorial assistance and advice. I wish to thank in particular Juliet Mabey for encouraging me to undertake this project, and Rebecca Clare and Alaine Low for examining the manuscript meticulously to ensure that what I have written is clear and accurate. Needless to say whatever errors and flaws still remain are due to my own carelessness.

Introduction

Japan ranked eighth in the world in population in 1998. Over 126.4 million people are crowded into an area about as large as the state of Montana. The islands that constitute the nation are mountainous, and only slightly over thirteen percent of the land is arable. Although the country is poor in natural resources, it is the world's second most productive industrial nation. Until the nineteenth century it was an island nation virtually isolated from the rest of the world although historically it had close cultural ties with Korea and China. Its political, social, and economic life has been molded essentially by internal factors and developments.

For historical periodization the pre- and proto-historical periods have been classified into the early Jōmon (*c.* 8000 B.C.E. or earlier to 250 B.C.E.) and Yayoi (*c.* 250 B.C.E. to 250 C.E.) periods. The former is named after the potteries with cord markings and the latter after the place where potteries belonging to this era were found. The next era is the Yamato period, *c.* 300–710 C.E., with the political center located in the area around Kyoto, then known as Yamato. This era is followed by the Nara period (710–784) named after the capital city. For a decade the capital shifted to another city. This was followed by the establishment of the capital in Heian (present-day Kyoto), hence the Heian period (794–1185). Then the Minamoto clan established its headquarters, the shogunate, in Kamakura (1185–1333). This was followed by the era of the Ashikaga shogunate from 1338 to 1573. After a quarter-century of ascendancy by two Chieftains (Oda Nobunaga and Toyotomi Hideyoshi) national unity and hegemony was established by the

Tokuagawa clan whose regime lasted from 1600 to 1867. Since then the eras have been named after the reigning Emperors: Meiji (1868–1912), Taishō (1912–1926), Shōwa (1926–1989), and the current Heisei era (1989–).

Politically, after the migration of peoples from the continent and possibly South East Asia, the story is the struggle among various tribal and clan chieftains to establish hegemony over the islands. Eventually the clan that gained ascendancy established the imperial dynasty around the late fifth and early sixth century C.E. The actual wielders of power during the ascendancy of imperial rule to the twelfth century were the court aristocrats. The Emperor remained essentially a figurehead and was put on a pedestal. But throughout history no one dared to eliminate the Emperor system and outwardly treated it with honor. In the twelfth century the court aristocracy were challenged by the increasingly important warrior class and samurai rule was established. From the late twelfth to the nineteenth century different warrior clans retained political control and exercised power by providing the command-ing general, the shogun. These leaders were challenged periodically by other military chieftains but from the early seventeenth century to the mid-nineteenth century firm political control was sustained by the Tokugawa shogunate. The imperial court was allowed to remain in Kyoto as the symbolic ruler of the land. Thus until the mid-nineteenth century when the country was opened to the West there were, in essence, two political forces, the military caste and the court aristocracy. In 1868 in theory imperial authority was restored but political power continued to be wielded by different political cliques, including the military, until Japan's defeat in the Second World War.

The economy of Japan until the nineteenth century remained essentially agrarian. Rice culture was introduced to the islands around 100 B.C.E. and the peasants struggled to eke out a living, tilling the sparse land areas, growing rice in tiny paddies in the flat land and carving out terraces on the hillsides to grow other cereals and vegetables. Tea and silkworm cultivation also became an important source of income for the villagers. Eventually arts and crafts came to flourish with the introduction of the crafts from Korea and China from the fifth century on. The land worked by the peasants provided the ruling class with its material necessities.

Thus the power struggle by the clan and tribal chieftains was a struggle to control the farm land and keep the peasants working it. Local commerce prevailed but in the thirteenth and fourteenth centuries trade with China was fostered. This stimulated greater commercial activities and greater external contacts, including the advent of Western traders and missionaries. With the country virtually sealed off by the Tokugawa shogunate in the seventeenth century foreign trade declined but domestic commerce flourished and numerous commercial centers emerged.

There was from the outset a hierarchy of the wielders of power and those subjected to serve them in various capacities. With the introduction of Confucian concepts in the fifth to sixth centuries the case for maintaining a hierarchical social order was strengthened. Hence the Confucian emphasis on preserving the hierarchical order between the "superior" and "inferior" persons and the maintenance of proper relationships to ensure social harmony (which meant compelling the "inferior" persons to behave in accordance with his or her station in the family and society) came to be staunchly embedded in Japanese mores. This social imperative was reinforced by the emergence of the samurai as the dominant force in the late twelfth century. They reinforced the sense of hierarchy by the edge of the sword. The Tokugawa shogunate instituted a legal class-order of samurai, peasants, artisans, and merchants (based on the Confucian hierarchy of scholars, peasants, artisans, and merchants). Outside this classification were the so-called "unclean" class, the outcastes. What this meant was the samurai caste at the top and the others below. Even after the end of Tokugawa hegemony and the advent of the modern Meiji era, class distinctions were retained with people in registries identified as *shizoku* (former samurai class), and commoners. The special status of the old aristocracy was preserved with their classification as *kazoku* (nobility). The discrimination of the outcaste group was also sustained with the classification: new commoners. After the end of the Second World War legal class distinctions were eliminated though social discrimination persisted.

This evolving sense of status distinctions came to influence the place of women in Japanese society also. There is evidence that early Japan was a matriarchal society, or at least a matrilineal society. The acceptance of the Confucian social philosophy, and the ascendancy of the samurai class resulted in a steady decline in the social standing of women. In the Tokugawa era gender discrimination came to be enforced most stringently among the samurai class but relationships between men and women among the townspeople remained less rigid.

As for the Japanese mode of thinking, the island environment produced a strong sense of ethnocentrism and ultimately nationalism. This sense of being a unique and, in essence, a superior race was fostered over time by the imperial clan and its supporters. Japanese distinctiveness and superiority came to be asserted in part as a reaction against the powerful Chinese cultural influence. This, as noted below, took the form of cultural nativism in the Heian period (794–1185), Buddhist nationalism of Nichiren in the Kamakura period, and the rise of National Learning (*kokugaku*) in the Tokugawa period. This nationalism burgeoned with the opening of the country to the West as it induced a movement to assert Japan's autonomy against the onslaught of Westernism. Then it turned to militarism and imperialism against Japan's neighbors.

Another characteristic of the Japanese mode of thinking is the sense of group identity, starting with family, clan group, community, province, and eventually the nation as a whole. But in immediate terms it was identity with the close social circle. Hence individualism in traditional Japan never developed into an acceptable mode of behavior. This practice of suppression of individual interests for the good of the group was reinforced by the advent of Confucianism with its moral code built around the family system. The emphasis on group interests led to the idealization of such values as submissiveness, obedience, self-sacrifice, responsibility, duty, and so on. At the same time the emphasis on group interests resulted in a parochial outlook with a strong sense of division between the in-group and the outsiders. This in-group versus the "other" mentality applied not just to the family versus others, but ultimately to "We, the Japanese" versus foreigners.

In the realm of cultural, religious and intellectual development the most significant force that molded traditional Japanese cultural life was Chinese culture which initially came in by way of Korea in the fourth century. Its impact became increasingly extensive. The writing system, learning, literature, philosophy, religion, arts, crafts, architecture, and so on were all either direct imports or were adapted and incorporated into Japanese life and society. As a result of Chinese cultural impetus, indigenous culture and literature began to flourish in the Heian period and after.

In religion there was the indigenous Shinto, essentially an animistic religion with a close identity with nature. Many elements in nature were seen to possess sacred spirits. Politically it came to be embraced by the imperial family to justify its right to rule as the descendant of the Sun Goddess. Thus politicized Shinto came to be the foundation for nationalism while for the masses it remained the focal point of animistic worship. With the advent of Chinese civilization came Buddhism which was embraced by the Heian court. In the Kamakura period popular sects spread the religion widely among the masses and it remained the dominant religion of the people. Artistically the Zen sect influenced Japanese aesthetic life from the Kamakura period to the present. Confucianism constituted the heart of learning and in the Tokugawa period was embraced by the shogunate as the official credo. In the modern period, together with Shinto nationalism, it formed the moral underpinning of the education system.

The other credo that came to influence the Japanese mind was the code of the warriors (*bushidō*) that evolved with the rise of the samurai caste in the late Heian period. The "militaristic" side of Japan emerged as the antipode to the civilian side that had been nurtured and fostered by the Heian court aristocrats who had adopted the Chinese code of propriety, decorum, moderation, composure, and so on. The samurai favored direct action and decisiveness, and the code of the warriors and its Spartan values functioned as counterpoints to the genteel ways of the court aristocrats as well as to the freer and more hedonistic ways of the townspeople that emerged in the Tokugawa era. Thus the Japanese value system, like those of other societies, evolved in a multi-faceted fashion.

In the modern period, from the mid-nineteenth century, Japan was influenced extensively by Western civilization although liberal, democratic thinking did not gain popular acceptance until the post-Second World War era. But since the nineteenth century traditional culture and mode of thinking, and Westernism have been developing in a distinctive Japan character.

ONE

From Early Years to the Heian Era

Archaeologists and historians have so far failed to determine exactly where the Japanese people came from. It is assumed that various tribal groups entered the islands in different periods. Some of the early immigrants are believed to have been Tungusic people from the northeastern region of the Asian continent. It is also believed that some came from the south, from South East Asia or South China. There is general agreement that contingents of Mongoloid people entered the islands by way of Korea. Among the early inhabitants of Japan were the ancestors of the current Ainu people who are located primarily on the island of Hokkaido. The Japanese language has links to Polynesian and Altaic languages.

The early stage of the neolithic age in Japan is referred to as the Jōmon period. Until recently it was assumed that the Jōmon era started around 4500 B.C.E. and extended to about 250 B.C.E. But recent archaeological discoveries have extended the origin to about 8000 B.C.E. Archaeological finds in 1997 have led some to believe that Jōmon culture was present around 10,000 B.C.E. Formerly it was believed that Jōmon people hunted, fished, and gathered food but recent discoveries have indicated that they were also engaged in farming about six thousand years ago. Evidence of simple housing has been uncovered which reveals that they were not simply pit-dwellers. Their earthenware had a distinct style with high reliefs made with cord impressions, *jōmon*, hence the designation of the style and the period.

The later stage of the neolithic age in Japan is known as the Yayoi period because potteries of this time were discovered in

1884 in Yayoi in Tokyo. The Yayoi potteries were different from Jōmon potteries. Pots were wheel-made, reddish in color and less elaborately decorated. The Yayoi period is assumed to have started around 250 B.C.E. in northern Kyushu and lasted until about 250 C.E. In this period rice culture was introduced from South East Asia or China and the distinctive economic, and socio-political life based on rice culture governed Japanese life until the modern industrial age.

In the Yayoi period there were two population centers, one in northern Kyushu and the other in central Japan (the area around Kyoto known as Yamato). It is believed that Koreans, led by clan chieftains, began entering Japan with increasing frequency in the later years of the Yayoi period. With superior military weapons and, perhaps with warriors on horseback, they were able to extend their political influence into northern Kyushu and eventually to central Japan.

Traditional Japanese historians had regarded the early immigrants from Korea as aliens who had to be "Japanized". With recent information from Korea it is now believed that the Koreans were not regarded as aliens but were seen as people similar to others who preceded them to Japan, and they melded into the population, playing an increasingly important political, cultural and economic role in early Japan. In fact many of the Emperors listed in the imperial lineage were actually Koreans. The influx of Koreans and Chinese continued down into the sixth and seventh centuries.

There are no written accounts of early Japanese history because Japan had no writing system. It was not until Chinese learning and culture was introduced on a large scale in the fifth and sixth centuries that historical accounts came to be written. The Chinese historical records provide the earliest accounts of early Japan. Reference to Japan is found in the *History of the Kingdom of Wei* written in 297 C.E. Next, Japan is noted in the *History of the Later Han Dynasty* compiled around 448 C.E. These histories indicate that Japan underwent a period of civil strife during the second century C.E. and mention a queen named Pimiku (Himeko in Japanese), a shaman who practiced magic and sorcery. It is assumed that she was one of the early political leaders but the imperial historians have not claimed that the imperial dynasty originated with her. There is no conclusive proof as to where she lived. Some contend it was northern Kyushu, others assume it was in central Japan around present-day Kyoto.

The official national history before Japan's defeat in the Second World War asserted that the imperial dynasty was descended from the Sun Goddess, Amaterasu. The grandson of the Sun Goddess sent her grandson, Ninigi, to Japan to rule the earth. Ninigi settled in northern Kyushu and his great grandson, Jimmu, the mythical first Emperor of Japan, then left Kyushu to reign over the rest of Japan. After subduing foes along the way he settled in the Yamato area, and ascended the throne in 660 B.C.E. Historically, however, it is thought that there were a number of clans that contended for power. There is strong historical evidence that many of the clan leaders came from the Asian continent by way of Korea, and eventually the leading clan settled in the Yamato area. For this reason the period from about the third century C.E. to the early eighth century is known as the Yamato period.

THE YAMATO AND HEIAN ERAS: POLITICAL DEVELOPMENTS

The actual founder of the imperial dynasty, some historians have concluded, was Emperor Sujin who ruled in the latter part of the third century C.E. Others, however, contend that Sujin too was a mythical figure and the first historical political ruler was Emperor Ōjin who is believed to have reigned around 400 C.E. Ōjin was actually a Korean from the Korean kingdom of Paekche, known as Homuda in his era. Many historians hold that only the kings or Emperors from Ōjin on were actual historical personages. In Ōjin's time there were other clan leaders who were seeking to gain ascendancy. There is strong indication that the person who gained control of the Yamato region and managed to establish the imperial dynasty that survived to the present was Emperor Keitai of the early sixth century. Thus it is likely that there were three major houses in the Yamato period: the Sujin, the Ōjin, and the Keitai clans. The imperial dynasty that extended its control over the greater part of Japan then was most likely Keitai's successor.[1]

Following Keitai the imperial clan sought to centralize authority and strengthen its political foundation. From the fourth and fifth centuries Korean and Chinese influence became extensive as cultural, intellectual, religious and political concepts reached

Japan. Politically the ruling clan sought to strengthen its position by adopting Chinese political institutions and practices. The person credited with facilitating this process was Prince Shōtoku (574–622), regent to the Empress from 593 until his death. Some believe that the actual reformers were members of the Soga clan who were of Korean descent.

The Shōtoku reforms saw the promulgation of the "Constitution of Seventeen Articles" in 604. This "constitution" does not entail political or administrative provisions but embodies moral injunctions designed to strengthen the authority of the imperial family. Confucian ideals of propriety, good faith, and harmony were emphasized. From this period the Emperor came to be referred to as "kami (god) appearing as man," that is a living god. The term *tennō* (heavenly prince) was adopted from China sometime in the seventh century. During the same period the term *Nihon* was adopted as the name for Japan. In order to foster closer contacts with China missions were sent frequently and students and monks were encouraged to go there to study.

The Shōtoku reforms resulted in the Soga clan entrenching itself in power. Led by the founder of the Fujiwara family that came to dominate the imperial court during the subsequent five centuries and more, the Soga clan remained in power until 644, and the new wielders of power introduced reforms known as Taika Reforms. The Taika Reforms (mid-seventh century) and the early eighth-century Taihō legal and administrative reforms, based on the Chinese Tang institutions, resulted in the establishment of a centralized administrative system. In the realm of local administrative reforms the country was divided into sixty-six provinces in order to offset the control of the regional clan chiefs. This did not result in their displacement, however, because many were appointed provincial governors.

In the economic realm, the Tang landholding system was adopted. Land was nationalized and landholding was to be equalized. In theory the average holding was to be two *tan* (one tan equals 0.245 acre) but here again exceptions were made for the imperial family and nobility. Moreover not all land was nationalized and upper level clansmen were allowed to hold special estates. These were tax free for court members and the aristocracy. These tax-free estates were known as *shōen* and over the years shōen holdings continued to grow. This policy of bringing the land into the public domain and instituting equal landholding was not fully implemented and was eventually abandoned, enabling local leaders to increase their holdings.

Other reforms included systematization of tax collection, the adoption of a military conscription system (which was abandoned in 792 because of its inefficiency), and the establishment of checkpoints at strategic places to restrict the movement of people such as peasants fleeing tax collectors. Another Chinese practice that was adopted was the establishment of a permanent capital at Nara in 710. Prior to this the political center was wherever the Emperor resided. Now for the first time an elaborate capital city patterned after the Tang capital of Zhang-an was constructed. In 784 the Emperor Kammu (737–806) moved the capital to Heian-kyō (Kyoto). The era known as Heian period commenced in 784.

The policy of adopting Tang administrative and legal practices in order to strengthen the imperial court resulted in the centralization of authority under the imperial government. Emperors, however, seldom exercised authority directly; they relied on the court officials to oversee the administrative affairs. Imperial regents also emerged as powerful leaders. Initially regents served during the minority of the Emperor or during the reign of an Empress but toward the end of the ninth century the regency came to be occupied by members of the Fujiwara family, descendants of a court official who helped to institute the Taika reforms. The Fujiwara members served as regents regardless of the Emperor's age, and came to monopolize the post. They remained as top court officials even after the imperial court lost real power with the rise of the warrior class at the end of the Heian period. Their descendants emerged as key figures in the modern period.

Fujiwara family members extended their power by intermarrying with the imperial family, and by increasing their holdings of tax-free estates. The sumptuous lifestyle of the Fujiwara clan and the emergence of the Heian court as the nerve center of Japan resulted in a flourishing of cultural and intellectual life.

While the Fujiwara clan was exercising power at the center, the outlying regions were beginning to witness the rise of military chieftains who were gradually extending their control by increasing their shōen holdings. At the court Fujiwara political monopoly was beginning to be challenged by the Emperors. The first Emperor who sought to exert direct authority was Emperor Shirakawa (1053–1129) because during his reign there were no dominant Fujiwara family members. After he retired he sought to exclude the Fujiwara family from the government by acting as the guardian of his successor who was a child. This practice was continued by subsequent retired Emperors who usually entered a monastery. This political practice came to be known as "cloister government."

By this time the Emperor system appears to have been firmly established. The Fujiwara family began to exercise power at the center by the late ninth century but they made no attempt to replace the imperial family. Instead they sought to shore up their position by intermarrying with the imperial family. This tendency to pay outward homage to the Emperor persisted even after the real power was taken over by the shoguns in the late twelfth century. The prevalence of the mythological origin of the imperial dynasty that came to be propagated from around the fifth and sixth centuries may account for this. The *Kojiki* (Records of Ancient Matters), whose compilation was initiated by Emperor Temmu (673–686) to enhance the position of the imperial government, reinforced the myth. It is based on oral tales, and Chinese and Korean historical accounts.

The Shinto underpining of imperial rule emphasized the religious role of the Emperor. The unity of religious and political functions is seen in the use of the word *matsuri* which meant performance of government duties and worship of the gods. Shinto prayers are called *norito* and *nori* means law. With the Emperor as the high priest Shinto was able to survive through centuries of shogunate rule. Also upon the entrance of Confucianism, it was utilized to underpin the imperial system. This is reflected in Prince Shōtoku's Constitution of Seventeen Articles which emphasizes the Confucian concepts of proper conduct and stresses the ideal of the lord-subject relationship whereby "the lord is Heaven, the vassal is Earth." And instead of using the term *ō* (king) in refering to the ruler the Chinese term *tennō* (heavenly prince) was adopted, a term that applies to the Emperor to the present. The sense of reverence and respect inculcated in the people reached to the masses and was long-lasting.

In order to curb the Fujiwara clan Emperor Shirakawa initiated the practice of bringing the emerging military forces into the capital to assist him. This was an ominous portent for the central government – a sign of power shifting to the regional forces. The Taika reform's objective of enforcing equitable landholding was never fully implemented and land became concentrated in the hands of local magnates, Buddhist monasteries, court aristocrats, and high government officials. The estates held by them were tax-free and were also free from the jurisdiction of government officials. As a result the owners of these estates began to form their own militias to protect their estates. Many local magnates began expanding their holdings by encroaching on the areas under the jurisdiction of the provincial governors, and also by taking over the land held by weaker neighbors. By the twelfth century it was estimated that only about one-tenth of the land remained under the authority of local governors responsible to the Heian court. This process resulted in a gradual decrease in tax revenues for the government and weakening of its police and military authority.

The military conscription system introduced in the early eighth century was abandoned in 792, and the power of the local magnates began to increase. An arrangement akin to the European feudal master-follower relationship began to emerge among the local leaders. The personal bonds were based on kinship ties, and relationship between shōen chiefs, and local residents and workers. In return for loyal service the master was expected to provide the follower with land or the right to collect some form of income from the land. The peasants working the land, however, were not serfs and were not bound to the soil.

The local chiefs and their followers came to constitute a warrior band, a sword-bearing samurai class. As the more powerful chiefs began to extend their control over the local areas large regional power blocs began to emerge. By the twelfth century two major clans, the Taira and Minamoto families, came to dominate the outlying regions. They both claimed descent from Heian Emperors (again indicative of the importance of the imperial family in the people's mind) and sought to establish close ties to the Heian political interests, especially the Fujiwara family. The Minamoto clan began to consolidate its power base in the Kantō region (the area around current Tokyo) while the Taira family began to build up its power base to the west of the Heian capital. The shift in power from the Heian court to the local clans was demonstrated by the intervention by Tairas in the struggles for power at court. In 1156 a power struggle surfaced between the reigning Emperor and the retired Emperor. The Taira leader Kiyomori (1118–81) supported the reigning Emperor and defeated the opposing faction. This resulted in the political ascendancy of Kiyomori who became chancellor and virtual dictator. Like the Fujiwaras he sought to shore up his power base by having his daughter marry the Emperor. His grandson then became heir to the throne. These developments then presaged the advent of a new political paradigm, the shift of power from the court to the military clan.

SOCIAL AND ECONOMIC DEVELOPMENTS

After the introduction of rice culture, rice production came to constitute the mainstay of Japanese agriculture. Rice paddies were constructed wherever water could be drawn in. Wooden tools were replaced with iron implements. The practice of using water buffalos to draw plows was adopted, and along the hillsides terraced plots were constructed for cereals and vegetables. Fishing in coastal regions remained an important source of subsistence. As the local Chieftains extended their control and tax-free estates became more common-place the peasants' freedom of movement became restricted.

In arts and crafts functional, hereditary groups known as *be* were organized and were kept under the control of the different clans They were similar to the hereditary guilds of the Roman Empire. Skilled artisans, such as weavers, who came from Korea and China constituted important functional groups. As the imperial family extended its authority over the clans it began to curtail clan control of the *be* and extended its own. But as regional warrior Chieftains extended their power the workers too came under their control.

In social practices and beliefs the old way of life prevailed. Early Japanese beliefs about life and death and one's relationship with external forces were based on animistic concepts. Early Shinto, the indigenous religion, was basically animism. Upon death one went to the land of darkness and pollution. As a result death was viewed as being defiling. Before the advent of Buddhism in about the sixth century the dead were buried. With Buddhism the practice of cremation became common. When Emperors and great chieftains died they were entombed in huge sepulchral mounds. They were buried with various personal belongings such as swords, bronze mirrors, and armor. A large number of clay images known as *haniwa* were also placed around the mound.

In marital relations, polygamy was prevalent, and marriage between close relatives such as cousins, half-brothers and sisters, aunts and uncles was common. Even today marriages between cousins is accepted. Japan, as noted above, originally appears to have been a matriarchal or, at least, a matrilineal society. The mythical founding deity of the imperial clan was the Sun Goddess, and the ruler was a woman, Pimiku. Until the late-eighth century the imperial throne was frequently occupied by female members of the imperial family. This practice persisted even after the samurai class became dominant and imposed a stringent masculine orientation in society. Even in the Tokugawa period two of the occupants of the imperial throne were women.

In the Heian period husband and wife lived apart and the children remained with the mother's family. The husband was not an immediate member of the household; he came virtually as a visitor. The head of the family was thus a woman. This situation began to change as the samurai class became the dominant political-social force. In the twelfth century husband and wife began to live together, and the patriarchal system became stronger. The Confucian philosophy reinforced the patriarchal, male-dominant character of Japanese society. This is reflected in *The Tale of Genji*. The author, Lady Murasaki, has the hero Prince Genji conclude: "women were creatures of sin. He wanted to be done with them."[2] Women came to be regarded as incapable of mastering the difficult Chinese writing system and were expected to rely on the simpler phonetic system (*kana*) that was formulated in the Heian period. However, remnants of the matriarchal practice did not disappear completely. When a family had only daughters, the oldest daughter took a husband into the family, and the latter adopted the wife's family name. The significant role that women played in the cultural realm is seen in the many creative writers of the Heian period.

CULTURAL AND RELIGIOUS DEVELOPMENTS

In the early years before Chinese writing and learning entered Japan only the oral tradition prevailed. Some of the stories as well as the poems from the early years were presumably incorporated into the historical accounts and collection of poems that were compiled in the seventh and eighth centuries.

The general cultural and religious outlook that prevailed in the early years can be discerned in early Shinto. A Western scholar concluded that Shinto "was not advanced beyond crude polytheism; its personifications are vague and feeble; there is little of the conception of spirit; it has scarcely anything in the shape of a moral code."[3] The natural world was believed to be possessed by gods and spirits. Trees, streams, mountains, animals such as snakes and foxes were linked to gods or spirits. Many of the Shinto shrines are dedicated to the fox. The sun is viewed as being sacred because it is the Sun Goddess itself. It is said that a villager was blinded by the divine sun for having cursed her for causing a drought. Shinto emphasized cleanliness and purity. The grounds of Shinto shrines are kept pristine clean, and those entering Shinto shrines must cleanse themselves by rising their mouths and washing their hands. This emphasis on purity was linked to the moral outlook. What is good and agreeable is clean; what is unclean is bad and disagreeable. Hence the admiration for a clean mind, a clean spirit. Shinto, however, did not develop a well-formulated moral code.

Each tribe or clan (*uji*) had its own god (*kami*), a founder of the clan or a prominent ancestor. Hence in Shinto human beings can become a *kami*. Many historic figures and recent generals and admirals, not just Emperors, are enshrined in Shinto shrines. The war dead are enshrined in the Yasukuni Shrine in Tokyo.

The products of Chinese civilization were introduced to Japan primarily by way of Korea before the fifth century but during the fourth and fifth centuries a large number of Korean artisans and craftsmen emigrated to Japan. In addition Chinese who had fled to Korea during the turmoil that followed the fall of the Han Dynasty (206 B.C.E.–221 C.E.) entered Japan in the early fifth century. Aside from the practical knowledge they brought from China and Korea, they introduced the Chinese way of life and culture. According to the chronicles at the end of the fourth century a Korean from Paekche, Wani, brought to Japan the *Confucian Analects* and the *Thousand Character Classics*, so introducing the Chinese writing system. The Chinese writing system in fact had entered Japan before this. Its introduction was a revolutionary cultural event. Henceforth records were kept, chronicles were compiled, literary works were produced, and Chinese learning was accessed and studied.

Confucian moral concepts were adopted and Confucian virtues such as benevolence, justice, propriety, knowledge, and good faith, and the importance of maintaining proper hierarchical relations were emphasized by the ruling class that endeavored to keep those below them in their place. Access to historical accounts and stories from China and Korea helped the Japanese to develop their own literary and cultural tradition.

Among the written accounts forged by the ruling cliques to justify and fortify their political standing were the *Kojiki* (Records of Ancient Matters) and the *Nihongi* (Chronicles of Japan), completed in 712 and 720. These were claimed to be records of tales and legends passed down orally from the founding days of Japan. The legendary accounts of the *Kojiki* are presented as actual historical records regarding the creation of the Japanese islands by the founding deities, and the life of the Sun Goddess. The *Nihongi* focuses more on history proper. The orthodox national historians have presented the accounts as factual truth. The history, however, was compiled under the direction of Emperor Temmu (reigned 673–686) in order to justify and glorify his dynastic lineage. Both histories incorporated materials from Chinese and Korean sources. Korean historians have pointed out that many of the legendary tales are similar to those found in early Korean tales. These histories became sacred accounts used to assert the divinity and sanctity of the imperial dynasty, especially after it regained its political authority in 1868.

The other significant cultural import from Korea and China was the introduction of Buddhism during the mid-sixth century. In fact it may be that the religion reached Japan earlier as immigrants from Korea and China entered the country. But the official version holds that it was introduced in 538 with the presentation of Buddhist images and scriptures by the king of

Paekche. Buddhism's acceptance, it is believed, was facilitated by the beautiful artifacts that accompanied the religion.

In the Heian period more serious study of Buddhism was pursued. The branch of Buddhism that had flourished in China, Korea, and Japan was Mahayana Buddhism. This held that salvation is to be achieved by faith in merciful Buddhist deities, the *bodhisattvas*. The other branch, Theravada Buddhism, taught that *nirvana*, the state of bliss, is to be attained by self-knowledge and self-mastery. The latter spread into South East Asia while the former entered China, Korea, and then Japan. The two major sects that emerged in the Heian period were the Tendai (Heavenly Platform) and Shingon (True Word) sects. The former based its teaching on the Lotus Sutra which teaches the unity or oneness of all. The founder of the Shingon sect in Japan was Kūkai (774–835) who had studied in China. This sect emphasized esoteric rituals, chants and prayers. Although it cannot be verified with certainty, Kūkai has been credited with inventing the phonetic system to transcribe Japanese.

During the Heian period Buddhism did not spread widely among the people and it remained a doctrine and practice engaged in largely by the upper classes. An attempt to syncretize Buddhism and Shinto emerged. All deities including Shinto gods, it was held, were manifestations of the primordial Buddha. This school was known as Dual Shinto. In a way this is in tune with the non-exclusive attitude that has characterized Japanese mores. One can believe in Shinto, Buddhism or any other religion at the same time.

LITERATURE AND POETRY

In literature and poetry, the first major creative work was the anthology of poems, the *Man'yōshū* (Collection of ten thousand poems) compiled in the eighth century. It consists of over four thousand long and short poems from the period before writing was introduced as well as those composed from the fifth century to about 760. The composers include nameless peasants, court aristocrats, and Emperors. The poems not only have literary merit but they reflect the moral and intellectual values of early Japan. Critics see in the poems expressions of natural human sentiments that prevailed before the Confucian ideals of propriety and restraint became influential. Sentiments of love of wife and family which later came to be regarded as "unmanly" were freely expressed. For example, "My wife and I are one in heart/ However long we are side by side/ She is charming all the more/ Though face to face we sit/ She my cherished love, is ever fresh as a new flower."[4]

A literary work that ranks among the classics in world literature is *The Tale of Genji* written by Murasaki Shikibu (978–1016), a lady-in-waiting to the Empress. The setting is the Heian court. Prince Genji and his love life is the story line but what makes this a remarkable classic is the overall aesthetic effect created by the author's graceful poetic style. It is more a work of poetry than prose. The mood that permeates the entire novel is the sense of pathos, *mono-no-aware*. Genji says "Nothing in this world is permanent. Life is uncertain for all of us."[5]

Murasaki Shikibu was writing at a time and place when form, appearance, and decorum were stressed. How one was perceived by others became an obsessive concern. This excessive sensitivity to appearance and form seemingly became a part of the Japanese national character. The Heian court circle was also a highly status-conscious, snobbish society. The common people, ignorant of the delicate rules of decorum, were looked down upon. The emphasis on politeness and refinement came to characterize the language. Proper use of polite and honorific terms became embedded in the language. Sei Shōnagon, another accomplished literary stylist of this period wrote in *The Pillow Book*: "It is particularly unpleasant to hear some foolish man or woman omit the proper marks of respect when addressing a person of quality."[6]

With the introduction of Chinese culture, Chinese poetry and literature was perused and poetry in Chinese style was composed. But by the ninth century a move to free Japanese culture from excessive reliance on Chinese literature began to develop, and the *waka* (literally Japanese songs), a thirty-one syllable Japanese poem, came to be composed. In the tenth century an anthology of eleven hundred waka, *Kokinshū* (Collection of Ancient and Modern Poems) was compiled. One of the editors wrote: "The poetry of Japan has its roots in the human heart and flourishes in the countless leaves of words."[7] For example, a twelfth-century poet mused: "In a tree standing, Beside a desolate field, The voice of a dove, Calling to its companions – Lonely, terrible evening."[8]

ART AND ARCHITECTURE

During the early years of the Yamato era the distinctive architectural style seen in Shinto shrines evolved. They were boxlike structures built in plain, unadorned style to fit in with the natural surroundings. The prototypical Shinto shrines are the Ise shrines in central Japan. The Inner Shrine is dedicated to the Sun Goddess and the Outer Shrine to the goddess of agriculture and sericulture.

With the advent of Chinese civilization Buddhist temples and monasteries came to be built throughout the land. One of the most renowned Buddhist structures is the monastery of Hōryūji in Nara. Originally built in 607 it was destroyed by fire and rebuilt at the end of the century. The five-storied pagoda and the Golden Hall stand out in the compound. The structures reflect a sense of balance, order, and cohesion. The Tōdaiji in Nara built in the same century houses a great bronze Buddha over fifty feet tall. The move to build Buddhist monasteries in all the provinces commenced in the Yamato period and continued into the Heian years. The ground-plans tended to become more asymmetrical since the buildings were designed to fit in with the lay of the land. The temples and monasteries were adorned with frescoes and statues. Thus the adoption of Buddhism with its accompanying art and architecture enhanced the artistic creativity of the Japanese society. In dwellings also distinctive structures came to be constructed with raised wooden floors, unpainted pillars, removable panels, sliding doors, and screens to partition rooms.

The emergence of a distinctive Japanese painting style, known as *Yamato-e*, flourished in the Heian period. Initially Buddhist subjects tended to predominate but soon Japanese scenes and tales came to be portrayed. The subjects were outlined with thin lines and filled with bright colors. Sliding door panels, screens and horizontal narrative scrolls (e-makimono) were painted in the Yamato-e style.

Also an art learned from the Chinese masters, calligraphy, that is, brush-writing, gained eminence as a graceful aesthetic pursuit.

TWO

The Age of Samurai Ascendancy, 1185–1600

POLITICAL DEVELOPMENTS

After Taira Kiyomori gained political control at the capital he sought to preserve his position by stifling any opposition. The stringency of Taira control led people to say "If one is not a Taira, one is not a human being." But opposition was brewing in the eastern Kantō region led by the Minamoto clan headed by Yoritomo (1147–99). Yoritomo began his uprising in 1180. About the same time severe famines occurred (1181–82) causing thousands to starve to death. A contemporary account related that, "Beggars swarmed by the roadsides and our ears were filled with the sound of their lamentations ... Everybody was dying of hunger."[1] This state of affairs coincided with Kiyomori's death, which weakened Taira's political standing. Yoritomo was able to take advantage of this situation and defeat the Taira forces. He executed all members of the Taira family, even little children. Ironically as a child himself he had been saved from execution by Kiyomori by the intercession of Kiyomori's stepmother. Thus in 1185 Yoritomo gained political ascendancy. In order not to be influenced by the flaccid lifestyle of the Heian court Yoritomo decided to establish his headquarters in Kamakura, his original power base. Then he set about consolidating his control over the land. When samurai warriors engaged in combat the leader usually directed the campaign from a tent. The tent headquarters were referred to as *bakufu*. Thus the political and military headquarter established by Yoritomo as well as all the military controlled government that followed until 1867 was identified as *bakufu*. In 1192 Yoritomo was appointed *seitaishōgun*, generalissimo. In this way he and his successors ruled the land as *shōgun*.

The warrior control established by Yoritomo and sustained by his wife's family, the Hōjō clan, lasted until 1333. The period from 1185 to 1333 is referred to as the Kamakura period. The power then shifted to the Ashikaga clan a member of which occupied the shōgun's position from 1338 to 1573. In reality from the mid-fifteenth century the regional warlords contended for power and the country entered a state of civil strife, that is, a period of "warring states." Even though centralized control was re-established by two warlords, Oda Nobunaga and Toyotomi Hideyoshi, for the last quarter of that century, it was not until Tokugawa Ieyasu gained control in the early seventeenth century that the country entered a period of stability and order which lasted until 1867.

The imposition of samurai rule changed the social and cultural complexion of the country drastically from the ostensibly refined, cultural life of the Heian society. It was not just a change in political order. The cultural, moral and intellectual core of Japanese life came to be permeated deeply with samurai mores. The two contrasting faces of Japan, the Heian elitist gentility, and the tough-minded samurai mode came to characterize the lifestyle of Japan.

Although he became the *de facto* wielder of power Yoritomo retained the imperial system. Ostensibly he was serving as military chief or shōgun, on behalf of the Emperor. He obtained imperial sanctions for his policies and was appointed as supreme constable and supreme land steward of the sixty-six provinces. In the former capacity he held military and police power over the land, and in the latter capacity he had the right to collect taxes on public domains. He also appointed provincial constables and land stewards. In the Kantō region where he retained direct control he appointed provincial governors. He also owned a large number of *shōen* throughout the country, having confiscated the former Taira shōen. The bulk of the shōen were still held by the imperial court, the court nobles, monasteries, and some local magnates. Thus a pattern of divided authority prevailed in the provinces.

In effect a dual government of sorts prevailed with the pattern of control differing from area to area. The Kamakura system cannot be defined simply as feudalism because it was not like the European feudal system. However, a personal master-vassal or lord-follower relationship characterized the relationship between the samurai chiefs and their followers. It was not bound, however, by the lord granting fiefs to the vassals. The practice of granting what in essence were fiefs emerged later but, just as in Europe, the practice was not uniform. Initially when the lord-follower relationship developed it was based on kinship ties. As the lord expanded his power base non-family members joined the circle. The relationship was formalized by a ritual with the follower presenting a name plate to the lord. In return for the vassal's services the lord granted him the right to collect taxes or rents from the land or a piece of land (not a fief with political rights over the land). For convenience the term feudal will be used but it should be understood that it does not signify a European-type system.

Minamoto rule did not prevail very long because after Yoritomo's death his wife Masako's family, the Hōjō clan, exercised power as regent to figurehead shōguns. When the Minamoto family control was being replaced by the Hōjō clan, ex-Emperor Gotoba sought to reassert imperial supremacy and called for the support of military chiefs and constables in the Kyoto area and rallied in all about ten thousand warriors in 1221. Masako led a large samurai contingent and swiftly crushed the imperial forces. This enabled the Hōjō leaders to strengthen the Kamakura bakufu's position against the imperial court and also to take control of the rebels' shōen.

The Gotoba move was not a major threat to Hōjō rule. The big threat came from abroad with the Mongols' attempt to invade Japan. Relations established with China under the Sung Dynasty (960–1279) continued during the Heian era. Taira Kiyomori fostered trade with China, and this policy was continued in the Kamakura period. Sung influence was seen in painting, literature, and in Zen (Chan) Buddhism. This amicable relation was interrupted with the Mongol conquest of China in 1260. In 1274 Kublai Khan sought to invade Japan but the Mongol fleet was destroyed by a typhoon, the so-called *kamikaze*. The second attack in 1281 resulted in the landing of Mongol troops in northern Kyushu but the Japanese forces were able to drive them out.

Even though the Mongol invasion failed, the defensive efforts strained the Kamakura government's financial resources. Furthermore the warriors who rallied to defend the land expected some sort of remuneration but the Bakufu did not have the means to reward them since there were no fruits of victory to share. This resulted in a growing disaffection with the Hōjō leadership. The rise of a money economy, stimulated in part by the importation of Sung coins, also increased the financial strain on the samurai who began to fall into debt. The Bakufu sought to ease their plight by issuing an edict cancelling all debts but this did not solve the basic economic problems. As the Bakufu was weakened by financial strain and the growing samurai discontent, local leaders such as provincial constables, land stewards, shōen owners, and Bakufu vassals began to contend for land and power. The power disruptions resulted in the rise of brigands and thieves who began the pillage of the countryside.

Perceiving the growing discontent toward the Bakufu, the imperial court moved to regain political control. In 1331 Emperor Godaigo (1288–1339) staged a rising against the Bakufu with the support of military chiefs around Kyoto and western Japan. Initially the insurgency seemed to be a failure but one key leader, Ashikaga Takauji (1305–58) decided to defect to the imperial side and he helped to topple the Hōjō government. Thus imperial rule was restored briefly in 1333 but it lasted only until 1336.

Godaigo failed to extend his authority over the land. Samurai discontent turned against the imperial government because they were not properly rewarded. Land and power disputes continued in the provinces. Seeing the unstable state of the imperial court Ashikaga Takauji, who had helped to overthrow the Hōjō government, decided to take power himself. In the ensuing power struggle Takauji succeeded in winning the support of the discontented elements and gained control of Kyoto. He then placed a member of the collateral line of the imperial family on the throne. When he saw pro-imperial forces rising against Takauji, Godaigo decided to join them and fled south to the Kii peninsula. He established a rival government in Yoshino in 1336. Thus there were two imperial courts, the northern court and the southern court. This system of dual imperial dynasties lasted until 1392.

ASHIKAGA SHOGUNATE (1338–1573)

In 1338 Takauji was appointed shōgun by the northern court, and he and his successors sought to subdue the opposition forces and consolidate Ashikaga rule. The third Ashikaga shōgun, Yoshimitsu (1358–1408) succeeded in persuading the southern court to return to Kyoto and merge with the northern court in 1392. The descendants of the two courts were to occupy the throne alternately. But this agreement was not kept and the northern court descendants have occupied the throne to the present.

Although Yoshimitsu had united the two courts and had established fairly firm control over the country the local chieftains, constables, and land stewards remained entrenched in the provinces. The Ashikaga shōen holdings were not as large as the Hōjō holdings so the Ashikaga government had to rely on taxes to meet its financial needs.

After Yoshimitsu's death in 1408 the shogunate began to experience increasing difficulty in keeping the major constabulary houses under control. These elements had extended their control in the outlying provinces during the years when the country was split between the northern and southern courts. By the middle of the fifteenth century a large number of constables had gained hereditary possession of their posts and began to extend their control over other provinces. They began to take possession of the shōen in their provinces which were formerly held by the imperial court, court nobles, monasteries, and local owners. They had gained taxation rights as well as the power to impose *corvée* on the people in the shōen. To strengthen their power position they began to convert local officials and independent landholders into their vassals. By the middle of the fifteenth century the shōen holders had virtually lost control of their manors and the constables were emerging as provincial landholding magnates, the *daimyō*, the big names.

By the mid-fifteenth century four major constabulary houses emerged. Their rivalry ended in a major civil conflict instigated by two major houses, the Yamana and Hosokawa families. This power struggle, known as the Ōnin War, split the country into two warring factions. The conflict lasted a decade from 1467 to 1477 but more importantly it turned out to be the beginning of the time of troubles known as the Age of the Warring States (in emulation of the Chinese era of Warring States, 403–221 B.C.E.). This period of internal strife engaged in by regional chiefs, the daimyō, lasted for a century until centralized control was more or less established by one of the major warlords, Oda Nobunaga (1534–82).

During the century of civil strife rank and status meant nothing. Only military skill and ruthless determination to crush the opposition counted. Many local warrior chiefs gained regional control by overthrowing the dominant constabulary families. Numerous deputies and vassals of constables as well as lower level samurai organized contingents of warriors and peasants and built up their power base and extended their control over larger and larger areas. By 1563 the country was divided among 142 major daimyō. The daimyō began to build castles in their power bases and many of these developed into major cities.

During this period the practice of granting fiefs to the vassals had become common. In return for the fief the vassal had to provide the lord with a fixed number of warriors. To prevent the fiefs from being divided into smaller and smaller units by subdividing the land among the sons, the practice of primogeniture began to prevail. This weakened the status of women because hitherto women had the right of inheritance. In an age when only military might counted, women lost their rights and came to be used as political pawns by their fathers or brothers who compelled them to marry into families that would strengthen their power position.

SOCIAL CLASS: THE PEASANTRY

The condition of the peasantry varied from place to place during the Kamakura-Ashikaga period. The peasants were not serfs, but impoverished peasants were often driven to sell their wives and children as slaves to serve as household or farm workers. There were also tenant farmers and hired workers. The most well-off held title to the land under the jurisdiction of the shōen owners. During the years of civil strife in the early Ashikaga years the control over the peasantry by the constables and shōen owners weakened, and the peasants were able to gain greater freedom. Many acquired their own plots. The independent farmers became leaders of the peasantry, and some became warrior-farmers and began to serve the rising warrior chieftains. Unlike the ordinary peasants who were known only by their first names or were identified by their locale, the warrior-farmers were allowed to use surnames. As law and order began to weaken the peasants were confronted with brigands and plunderers so they began to band together to defend themselves.

The burden on the peasantry grew heavier as the Ashikaga Bakufu increased taxation in order to resolve its economic difficulties. As a result the peasants had to turn over seventy percent of their produce as taxes and rents. In times of famine the peasants were reduced to starvation. Many sold their daughters to brothels and sons to monastic priests. During 1459–61 serious drought, floods, and typhoons occurred together with a plague of locusts. As a result mass starvation occurred during this period. It is estimated that eighty-two thousand people starved to death in Kyoto.

Faced with natural calamities, heavy taxation, and increasing debts the peasants began to rise up in protest. These were staged against the Bakufu, the shōen owners and the urban moneylenders who were becoming more active as commerce and the money economy began to expand. In the fifteenth century a growing number of peasant uprisings began to occur. During a thirty-year span in mid-century eighteen peasant uprisings broke out. These were often led by lower-class samurai or independent farmers. As the local military chiefs began to gain power in the provinces many of these men became retainers of the ascending daimyō. They abandoned the cause of the peasantry and as sword-wielding samurai helped their new masters keep the peasants under control. The unsettled conditions enabled some peasants to serve the military chiefs as warriors and rise up the social hierarchy because no rigid caste system existed during this time. The most notable example of this was Toyotomi Hideyoshi (1536?–98) who rose from the peasantry to become the dictator of the entire country in the sixteenth century.

In the late-fifteenth century one Buddhist sect, the True Pure Land sect, discussed below, organized peasants and staged uprisings in some regions to challenge the local lords. These were inclined to be more political and religious in nature than uprisings designed to improve the condition of the peasantry.

THE STATUS OF WOMEN

As noted earlier, in early times, Japan was most probably a matriarchal society. But with the influence of Chinese civilization and Confucianism the idea of a hierarchical family relationship of husband and wife, male and female came to be accepted. Buddhism also placed women in an inferior position to men. It taught that salvation was not possible for women. This teaching changed in the Kamakura period with the rise of the popular Buddhist sects. With the rise of the samurai class, military valor and physical strength came to be valued and women were placed increasingly in an inferior position relative to men. Distinctions in speech between men and women began to become more pronounced. Women were expected to speak in a polite, refined, deferential manner. Women's right to inheritance came to be eroded as primogeniture became the common practice. But in the Kamakura period daughters still had the right of inheritance and widowed mothers controlled the family property. Daughters of samurai were trained in the martial arts and widows of samurai were expected to perform the duties of a vassal and, if necessary, engage in combat. A notable example of this is Yoritomo's widow Masako who led the Minamoto army against the imperial forces.

ECONOMIC DEVELOPMENTS

In the fourteenth and fifteenth centuries significant economic growth transpired with improvements in agricultural production, and increase in commerce and industry. Better tools, improved methods of farming, greater use of draft animals, utilization of animal and human waste as manure, better methods of irrigation using water wheels, a two-crop system, better strains of rice, and the opening-up of new land for farming all contributed to the increase in farm production.

Agricultural growth stimulated commerce and industry. Market towns came into being and grew in size. Merchant guilds for a host of commodities, and craft guilds of artisans and workers were organized. The growth in commerce was accompanied by the rise of a money economy. Trade with China stimulated the use of coins, and moneylenders, as well as wholesale merchants, became more active. Port cities, market towns, and castle towns emerged as important centers of commercial activity. A number of commercial communities, like Sakai near Osaka, began to emerge as autonomous cities. They were unable to retain their autonomous standing, however, as more powerful daimyō began extending the power base in the sixteenth century.

Ashikaga Shōgun Yoshimitsu was interested in increasing trade with China. In 1404 he concluded a commercial treaty with Ming China, and he sought to curtail the Japanese pirates who were attacking the coastal towns of Korea and China. Trade with Korea was more extensive than trade with China. The daimyō in western Japan fostered trade with China and Korea as well as with the Ryukyu [Okinawa] Islands. Commercial relations with South East Asia were established for the first time with Ryukyu merchants functioning as middlemen. These commercial activities enabled the daimyō in the western provinces to establish a strong financial base and become major players in the civil conflict in the fifteenth and sixteenth centuries.

CULTURAL AND INTELLECTUAL DEVELOPMENTS: THE ETHOS OF THE SAMURAI

We saw the rise of the master-follower, or lord-vassal relationship during the Heian years when provincial warlords began to emerge. With the establishment of the Kamakura Shogunate the era of samurai ascendancy began. For the masters the ideal code of behavior for the samurai followers was loyalty, diligent performance of duty, courage, and honor. Generally speaking the samurai master-vassal system was based on a reciprocal relationship of services and rewards. In essence the samurai were motivated by self-interest and in time of turbulence and power struggles many were willing to change masters to be on the winning side. During the fourteenth century when the imperial court was split into two factions the "great age of turncoats" came about. A similar situation came about in the late fifteenth and sixteenth centuries when a period of contending warlords prevailed. When strong personal ties and a sense of loyalty bound the samurai to the lord, however, they were willing to fight to death for the lord, and in case of defeat, die with the lord.

When the Hōjō clan was defeated by the imperial forces in 1333 thousands of loyal samurai committed *harakiri* (disembowelment with the sword) to share the fate of their Hōjō masters.

Since the main function of the samurai was combat they were expected to harden themselves under tough Spartan regimentation. They were trained to fight with the bow and arrow and also engage in combat with the sword. As a result sword-making became an important craft and numerous master swordmakers emerged in this period.

In theory the code of the warrior called on the samurai to be chivalrous and protect the weak, the helpless, and the defeated but in reality the samurai was trained to kill so they usually behaved as ruthless killers. It was not until the Tokugawa era when firm control was established by the Tokugawa shogunate and there were no violent conflicts that the code of the warriors on chivalrous, honorable behavior came to be spelled out.

BUDDHISM IN THE KAMAKURA-MUROMACHI YEARS

While Buddhism gained popularity among the upper class during the Heian period, it spread more rapidly among the common people in the Kamakura period and after. This development may have been the result of the chaos and conflict, and power struggles that developed in the later part of the twelfth century and prevailed into the sixteenth century. People were also beset by natural calamities periodically. Thus the "end of the world" as envisaged in Buddhist thinking may have appeared to be near at hand. This sense of despair and pessimism may have led people to seek spiritual comfort in the emerging Buddhist sects that reached out to the common people. The Mahayana branch of Buddhism which flourished in China, Korea, and Japan envisioned the rebirth into the Land of Bliss. In the Heian period emphasis was placed on rituals and recitation of spells and magical formulae. The more often the mantras were repeated the better the chances of salvation. One person, it is said, set aside one bean for every mantra he cited and accumulated 3.6 billion beans.

In Mahayana Buddhism people were taught that salvation was to be achieved by faith in the merciful Buddhas and Bodhisattvas (those who have achieved enlightenment but remain on earth to help others gain salvation). Amida Buddha, the Body of Bliss, became the most popular Buddha in Japan. Rather than comprehension of Buddhist doctrines and recitation of mantras the Buddhist leaders who emerged in the Kamakura period emphasized devotion to Amida Buddha and other merciful Buddhas for salvation. These new leaders founded their own sects.

Among the Kamakura Buddhist leaders was Hōnen (1133–1212) who founded the Pure Land (*Jōdo*) Sect; he taught that all that was needed to gain salvation was reliance on the saving power of Amida Buddha. Hōnen's disciple Shinran (1173–1262) made salvation even easier by insisting that all that was necessary was one sincere invocation of Amida's name. This contrasted with Hōnen who taught that the more often Amida's name was invoked the better the chances of salvation. Shinran also taught that moral conduct was irrelevant to salvation. Everybody, good or evil, would be saved if they relied wholly on Amida Buddha. In fact an evil person who realized that he could not save himself might have a better chance of salvation than the good person who felt his good conduct ensured him salvation. By giving oneself over completely to Amida Buddha Shinran taught that one would become a moral person. He called his sect the True Pure Land Sect (*Jōdo Shinshū*) and it won a wide following among the downtrodden. Since external conduct was not relevant to salvation Shinran contended that adherence to injunctions against the consumption of certain food and drink, such as beef and alcohol, was not necessary for salvation. He also believed that the clergy need not lead a life different from the laity and rejected monasticism and clerical celibacy. He set out to reach the common people and went to outlying, impoverished regions to spread his message to aid the downtrodden people, and gained a wide following among the peasantry. Thus the True Pure Land Sect gained a popular following and retained the faith of the masses to the present day.

The other sect that gained a popular following was the Nichiren Sect (Lotus Sect) founded by Nichiren (1222–82). He held that the three bodies of Buddha emphasized in the Lotus Sutra, that is, the Body of Essence, the Body of Bliss (Amida Buddha) and the historical Buddha are a unity and equal in importance. Recitation of the Lotus Sutra would enable one to gain salvation. He condemned the other sects as propagating false teachings and set out to replace them with his doctrine. His dogmatism and intolerance set him apart from the other sects which tended to be more tolerant of diverse beliefs. Nichiren also tended to be nationalistic and his thinking was akin to Shinto nationalism. Beside helping people to gain salvation he set out to be "the Pillar of Japan, the Great Vessel of Japan." He stressed service to the country and obligation to the sovereign. Japan, he asserted, was the land of the gods destined to be the universal center of the Nichiren Sect. His militant viewpoint won over many samurai but his sect also won a wide following among the masses and has remained a vibrant sect.

Zen Buddhism also emerged as a significant movement in this period. It tended to influence the cultural sphere of Japan more than the other sects. As Chan Buddhism it was introduced to China from India in the sixth century or earlier. It entered Japan in the Heian period but did not become an influential sect until the Kamakura period when its teachings appealed to the samurai class. Unlike the other sects Zen does not preach salvation through faith in the Buddhas or Bodhisattvas. By means of meditation and concentration "enlightenment" (*satori*), becoming one with the underlying reality unencumbered by surface illusions, will be achieved. Reason, knowledge, scriptures, mantras will not aid in achieving *satori*. One has to probe directly into one's soul to grasp reality and one's Buddha nature. Once one achieves *satori* one cannot transmit this reality to others by words. Bodhidharma who brought Chan Buddhism to China said, "A special transmission outside the scriptures; No dependence upon words and letters; Direct pointing at the soul of man; Seeing into one's nature and the attainment of Buddhahood."[2]

Two Zen sects emerged emphasizing different approaches to achieve *satori*. One stressed *zazen*, sitting in meditation. The other emphasized *kōan*, enigmatic, paradoxical themes, to break one's habit of relying on reason to liberate the unconscious, for example, "What is the sound of one hand clapping."[3]

Because Zen required discipline and concentration it did not gain a mass following among the populace. But it won a strong following among the samurai who had to face life and death on the battlefield. A sixteenth-century warlord told his followers to devote themselves to Zen. "Zen has no secrets other than seriously thinking about life and death."[4] Many samurai and modern warriors entered Zen monasteries to discipline themselves and rise above the fear of death. Zen emphasis on grasping the essence of the nature of things had a significant impact on cultural developments.

ARTS AND LITERATURE

Scroll paintings and portrait paintings that emerged in the Heian period continued to flourish during the age of the warring samurai. In the sixteenth century when the rising warlords began to build huge castles, they embellished the interior with painted walls, sliding doors, and folding screens. The sliding doors and folding screens were painted in bold, bright colors against backgrounds of gold leaf. Among the renowned artists of this genre was Kanō Eitoku (1543–90).

Buddhist architecture that began in the Heian period continued to embellish the countryside. In sculpture huge Buddhist figures were created, such as the Deva kings that guard the Tōdaiji temple in Nara and the forty-two foot Great Buddha of Kamakura. In the late fourteenth century Ashikaga Shōgun Yoshimitsu built the Golden Pavilion, a three-storied building set among trees, rocks, and a lake in Zen-like style. During the period of the "warring states" daimyō began to build huge castles as fortresses and power bases. Among the most notable of these is the Fushimi castle near Osaka that Toyotomi Hideyoshi built in the sixteenth century.

With the rise of the samurai, sword making became an important profession. Many skilled swordsmiths emerged in the Kamakura period and after. Among the most renowned master swordsmiths was Masamune (1264–1344) whose creations are valued as rare treasures today. The art of ceramics also began to gain prominence in this period, especially as the tea ceremony came to be linked to the pursuit of Zen aesthetics. Sung ceramic art with its highly finished style, and Korean ceramics of crude simplicity influenced Japanese ceramists.

In literature the narrative style that developed in the Heian era known as *monogatari* flourished. The topic of the tales naturally had to do with the clans contending for supremacy like the *Tale of*

Heike. Quite naturally the ethos of the samurai are reflected in these tales but the Buddhist sense of the ephemeral nature of life also permeates the narrative. The *Tale of Heike* which deals with the rise and fall of the Taira clan opens with the lines: "In the sound of the bell of the Gion Temple echoes the impermanence of all things ... The proud ones do not last long, but vanish like a spring-night's dream. And the mighty ones too will perish in the end, like dust before the wind."[5]

A number of prominent histories or chronicles were written in this period also. The *Gukanshō* (Jottings of a Fool) written by a monk in the early thirteenth century interpreted Japanese history in terms of the periodic decline of the Law of Buddha. His age was in the period of decline represented by the decline of the imperial house. In 1339 a supporter of the Southern Court, Kitabatake Chikafusa (1293–1354) wrote a Shintoist interpretation of the imperial court entitled *Jinnō Shōtōki* (The Records of the Legitimate Succession of the Divine Sovereign), which came to be cited by the defenders of the imperial court down through the ages.

Zen Buddhism became a significant cultural force during the Ashikaga years and molded the aesthetic taste of the Japanese to the present. The appreciation of the simple and the austere, imbalance and asymmetry came to be reflected in many cultural spheres: landscape gardening, Noh plays, flower arrangements, the tea ceremony, ceramics, painting, poetry, and architecture. It also influenced swordsmanship and archery. Zen aesthetics are embodied in the tea ceremony in which a sense of simplicity, austerity, melancholy, solitude, serenity, restraint, and composure prevail. The daimyō of the warring states period took a fancy to the tea ceremony and a number of tea houses, located in a natural surrounding where Zen aesthetics of simplicity and rusticity prevail, were constructed.

Gardening also became a fine art, designed to reduce nature to its bare essentials. Among the renowned Zen-style gardens is the Rock Garden of Ryōanji Temple in Kyoto. It consists of white sand and fifteen stones symbolizing sea and rocks.

Zen influence also extended to painting. The paintings of a Zen monk of Sung China, Mu-chi, fostered a distinctive *sumie*, ink drawing, in Japan. Sumie painters did not endeavor to paint a realistic picture of nature but sought to depict the essence of things, leaving out unessential details. The dynamism and vigor of the sumie painters and calligraphers are seen in the bold, forceful strokes and rhythm and movement of the brushwork.

Noh drama had developed as folk dance plays performed at Shinto festivals. In the Ashikaga period Noh drama became more refined and embodied Zen simplicity and restraint. The stage is virtually devoid of scenery and props. The all-male cast performs in a highly stylized, formal, measured manner, with gestures and movements having symbolic meaning. Noh performances seek to depict a sense of *yūgen*, "what lies beneath the surface ... the subtle, as opposed to the obvious, the hint, as opposed to the statement."[6] Noh remains a drama form considered to be an art appreciated by the cultural elite, a significant shift from popular folk dances of earlier centuries.

Learning had remained a special privilege of the Heian cultural elite but the samurai and better-off peasants began to send their children to the temple schools (*terakoya*) in the Ashikaga era. It was not until the Tokugawa period that this practice became more widespread but the beginning of this institution, an important means for the masses to acquire some degree of learning, emerged in this period.

ENCOUNTER WITH THE WEST

In the late fifteenth century Portugal and Spain began overseas exploration. The Portuguese ships sailed east and Vasco Da Gama arrived in India in 1498. In 1513 the Portuguese traders arrived in Canton, China and then in Japan in 1543. They were followed by the Spanish traders in 1584. The English and the Dutch began overseas exploration and eventually arrived in Japan also, the Dutch in 1600 and the British in 1613.

Among the items introduced to Japan by the Portuguese were muskets. The item sought by Westerners in Japan was silver. The most important cultural development in Japan's encounter with the West in the sixteenth century was Christianity which was introduced by the Jesuit St. Francis Xavier who arrived in Japan in 1549. The daimyō in Kyushu were receptive to the Jesuit missionaries because they believed this would facilitate trade with the Western nations. Also Oda Nobunaga, who was gaining political ascendancy in the 1560s, supported the missionaries because he sought to curb Buddhist elements who were antagonistic to him. With the conversion of some Kyushu daimyō and Nobunaga's support the number of converts began to increase. By 1582 it is estimated that there were about one hundred and fifty thousand Christians and two hundred chapels in Japan. The number of Christian converts continued to grow and by 1614, when the founder of the Tokugawa Bakufu banned the religion, it is estimated that were over three hundred thousand Christians (some estimates run as high as seven hundred thousand). The nation's population at that time has been estimated at between eighteen and twenty million.

After the initial favorable response to the Christian missionaries the ruling authorities began to grow somewhat concerned about the loyalty of the Christian vassals who ultimately owed their loyalty to a higher authority than the daimyō masters, God. Hideyoshi, who became the dominant power following Nobunaga's demise, issued an edict in 1587 ordering the missionaries to leave the country. Initially he did not enforce the ban but when some suspicion was aroused that the Franciscans, who arrived in 1593, were precursors to Spanish political incursion Hideyoshi crucified twenty-six Franciscan missionaries and Japanese converts in 1596. Ieyasu too was initially tolerant of the Christians but he also became concerned that loyalty of the Christians could not be counted upon and he banned the religion in 1614. He ordered everyone to become a member of one of the major Buddhist sects. Missionaries were ordered to leave the country and the daimyō were ordered to purge their domain of Christians. Christians who went into hiding were rooted out and executed. The third Tokugawa shōgun, Iemitsu ruthlessly forced Christians to become apostates by torturing them. Between 1614 and 1640 five to six thousand Christians were executed. During 1637 and 1638 the peasants of Shimabara Peninsula and Amakusa Island in Kyushu rebelled under the leadership of a Christian youth, Amakusa Shirō (1621–38). About thirty-seven thousand people resisted the one hundred thousand Bakufu forces but they were crushed. The Christians who refused to apostatize concealed their faith and became "hidden Christians."

PRELUDE TO TOKUGAWA HEGEMONY

Among the contending daimyō of the sixteenth century the warlord who emerged as the potential ruling power was Oda Nobunaga whose domain was the area around Nagoya. Nobunaga formed alliances, used new tactics, engaged in surprise attacks, and was the first to make effective use of firearms when they were introduced by the Portuguese. In 1568 he occupied Kyoto and in 1573 he put an end to the Ashikaga shogunate.

Nobunaga was a ruthless warlord. He was opposed by a number of Buddhist groups, including peasant forces (Ikkō) tied to the True Pure Land Sect. In one campaign against the Ikkō forces he captured and massacred tens of thousands of Ikkō peasants. Facing opposition from the monks of Mt. Hiei near Kyoto he burned down the monastery and seized and executed about sixteen hundred people not just monks but villagers, including women and children. On another occasion he had 150 monks burned to death because they had conducted funeral services for one of his foes. It is said he executed a young maid for not cleaning the room thoroughly, she had left a stem of fruit on the floor.

Nobunaga too became a victim of the dog-eat-dog world of turbulence. One of his followers turned against him and he perished. He was succeeded by a former follower, Toyotomi Hideyoshi, a peasant, who began his career as Nobunaga's sandal carrier, and rose to become one of his top generals. He succeeded in subduing his rivals and gained supremacy over the land. He was appointed regent and chancellor by the Emperor but he could not become shōgun because it had become customary to appoint only descendants of the Minamoto clan to that position. After establishing control over Japan he turned his eyes to the continent and in 1592 he launched a campaign against Korea, aspiring to conquer Korea and China. As his forces moved north toward China the Ming government intervened and his campaign stalled, and a truce was negotiated. When he misinterpreted the agreement and concluded the Ming government had reneged on the agreement, Hideyoshi sent another force into Korea in 1597. He died the following year before he gained his objective and the troops were withdrawn.

His Korean campaign caused desolation in Korea and led to famine and death among the Korean population.

In his domestic policy, despite his own peasant origin, he set out to keep the peasants from causing future disturbances. He issued a decree forbidding the peasants from leaving the soil, and ordered them to turn over all their weapons to the authorities. In effect he laid the basis for serfdom that was instituted in the following Tokugawa era. During the years of contending warlords there was less social rigidity and peasants were able to join the warlord-fighting force, a course that Hideyoshi himself pursued. He also conducted a cadastral survey to determine land value and ownership, and fix the peasants' tax payments. The land value was determined by the amount of rice it produced. The measurement used was the *koku* (9.8 cubic feet). This became the unit to determine the size of the daimyō and samurai holdings until the Meiji era.

THREE

Tokugawa Rule

Upon Hideyoshi's death a power struggle among the leading daimyō ensued. Tokugawa Ieyasu (1542–1616), who had retained a large holding in the Kantō region with his base in Edo, succeeded in defeating his rivals, crushing the supporters of the Toyotomi forces, and establishing Tokugawa hegemony in 1600 that lasted until 1867. Ieyasu was as ambitious as the other daimyō and could be just as ruthless. When he was ordered by Nobunaga to do so he executed his wife and compelled his son to commit *harakiri*. He claimed descent from the Minamoto clan and was appointed shōgun in 1603. He remained in Edo which became the center of government. Like previous shōguns he allowed the imperial court to survive in Kyoto but the Emperor had no political authority although he remained the chief of the imperial Shinto cult.

Two-and-a-half centuries of Tokugawa rule molded the Japanese mode of thought, value system, social behavior, and institutions much more significantly than previous forces that had forged the Japanese way of life. Comprehension of Tokugawa society is essential to the understanding of modern Japan.

To ensure the security of his regime Ieyasu instituted a number of measures. The daimyō were allotted landholdings as their fiefs but the Tokugawa family retained the largest holdings as their demesne. The yield of the entire country was estimated to be thirty million koku at that time. The Tokugawa holdings came to about seven million. The Bakufu's holdings were located in the Kantō region and other strategic areas. Ieyasu granted fiefs from his demesne to the liege vassals and direct retainers. The remaining twenty-two to twenty-three million koku were held by the daimyō. The number of daimyō varied during the Tokugawa era but it averaged about 270. The minimum holding for a daimyō was ten thousand koku. The vast majority held less than one hundred thousand koku but a few held as much as three hundred thousand koku or more. The largest held 1.02 million koku. The imperial court initially was granted twenty thousand koku.

There were three categories of daimyō: relatives of the Tokugawa family, including three collateral houses established by Ieyasu's sons; the daimyō affiliated through lineage to the Tokugawa family; and those who submitted to the Tokugawa clan after its victory, the "outside" lords. The hereditary lords were placed in strategic areas while the outside lords were located in outlying regions or were placed between hereditary lords. The daimyō were prevented from establishing marital ties or repairing castles without the Bakufu's approval. They were required to spend every other year in Edo, and their family members had to remain in Edo.

The daimyō were allowed to govern their own domain (*han*) freely but the Bakufu retained control over foreign relations, coinage, and inter-han transportation. Each daimyō had his castle town as his headquarter, and exercised power over his vassals and the people living in his domain, primarily peasants. This division of the country into distinctive daimyō domains molded Japanese regional identity and fostered a sense of alienation toward other areas.

In order to ensure political and social stability the Tokugawa Bakufu set out to fix a rigid class system. Before the era of the contending warlords there was no strict distinction between samurai and peasants. In time of peace samurai engaged in farming and when called upon went to fight. Peasants were able to join warrior groups. During the period of the "Warring States" the samurai began to devote more time to fighting and settled where their lord established his headquarters. Then Hideyoshi set out to bind the peasants to the soil. The samurai and peasant classes were beginning to become distinctive groups. The Tokugawa Bakufu formalized the class divisions and the status of samurai and peasants were fixed by birth. The Tokugawa rulers adopted the Chinese Confucian class divisions of scholars, peasants, artisans, and merchants but substituted the samurai for the scholars. The artisans and merchants were essentially a single class of "townspeople."

The samurai were the privileged, ruling class. They were paid fixed rice stipends rather than being granted landholdings. They were in effect political servitors who lived in castle towns, their lords' power bases. There was a big difference in the rice stipends that the upper and lower class samurai received, and intermarriage between the two groups was banned. The samurai were expected to be well-versed in Confucian learning and to conduct themselves in accordance with the code of the warriors which emphasized selfless service to the master. As a class above the common people the samurai were allowed to cut down with impunity any peasant or townsman who behaved insolently toward them. By the end of the Tokugawa era there were about 1.8 million members of the samurai class, thirty percent were lower-class samurai.

PEASANTS

The population at the outset of the Tokugawa years has been estimated at about twenty million. At the end of the Tokugawa era it was about thirty million. In the early eighteenth century the population of the commoners was about twenty-six million, eighty percent of these were peasants. The land belonged to the shōgun and daimyō. The peasants who worked the land were serfs fixed on the land. The acreage that they farmed varied but it averaged about one *chō* (about 2.45 acres). The levies imposed on them varied but generally they were taxed from forty to fifty percent of the crop. Some daimyō collected as much seventy percent of the yield. The general policy was to tax them as much as possible. One official asserted "Sesame seed and peasants are much alike. The more you squeeze them, the more you can extract from them."[1] Other miscellaneous taxes were imposed and the peasants were also expected to perform corvée for road maintenance and other public projects. The ruling class regulated the peasants' life stringently at the edge of the sword. They were, of course, forbidden to wear swords, a privilege reserved for the samurai, and they could not use family names. Frugality, diligence, self-denial, and submissiveness were virtues to be cultivated. They were instructed on what to raise, their work schedule, what to eat and wear, what leisure activities were permissible. Wives who wasted time flower-viewing and tea-drinking were to be divorced.

Of course very few had opportunities for learning and most remained illiterate. The ruling class believed that the less the peasants knew the better it was for them. A common saying among the ruling class was: "A good peasant is one who does not know the price of grain."

Most peasants led an impoverished, hand-to-mouth existence but some were better off and they served as village leaders. They helped the lord's officials collect taxes and kept records for them. Each village had five-man groups or neighborhood associations which were collectively responsible for payment of taxes and for any criminal acts committed by the members. The association also served as a mutual aid society to assist members in time of need and sickness.

TOWNSPEOPLE

It is estimated that the population of the townspeople in the eighteenth century numbered between three and four million. In theory the artisans and merchants were placed beneath the peasants in the Tokugawa social hierarchy, not only because of the Confucian influence but because the peasants were the backbone of the Tokugawa economy. The Tokugawa rulers also adopted the Confucian disdain of money-making. One Tokugawa Confucian scholar observed that enlightened kings of antiquity, "valued agriculture and curtailed industry and commerce. They respected the five grains and held money in disdain." Another Confucian remarked: "Merchants gain wealth without laboring, encourage luxurious living and undermine the people's minds."[7] This was the philosophical rationale but in fact the Bakufu and daimyō began to foster domestic commerce.

The daimyō sought to encourage the production of goods that could be marketed to other domains. Cities like Osaka became important commercial centers. Merchants, artisans, and craftsmen settled in castle towns of the daimyō, and pursued economic ends and developed a social and cultural life different from that of the peasants and the samurai. Money-making became their life goal. A writer who emerged in this environment, Ihara Saikaku (1642–93) remarked: "Money is the townsman's pedigree ... if he lacks money he is worse off than a monkey-showman."[3]

The growth of castle towns where the daimyō's samurai retainers as well as merchants and artisans congregated numbered about 130 cities and towns spread throughout the country. Between thirty and forty of these had populations of over ten thousand. The major centers had well over one hundred thousand residents. Edo's population in the early eighteenth century is estimated to have been between eight hundred thousand and one million. A large percentage of the Edo population consisted of samurai retainers of the Bakufu and daimyō. Osaka's population was about four hundred thousand and that of Kyoto 350,000. Many wealthy merchant houses emerged, such as the Mitsui and Kōnoike families whose business ventures continued into the post-Tokugawa era. The merchants and craftsmen were organized in guilds. Among the artisans and craftsmen a feudalistic relationship prevailed between the master and the workers.

OTHER CLASSES: OUTCASTES

There were groups of people who were treated as outcastes. The Tokugawa rulers classified the common people into "good people" and "base people." The majority of the commoners belonged to the former category but about 380,000 fell into the latter group. There were two categories of the "base people:" the "non-humans" (*hinin*) and the "extremely unclean" (*eta*). (Today they are identified as *burakumin* or hamlet people.) Before the Tokugawa era the two groups were not sharply differentiated but distinctions came to be made on the basis of occupational and social functions. Itinerant entertainers, beggars, prostitutes, and social offenders were classified as *hinin*. In some instances they could leave the status of "base people" and become "good people."

The "unclean" people were classified as outcastes by birth. The origin of this class is unclear but certain occupations were regarded as defiling such as slaughtering animals, butchering, and tanning. A person could be discriminated against because of ancestral racial or social differences, and certain diseases or abnormalities. By the Tokugawa period beside tanning and butchering and working with leather goods, other occupations unrelated to unclean work, such as making bamboo goods, candle wicks, baskets, and straw sandals, came to be regarded as work done only by the "unclean."

They were harshly discriminated against, not only in terms of occupation but living areas, attire (they could not wear wooden clogs or cotton clothing), social conduct (like the peasants who had to kneel when they encountered the samurai, the "base people" had to "bow and scrape" before the "good people"), and they were forbidden to intermarry with members of other classes. A contemporary burakumin said of his Tokugawa ancestors: "They were not allowed to wear any footwear ... They could use only straw ropes as belts, and only straws to tie their hair. They were forbidden to leave their hamlet from sunset to sunrise ... They were not allowed to associate with other people. When it was necessary to see others they had to get on their hands and knees before they could speak."[4] They were also forbidden to enter the grounds of non-outcaste shrines and temples.

This kind of discrimination in occupation, place of residence, marriages, and social relations continued into the post-Tokugawa era and virtually to the present. The Bakufu ignored them in official population surveys, and did not include their communities in official maps. In the late Tokugawa era when an *eta* was killed trying to enter a shrine an Edo magistrate held that, "the life of the *eta* is worth about one-seventh the life of a townsman. Unless seven *eta* have been killed, we cannot punish a single townsman ."[5]

WOMEN IN TOKUGAWA SOCIETY

The practice of relegating women below men which had commenced with the rise of the samurai class was formally institutionalized in the Tokugawa period. Even earlier, samurai women were treated like semi-slaves by their husbands. A Portuguese trader noted in the mid-sixteenth century: "her husband may kill her for being [lazy or bad]. For this reason women are much concerned about their husband's honour and are most diligent in their household duties."[6]

The Tokugawa rulers legalized the patriarchal family system, placing absolute authority over all family members in the hands of the male family head. Primogeniture was mandatory for the samurai class, and women lost the property rights they had held in earlier years. The husband could behave as promiscuously as he pleased but if the wife gave the slightest indication of infidelity the husband could execute her. Ieyasu's "Testament" stated that if the wife engaged in illicit intercourse the husband had the right to kill her and the man. In one of his plays the playwright Chikamatsu (1653–1724) has the samurai mother tell her daughter: "When you are alone with any other man – beside your husband – you may not so much as to lift your head and look at him."[7] Samurai women were expected to kill themselves if their chastity was threatened.

Marriages were arranged by parents, and daughters had no voice in the matter. A husband could divorce his wife at will while a wife could not. She had to endure hardships and abuses patiently and serve her husband and in-laws. Confucian scholar Kaibara Ekken (1630–1714) stated in his *Great Learning for Women*: "From her earliest youth, a girl should observe the line of demarcation separating women from men ... A woman should look upon her husband as if he were Heaven itself."[8]

Although the samurai ideal did filter down to the common people, especially the peasantry, the attitude that developed among the townspeople was less male chauvinist. One populist thinker asserted that in indigenous Japanese thought, "men and women are alike. There is no distinction of high and low, honorable and base." (The idea of regarding women as inferior to men was the misguided concept adopted from China.) "For the husband to love his wife, and the wife to be affectionate toward her husband and maintain a gentle and friendly relationship is the proper way." He believed that the cardinal human relationship was not the Confucian ideal of father and son but was that of husband and wife for "the way of humanity originated with husband and wife."[9] Primogeniture was not strictly adhered to among the townspeople. A younger son might be chosen to take over the family business, and family property could be divided among sons and daughters. However, the ruling class enforced primogeniture and the denial of property rights for women among the peasantry.

A practice that existed earlier but flourished in the Tokugawa period and continued into the modern era was the establishment of public brothels whose inmates were mostly girls from poor peasant families who were sold into prostitution by their impoverished parents. As Tokugawa society settled into years of peace and town life began to flourish, sections of the cities came to be designated as brothel districts. The most renowned of these districts was the

Yoshiwara district of Edo which was officially sanctioned by the Bakufu. Four further brothel districts were established at the main entry points to the capital as a recreational quarter for the daimyō retinues that travelled periodically to the capital. In addition public brothel districts were established nationally in twenty-five key cities. The brothel masters were given monopolistic rights in these districts but numerous "tea houses," not officially sanctioned, came into being throughout the land. The brothel masters treated the inmates inhumanely as virtual slaves but the authorities did nothing to protect them. Those who fled the houses and went to the magistrates for assistance found themselves sent back to the brothels.[10]

POLITICAL DEVELOPMENTS

The political order that was established by Ieyasu and his successors remained secure until the mid-nineteenth century when the established order was challenged by the advent of the Western powers. There was an orderly succession of shōgun. Some were more active than others but by and large administrative affairs were conducted under the direction of the councillors, in particular the great councillor. The primary objective of the Bakufu was to ensure political order and stability, so careful supervision of all segments of the society was maintained. Checkpoints were established at strategic locations, and people travelling from one area to another had to be inspected by the officials. The other concern was financial. The shōgun could not tax the daimyō. The Bakufu's source of revenue was income from their demesne. It usually collected forty percent of the harvest. It could levy special fees for public works, and for special projects. The daimyō were asked to contribute to these projects or undertake them for the Bakufu.

The area where the Bakufu had to implement new measures and enforce stringent controls was in foreign relations. Ieyasu and his successors adopted anti-Christian measures and this anti-Christian policy resulted in gradual restrictions being imposed in foreign contacts. In 1616 the Bakufu prohibited all Western merchants from entering Japanese ports other than Nagasaki and Hirado in Kyushu. Foreigners were allowed to reside only in Edo, Kyoto, and Sakai. In 1624 the Spanish were denied the right to trade with Japan. The British voluntarily ended their effort to develop trade with Japan. In 1636 the Bakufu prohibited all Japanese from leaving the country. Those who had gone abroad, to places such as the Philippines and Thailand, were not allowed to return home. Merchant ships from only three countries were allowed to enter Japanese ports; the Koreans at Iki Island; the Chinese and the Dutch at an island off Nagasaki. The Dutch were allowed to reside only on that island and could not travel to other parts of Japan without official permission. In order to exclude Christian concepts, Western books were banned until 1720 when non-religious books were allowed to enter. Thus the country was virtually secluded from the outside world, in particular from the West, at a time when significant developments, politically, intellectually, and scientifically, were taking place there.

By virtually sealing off the country from the external world the Tokugawa shogunate was able to preserve its political control by enforcing strict control over internal political forces. It did not encounter serious internal opposition until the early nineteenth century when pressure from the Western nations began to mount. Thus Japan constituted "a world state" for, according to Arnold Toynbee, "The smallest human community constitutes the whole world for the people inside it if it is insulated from all other human communities."[11]

INTELLECTUAL AND CULTURAL DEVELOPMENTS

In the Tokugawa period Confucianism virtually became the orthodox philosophy of Japan. Confucian moralism which emphasizes a social hierarchy of the superior and inferior persons based, in theory, on moral character, was embraced by the Tokugawa rulers. The samurai were the equivalent of the Confucian scholar-officials. Thus the Bakufu encouraged the samurai to be educated in the Confucian classics, and the vast majority of scholars in this period were Confucian scholars. The Sung or Neo-Confucian concepts as explicated by Chu Hsi (1130–1200) won the official imprimature by the latter part of the seventeenth century. Neo-Confucianism held that a universal principle, *li*, emanates from the Supreme Ultimate (*t'ai chi*). The Way of Heaven embodies li and t'ai chi. The ruler performs his duties in accordance with the Way of Heaven so he is, in effect, an agent of Heaven. Hence it is imperative for the people to obey the ruler. Japanese Chu Hsi scholars emphasized the concept of *taigi meibun*, grand justice, and one's name and place, that is the principle of justice defines one's place and duty in society. This doctrine was especially convenient for the shōgun and daimyō who demanded obedience and service of those below in the name of justice. It upheld the moral injunction that a person should "know his proper place."

Another school of Confucianism, the Wang Yang-Ming school was also embraced by a number of Tokugawa Confucian scholars. Wang Yang-Ming (1472–1528) of Ming China held that *li* is a product of the mind, not an objective universal principle. Truth which everyone is capable of grasping subjectively must be acted upon. This activist concept gained a strong following among the samurai and at the end of the Tokugawa era the samurai who saw truth in the sanctity of the Emperor acted upon their beliefs. Another group of Confucian scholars contended that rather than embracing the interpretations of later Confucian scholars people should go directly to the texts of Confucius and ancient Confucian philosophers. Among the scholars of this school of Ancient Learning was Ogyū Sorai (1666–1728). He rejected the Neo-Confucian thesis that the abstract theory of *li* governs all things and held that all rules, regulations and institutions are man-made. His thinking paved the way for later thinkers who began to contend that the existing order was created by man and hence can be changed.

The Confucian scholars who believed it to be their duty to instruct the common people on moral principles produced moral tracts for popular consumption. Among the most prominent of these was Kaibara Ekken who wrote readily comprehensible moral instructions. In his *Precepts for Children* he taught: "All men living in their parents' home should expend themselves in filial service to their father and mother; and in serving their lord should maintain single-minded loyalty to him." He also taught them to be kind toward others and not to abuse them. He admonished them not to kill any living thing wantonly, be it bird, beast, fish or insect. In a way he was a naturalist. He said that humans were products of nature and people should serve nature as repayment for the great debt they owed it.[12] But he was a firm believer in the hierarchical order as revealed in his *Great Learning for Women*. Many Tokugawa Confucian scholars sought to syncretize Confucianism and Shinto. This tendency persisted in the Tokugawa period but a Shintoistic nationalistic thinking that turned away from Confucianism also emerged. This was the school of National Learning.

NATIONAL LEARNING

As noted earlier, during the Heian era there was a movement to assert Japanese culture in reaction to the heavy reliance on Chinese culture. But because of the Tokugawa officials' emphasis on Confucianism the samurai class concentrated on Confucian learning. But some scholars began to react against this tendency and they turned increasingly to the study of indigenous Japanese history and culture. Out of this emerged the intellectual school of National Learning.

An early proponent of the study of Japanese history was Tokugawa Mitsukuni (1628–1700) of Mito han, one of the collateral houses of the Tokugawa clan. Mitsukuni initiated the compilation of the *Great History of Japan*. He and his disciples embraced the Neo-Confucian concept of *taigi-meibun* (great justice and proper place). They asserted that the Chinese owed supreme loyalty to the king, while in Japan the people owed supreme loyalty to the Emperor. Initially they saw no conflict in being loyal to the shōgun also because he was appointed to that post by the Emperor and hence was the Emperor's loyal minister. Eventually, however, loyalty to the Emperor came to be stressed above loyalty to the shōgun.

The school of learning that embraced a strong nationalistic and pro-imperial mode of thinking emerged in the latter part of the seventeenth century as some scholars of Japanese literature began to emphasize the importance of studying the *Man'yōshū*, the *Kojiki* and the *Nihongi*, not only for philological reasons but to comprehend the indigenous Japanese Way. One of these scholars, Kamo-no-Mabuchi (1697–1769) began to condemn Confucianism and the "artificial" Chinese way, saying it had corrupted the simple, natural way that had prevailed in Japan before its advent. This emphasis on the "natural" Japanese way and rejection of the

Chinese influence was embraced by Motoori Norinaga (1730–1801) who became the most influential philosopher of National Learning. His influence extended well into the twentieth century.

Starting with the study of the *Man'yōshū* Norinaga focused primarily on the *Kojiki* which, he believed, embodied the Way of the gods and was factual history. He rejected the "artificial" Chinese philosophy and learning that had misguided Japanese thought and culture. Japan was founded by the Sun Goddess (Amaterasu) who was the sun itself. The imperial dynasty descended from the Sun Goddess and was therefore a sacred institution. This theory concerning the imperial dynasty was made the official credo of Japan after the restoration of imperial rule in 1868, and was used to indoctrinate Japanese students until the end of the Second World War. However, Norinaga did not reject the Bakufu because the Bakufu's authority was derived from the imperial court. He rejected the notion of analyzing the Way of the gods by recourse to reason because "the acts of the gods cannot be fathomed by ordinary human reasoning." Thus he advocated acceptance of "mysterious things." The Way cannot be comprehended by learning. It is the inborn spirit of man; it is embedded in everyone's heart. So he rejected the Confucian emphasis on studying the sayings of the ancient sages to comprehend the Way. He held that "learning should be learning the truth instead of studying teachings."[13]

The other Japanese characteristic that Norinaga believed in was man's natural feelings. He rejected Confucianism which seeks to curb natural sentiments with artificial concepts of decorum and propriety. He pointed out that ancient Japanese poets expressed natural human feelings freely, and he cited poems from the *Man'yōshū* to make his point. For example, a warrior leaving his family cries, "having left my dear ones far behind / My mind knew no rest / While the pain of longing wrung my heart."[14] And, as noted earlier, expression of love for one's wife was freely expressed unlike the constraint against manifesting such sentiments that became the proper mode for the "manly male." He also perceived that Japanese sensitivity reflected a sense of sadness or pathos of life (*mono no aware*).

ANTI-ESTABLISHMENT THINKING

As learning was encouraged by the ruling authorities numerous schools of thought began to emerge. Since the Bakufu had embraced Chu Hsi philosophy as its official ideology, as diverse thinking began to rise it issued an edict in 1790 banning heterodox studies. The Bakufu could not, however, eradicate unacceptable schools of thought.

One school of thought that emerged was influenced by Western learning, namely Dutch learning. As the ban against Western books was lifted (except for Christian books) in 1720 a number of scholars began studying Western thought. They compiled a Japanese-Dutch dictionary and pursued Western learning, especially scientific topics. The Bakufu approved of and supported scientific studies. Western medicine in particular drew the interest of some scholars and they translated a Dutch medical text in 1774. Dutch studies were facilitated by a young German doctor, Philipp Franz von Siebold, serving in the Dutch factory in Nagasaki. Some scholars pursuing Dutch learning began to disagree with the Bakufu's policy of keeping foreign vessels away from Japanese ports and favored opening up the country.

One thinker, Honda Toshiaki (1744–1821) believed that the Bakufu should pursue a policy of bolstering the Japanese economy like the Western nations, and foster foreign trade and even engage in colonialism. The defeat of China in the Opium War in particular concerned some thinkers and led them to favor the adoption of Western military apparatuses. In effect, they were precursors of Meiji advocates of the policy of *fukoku kyōhei* (rich nation, strong military).

The other school of thought that began to sharpen the criticism of the Bakufu was that of National Learning. It began to emphasize respect for the imperial family but initially did not link this to anti-Bakufu sentiments. Followers adhered to the concept of "revering the Emperor and respecting the Bakufu." As long as pro-imperial advocates adhered to this line of thought the Bakufu tolerated them but those who manifested anti-Bakufu sentiments were exiled or even executed. As a result many who engaged in political commentaries were careful not to overstep the bounds, but faced with the possible threat from the West they began to express nationalistic sentiments which entailed emphasizing the unique Japanese national polity (*kokutai*) based on the imperial dynasty.

One of the key spokesmen for this mode of thought was Aizawa Seishisai (1782–1863), a member of the Mito-han. He became an early advocate of the policy of "revering the Emperor and repelling the barbarians" (*sonnō jōi*). He did not see any conflict between serving the Bakufu while being loyal to the Emperor because the Bakufu was also serving the Emperor. But he emphasized the importance of the imperial family members as descendants of the Sun Goddess; the imperial dynasty had survived inviolate through the ages. In face of the threat from the West he propounded a highly xenophobic viewpoint. "Today the alien barbarians of the West ... are dashing about across the sea, trampling other countries underfoot ... Our Divine Land is situated at the top of the earth...[America] occupies the hindmost region of the earth; thus its people are stupid and simple, and are incapable of doing things."[15] This kind of arrogant, chauvinistic writing came to underpin the ultra-nationalist thinking of post-Tokugawa Japan.

An influential proponent of National Learning, but not a xenophobe like Seishisai, was Hirata Atsutane (1776–1843). He was an ardent believer in Shinto and renounced Confucian and Buddhist influence on Japan. Like other proponents of Shinto nationalism he contended that Japan was founded by the gods and the Japanese people, being descendants of the gods, were superior to other people, and he advocated cultivating the Yamato [Japanese] spirit. However, he did not advocate "repelling the barbarians" and favored adopting Western science and technology.

THE LIFE OF THE COMMONERS

The peasants led a life of hard work and minimal material comfort. Their life was carefully regulated and the moral philosophy that governed it was the one imposed on them from the Confucian-oriented ruling class. So diligence, frugality, obedience, and self-denial became virtues embedded in peasant thinking. But when famine struck and starvation confronted them, they were reduced to painful measures such as infanticide, abortion or selling their daughters to the brothels. One writer, Satō Nobuhiro (1767–1850), who traveled about the countryside observed that infanticide was prevalent but also, "children are killed before their birth ... In [the northern provinces] the number of children killed annually exceeds sixty or seventy thousand."[16] In extreme cases of famine and starvation they were reduced to cannibalism. One scholar who traveled among the northern villages during the famine of 1785 encountered mounds of bleached bones. A peasant told him: "These are the bones of people who starved to death ... We used to catch horses roaming about ... cut into their flesh, cook the bloody meat and eat it ... When we ran out of animals we stabbed and killed our children, brothers and others on death's door... and ate their flesh."[17]

In the Tokugawa era there were thirty-five famines caused by bad weather and locusts. Many of the famines resulted in mass starvations. In the famine of 1732 it was estimated that 969,900 people starved to death. In the major famine of 1783–87, according to one contemporary, over two million people died in one province. This undoubtedly was an overestimation because of the practice of using units of ten thousand to indicate the magnitude of any development, but it is believed that several hundred thousand people perished in this famine.

A critic of the existing order and a champion of the peasantry emerged in the person of Andō Shōeki (1703–62). His views were virtually unknown until the twentieth century when his multi-volumed writings were discovered. He believed that the agrarian population constituted the foundation of the society and were the only ones engaged in "honest living by direct cultivation." He condemned those who consumed without doing any work, the chief offenders, he asserted, were the samurai. The Confucian scholars failed to criticize this situation because they themselves were "greedy consumers who do not cultivate the soil." Hence, Shōeki rejected the teachings of the ancient sages who propounded a hierarchical order of things, contrary to the world of nature. Espousing an egalitarian philosophy he asserted that before learning and civilization arose people were free, happy, equal, and moral. He renounced those who did nothing but talk without producing "a single grain of rice." In the true state of nature there will be no ruler, no privileged classes. Everyone will engage in "direct cultivation" and complete freedom and equality will prevail.[18]

While Shōeki condemned the existing order that exploited the peasantry, Ninomiya Sontoku (1787–1856) emphasized the virtue of selflessness, hard work, and thrift as a means to repay one's debt to the ancestors and society. Quite naturally the vested interests idealized him as the "peasant sage of Japan," and a model for the peasants to emulate. School children were taught that he was a diligent peasant youngster who read a book while transporting a heavy load on his back.

THE LIFE OF THE TOWNSPEOPLE

The population of the townspeople is believed to have numbered between three and four million in the mid-eighteenth century. They were placed at the bottom of the official Tokugawa hierarchy as, in line with Confucian values, the ruling class held money-making in low regard. But the townspeople who gathered in Edo and the castle towns strove diligently to make money. As noted above, Ihara Saikaku emphasized the importance of money-making for the townspeople. The kabuki playwright Chikamatsu has a merchant remark in one of his plays, "A samurai seeks a fair name in disregard of profit, a merchant, with no thought to his reputation, gathers profit and amasses a fortune. This is the proper way for each."[19] An early member of the Mitsui merchant house Mitsui Takafusa (1684–1748) admonished the townspeople that for them, "there is nothing that they can rely upon but the profits that accrue from gold and silver ... Never waste your attention on matters which have nothing to do with your work."[20] Ishida Baigan (1685–1744), who founded a school of philosophy called *Shingaku* (Teachings of the Heart) because he stressed the importance of grasping the heart of any book, asserted that for merchants money-making was in line with the Principle of Heaven.

Many townspeople embraced the philosophy of money-making and some emerged as wealthy merchants. Wholesale merchants, in particular, did well purveying to the major cities rice and other products, encouraged by regional daimyōs who wished to increase their own financial resources. Ordinary townspeople who engaged in trade, and arts and crafts also were economically better off than the impoverished peasants in the countryside.

TOKUGAWA CULTURE

The most significant cultural development in the Tokugawa period was the culture of the townspeople. The creative energy of the townspeople was manifested in all areas – prose fiction, haiku poetry, kabuki theatre, woodblock printing, and ceramics. The high point of the Tokugawa town culture was reached toward the end of the seventeenth and early eighteenth centuries, known as the *Genroku* era. The era represents the exuberant, colorful, ostentatious lifestyle of the materially well-off merchant class, especially in the major commercial centers such as Osaka and Edo. A German doctor visiting Osaka in the late seventeenth century said, "Even what tends to promote luxury, and to gratify all sensual pleasures, may be had at as easy a rate here as anywhere."[21] The world of this hedonistic lifestyle came to be known as *Ukiyo* (floating world).

The master of prose fiction who depicted the floating world was Ihara Saikaku of Osaka. He started out as a haiku poet, composing 23,500 haiku in twenty-four hours. He wrote dozens of humorous, erotic novels starting with *The Man Who Spent His Life in Love*. The hero started his amorous life at age eight and by sixty he had seduced 3,742 women. Unsatiated at age sixty he sails off in search of the fabulous Island of Women. Popular stories, entertaining as well as morally uplifting ones, continued to be written during the Tokugawa period, indicating the fairly broad level of literacy among the townspeople.

Haiku – a seventeen syllable poem – also emerged as a popular form of poetry among the townspeople. Its composition and appreciation were not limited to the townspeople. The greatest haiku poet, Matsuo Bashō (1644–94), a member of the samurai class, wandered around the countryside as a Buddhist monk. The brevity of haiku is explained by the Zen scholar Suzuki Daisetsu: "At the supreme moment of life and death ... feelings refuse to be conceptually dealt with ... haiku is not a product of intellection. Hence its brevity and significance."[22] For the haiku to be effective, Donald Keene explains that there should be two electric poles between which the spark leaps. For example, "The ancient pond. A frog leaps in. The Sound of the water."[23]

The other form of entertainment that flourished among the townspeople was the puppet and kabuki theatre. A leading authority on kabuki writes: "Kabuki fuses into a single form the arts of music, dance, acting, literature, as well as graphic and plastic arts."[24] The playwright who contributed most to the popularity of kabuki was Chikamatsu who produced 160 plays. The themes of his play often dealt with the conflict between love and duty, or human feelings (*ninjō*) and social and moral obligations (*giri*).

The art form that flourished among the townspeople was woodblock printing (*ukiyo-e*, paintings of the floating world). A host of artists whose works are appreciated worldwide today such as Moronobu (1618–94), Harunobu (1725–70), Utamaro (1753–1806), Sharaku (d. 1801), Hokusai (1760–1849) and Hiroshige (1797–1858) produced prints or illustrations for novels. Moronobu did some illustration for Saikaku; Harunobu is known for his delicate, coquettish female figures; Utamaro for his voluptuous women; Sharaku for the exaggerated poses of kabuki actors; Hokusai for his powerful landscape prints, and Hiroshige for his series of prints, *Fifty-three Stages of the Tokaido Highway*. Hiroshige was interested in the relationship between light and natural phenomena. "No one had revealed to us so freshly the beauty of the rain" writes an art historian.[25] Hokusai's dedication to his art is revealed in his remark, "Since the age of six I have had the habit of drawing forms of objects ... my pictorial works before the seventieth year none is of much value ... perhaps at eighty my art may improve greatly; at ninety it may reach real depth ... At one hundred and ten every dot and stroke may be as if living."[26] He signed his essay, "The old man crazy about drawing." The Japanese woodblock artists, particularly Hokusai and Hiroshige influenced the nineteenth-century French impressionists such as van Gogh.

Traditional decorative arts – screen paintings and paintings on lacquer and pottery also flourished in this period. Among the prominent artists in this medium were Ogata Kōrin (1658–1716) and Maruyama Ōkyo (1733–95) whose paintings on folding screens have remained national treasures.

EDUCATION

Literacy was widespread among the townspeople for it was necessary to conduct business. Children of merchants and artisans were taught reading and writing, and the use of the abacus for calculation. Learning among peasant children was limited but the well-off villagers sent their children to temple schools (*terakoya*) where they were taught by Buddhist and Shinto priests. Samurai children were taught by private tutors or attended han academies. It is believed that literacy among samurai men was almost a hundred percent. Overall it is estimated that by the end of the Tokugawa era forty percent of all boys and ten percent of girls were receiving some degree of education.

POLITICAL AND ECONOMIC PROBLEMS

The stability of Bakufu's reign was shaken from the latter half of the eighteenth century, as it began to encounter increasing difficulties, especially in the economic sphere. Financial difficulties mounted as expenditure outstripped revenue. The difficulties were compounded with the famines of the 1780s. This caused food shortages and high prices. The officials sought to cope with the problem by reducing expenditure, controlling prices, cancelling the debts of their retainers, and fostering frugality by issuing sumptuary laws, but the measures failed to resolve the difficulties. The Bakufu then debased the coinage, raised imposts and also pressured the rich merchants to donate money, but the difficulties continued. The daimyō and peasants also faced growing economic difficulties.

The daimyō's and samurai's economic underpinning remained, in theory, the agrarian economy. The castle towns and the major political and commercial centers like Osaka and Edo saw the emergence of a large population of townspeople who engaged in commerce and the production of numerous consumer goods. Consumption increased the financial needs of the daimyō and samurai beyond the income derived from the peasant-based economy. In order to meet their rising financial needs the daimyō encouraged the production of cash crops and industrial goods that could be sold to other domains. Thus certain areas came to be centers of tea, high quality rice, sake, pottery, textiles, handicraft goods, seafood, and so on. The merchants employed by the daimyō to serve as dealers, brokers, and shippers became wealthy members of the domain.

The financial problems of many daimyō were not resolved, however. Even though they were not taxed by the Bakufu they were asked to undertake public-work projects that were costly. The annual travels back and forth from their home base to Edo, mandated by the Bakufu, entailed considerable expenses because they traveled with a large retinue of retainers, maintaining a proper show of ostentatious decorum. Maintaining two suitable residences in the home domain and Edo was costly. The availability of luxury goods resulted in conspicuous consumption to keep up with their fellow daimyō. In addition the natural calamities and famines that occurred from time to time put heavy strains on the daimyō.

The samurai also began to experience economic difficulties. The life of austerity and frugality that was the old samurai ideal was not adhered to in the years of Tokugawa peace. The samurai's income was fixed in terms of rice stipends but their expenses grew as they adopted a less austere lifestyle. They tended to live in fine houses and wear quality clothes. Many pursued hedonistic lives attending kabuki performances or frequenting expensive brothels and patronizing "geishas."

The daimyō and the samurai began to fall in debt to the merchant houses from whom they purchased goods or borrowed money. In order to deal with their difficulties the daimyō began to increase the imposts on the peasants. Some of the daimyō began to withhold part of the retainers' rice stipends from time to time or ask them to "loan" a certain percentage of their stipends. Some asked their retainers to take stipend reductions as much as fifty percent. This of course aggravated the plight of the samurai. The other measure the Bakufu and daimyō resorted to was cancellation of debts they owed the rich merchant houses. By the early eighteenth century some of the merchant houses were owed huge sums by the daimyō. One house of legendary wealth had its resources confiscated by the Bakufu because of the huge debt the daimyō owed it. In 1789 the Bakufu cancelled the debts of ninety-six merchants houses.

Such measures made the merchants wary of extending credit to the daimyō and samurai. This resulted in the daimyō and samurai, in need of financial assistance, ceasing to behave haughtily toward them and in fact to pander to the rich merchants, granting them rights reserved for the samurai such as bearing swords. A role reversal seemed to have transpired. One observer noted both large and small daimyō feared "the sight of money-lenders as if they were devils. Forgetting that they are warriors they kow-tow to the townsmen." The samurai behaved more politely to the merchants. "Nowadays when a samurai writes a letter to a merchant who possesses some wealth, he addresses the latter ... like an exalted personage."[27]

The economic pressure confronting the ruling class affected the peasants. The money economy in the villages led to higher living costs for the peasants. Some daimyō began to make stringent demands on the farming population as their economic situation became acute. What affected the peasants most adversely was the increase in taxation that resulted from the growing needs of the ruling class. The Bakufu sought to retain a fixed tax rate of forty percent but some daimyō, especially in the poorer regions sought to extract as much as possible from the peasantry. Some extracted as much as seventy percent of the yield. In some cases the peasants were compelled to pay taxes several years in advance.

Ironically rice production had increased during the Tokugawa years. The area under cultivation had been enlarged by reclamation of wasteland, and production per unit of land increased as a result of better plant varieties, more use of fertilizers, and an improved mode of farming. In 1598 the area under cultivation in Japan was 1.5 million *chō* (1 *chō* equals 2.45 acres) while by the mid-eighteenth century it had increased to 2.97 million *chō*. Farm production in 1598 was estimated at 18.5 million *koku* and by 1834 it had risen to 30.43 million. The population did not increase significantly during the Tokugawa years. At the outset the overall population was about twenty million and by the end of the Tokugawa era it was about thirty million. The commoner population, over eighty percent peasantry, had increased to twenty-six million or so by the eighteenth century and remained more or less the same until the end of the era. But in time of severe famine the population dropped significantly, for example, following the famine of the 1780s the population dropped by over one million.

But overall it is estimated that there was increase in the commoner population of about three percent from 1721 to 1846. So with a fairly stable population and increased productivity even if taxation increased in some domains overall it may not have resulted in a severe drain on the peasantry's resources. But it was the wealthier villagers who benefited most from the increased productivity. They had gained possession of the reclaimed land so their landholdings were larger than the land farmed by the average peasant.

The fact that there was an increasing gap between the wealthier villagers and poorer ones is seen in the growing number of complaints directed against the wealthy village leaders. Although the ruling class sought to indoctrinate the peasantry about knowing their place and being obedient and submissive, peasant disturbances and uprisings broke out from time to time. Between 1590 and 1867 there were 2,809 peasant disturbances. In the later Tokugawa years these uprisings began to occur with greater frequency, indicating the growing pressure from the ruling class, the penetration of the commercial economy in the villages that increased the cost of living as well as enhanced the villagers' aspirations. The riots broke out most frequently after major famines like those of 1732–33, 1783–87, and 1833–36.

What was regarded as peasant "disturbances" included submission of petitions, flight from the villages, demonstrations and violent protests. The violent acts of protest were suppressed most harshly by the ruling class. The leaders were tortured and beheaded. Some were buried alive. Many of the violent actions involved attacks on the houses and warehouses of rich farmers, merchants, and moneylenders. The most common reason for the protests was taxation. Others included protest against the burden of the corvée, abusive officials and administrative measures, demand for aid and assistance in times of natural disasters and famine. The number of participants in these protests increased during the later Tokugawa years. For example, in 1754 168,000 peasants rioted in protest against excessive taxation in a province in Kyushu. In 1764 two hundred thousand peasants rose in protest against horse station corvée in the Kantō region. In most uprisings the peasants did not gain concessions or redress. The peasants' object was not political, rather the protest movements indicate the general malaise that was beginning to undermine Bakufu rule.

The urban population was much smaller than the agrarian population so there were not as many urban disturbances but they did occur in the latter part of the Tokugawa years, particularly in time of famine which resulted in rice shortages and high prices. The biggest disturbance occurred in 1837 in Osaka in protest against the officials' refusal to aid the city poor. One-fifth of the city was set on fire.

THE END OF SECLUSION

The Bakufu officials were aware of the incursion of the Western nations into Asia. They were familiar with Chinese sources about developments in other parts of the world. By the end of the eighteenth century Russia had extended its interests into eastern Siberia and its vessels began approaching Hokkaido, requesting the establishment of commercial relations. In 1818 the British sent a vessel to Edo asking for commercial relations. Whaling ships approached Japanese shores looking for food and water. The Bakufu responded negatively to such requests and issued an edict in 1825 ordering the ejection of all foreign ships from Japanese shores. This order was relaxed to allow aid to ships that drifted accidentally to Japanese shores but it did not revise its seclusionist policy.

The United States had become interested in the Far East and began sending clippers to China by the end of the eighteenth century. It was interested in engaging in whaling near Japanese shores as well as gaining protection for shipwrecked seamen. The Bakufu's policy was to treat such seamen as intruders. When the United States sent a merchant ship in 1837 to establish contact the ship was driven off. The same thing happened in 1846 when two warships under Commodore Biddle were sent to open Japanese ports. Then on July 8, 1853 Commodore Matthew C. Perry arrived off Uraga on Tokyo Bay with four warships. Perry refused to be cut off and gave the Bakufu three days to accept President Filmore's letter asking for the right of American ships to enter Japanese ports to obtain coal and supplies, and the establishment of trade between the two countries. Confronted with the "black ships" the Bakufu decided it had no choice but to allow Perry to land in Uraga and present the letter. Perry then left saying he would return early next year for the reply.

The Bakufu officials were aware of the dangers posed by the Western powers. They knew of China's humiliation in the Opium War of 1839–42. Faced with Perry's ultimatum the Bakufu leaders felt the need to seek advice from the daimyō and Bakufu officials. It also announced its willingness to listen to the opinions of the retainers of the daimyō, freelance warriors, and prominent merchants and villagers. In seeking broad-based advice they also felt obliged to solicit the views of the imperial court. Thus the Bakufu officials invited the court to make its recommendation. This is seen as a turning-point in Bakufu-imperial court political relations because the court was never given a voice in the Bakufu's policy-making process during the long Tokugawa rule. This gave a political opening to the court officials who wanted to assert the authority of the imperial court as well as those who were bent upon undermining the Bakufu's authority and possibly over-throwing it.

Opening up the decision-making process on Perry's demands did not strengthen the Bakufu's position. It could not arrive at a concensus. Of the seven hundred memorials submitted some advised acceding to Perry's demands but the majority advised that the seclusionist policy be continued but military confrontation must be avoided. A few even advocated going to war against the intruder. Among the latter, was the lord of Mito-han who contended that resorting to force would enhance the morale of the nation. Some advocated stalling Perry as long as possible. But this was not feasible because, as Perry had warned, he returned for a reply early in 1854 bringing with him eight "black ships" this time.

Lacking the means to oppose Perry's fleet the Bakufu acceded to his basic demands and signed the Kanagawa Treaty in 1854. It agreed to open two ports to American ships, Hakodate in Hokkaido and Shimoda on the Izu Peninsula along Tokyo Bay. It also agreed to provide proper treatment of shipwrecked American sailors and allow a consul to reside in Shimoda. The most-favored-nation clause was included in the treaty though there were no specific provisions on trade. A similar treaty was signed by England, France, and Russia. The arrival of Perry and accession to his demands mark a historic turning-point for Japan. It meant the end of the policy of seclusion, the birth of Japan as a modern state, and its emergence on the world scene.

In 1856 the U.S. government sent Townsend Harris to negotiate a commercial agreement. During the course of the protracted negotiation the Bakufu officials informed Townsend Harris that there was strong opposition to concluding a treaty with the U.S. The chief negotiator told Harris that only four of the eighteen major daimyō were in favor of the treaty, and of the three hundred daimyō only thirty percent were in favor of it. In order to get the opponents' consent the Japanese negotiators asked Harris for a two-month delay in finalizing the treaty "until a member of the Council of State could proceed as 'Ambassador to the Spiritual Emperor' at Kyoto to get his approval." This would compel those daimyō opposed to the treaty to withdraw their opposition. When Harris asked "what they would do if the Mikado refused his assent. They replied ... the Government had determined not to receive any objections from the Mikado." But the fact that the Bakufu had consulted the Emperor would allay the opposition, they contended.[28] Contrary to the Bakufu's expectations, however, the imperial court withheld its approval of the treaty because the court circle was dominated by the advocates of seclusion and "repelling the barbarians." Thereupon the Great Councilor Ii Naosuke (1815–60) decided to sign the treaty without imperial consent. Thus the Treaty of Amity and Commerce between the two countries was signed in July 1858. The treaty provided for the opening of three ports for trade and two more a few years later, and agreements were concluded on tariffs. Edo (Tokyo) and Osaka were to be opened for foreign residents in 1862 and 1863. American citizens were granted extraterritorial rights and freedom of worship. England, France, Russia, and the Netherlands followed with similar treaties. Thus Japan entered into full diplomatic and commercial relations with the Western nations. The treaties were unequal treaties in so far as it granted extraterritorial rights to citizens of the signatory nations.

The treaties settled the difficulties confronting the Bakufu in the realm of foreign relations but it resulted in serious internal problems. Signing the treaty without imperial consent gave the pro-imperial and anti-Western factions a cause to arouse public sentiments against the Bakufu.

DEMISE OF THE TOKUGAWA REGIME

Sentiment in support of the imperial court had been increasing since the rise of the school of National Learning but its chief exponent, Motoori Norinaga, did not see a conflict between the imperial court and the Bakufu. The advent of the Western powers and the concessions made to the West by the Bakufu, however, aroused nationalistic sentiments in the form of *sonnō* (révere the Emperor) and *jōi* (repel the barbarians). The chief proponents tended to be lower level, young samurai. Perhaps they were motivated partly by the frustration they felt under the hierarchical Tokugawa social order. The most vociferous activists tended to come from the domains of the "outside lords," especially Chōshū in the western mainland, Satsuma in southern Kyushu and Tosa on Shikoku island. But strong *sonnō* sentiments also prevailed in Mito, the collateral house of the Tokugawa family. The chief proponents tended to be fanatical, self-righteous activists who were willing to kill and die for their cause. They were referred to as *shishi*, men of high purpose. In a way they were precursors of the ultra-nationalist, superpatriots of the 1930s. Many of the *shishi* embraced the teachings of thinkers such as Aizawa Seishisai. Sakuma Zōzan (1811–64) who was also influential did not reject the West completely, because he recognized the importance of Western science and technology, but he emphasized the importance of traditional moral values and the "national polity." He favored "Eastern morals and Western science."

The doyen of the *shishi* fighting for *sonnō-jōi* was Yoshida Shōin (1830–59), a member of the Chōshū clan. He was well-versed in Chu Hsi and Wang Yang-ming philosophies, and had studied under Sakuma Zōzan. So he recognized the importance of Western technology. But he did not believe that "coastal defense" was the only way to cope with the threat from the West. He was convinced that the existing feudal order had to be transformed to unite the entire nation. His anti-Bakufu, *sonnō* beliefs had idealistic underpinnings. He asserted that "People throughout the country must all regard the affairs of the entire country as their business and serve the Emperor by sacrificing their lives if necessary. In this respect there should therefore be no distinctions of noble and base, superior and inferior." The existing political leaders were incapable of dealing with the national crisis. "It must be made clear that the present Bakufu and feudal lords are incapable of serving the Emperor and expelling the barbarians."[29] Here was his ideological rationale for advocating the establishment of a new order.

To educate young leaders capable of leading the new order Shōin started a private school in Chōshū. Out of this academy a circle of students emerged, not only fighters for *sonnō-jōi* but future leaders of Japan: Itō Hirobumi, Yamagata Aritomo, Kido Kōin, architects of the new Japan in the Meiji era.

Shōin became enraged at the Bakufu for concluding the treaty with Harris and ending the seclusionist policy in defiance of the Emperor's wishes. He declared: "All the gods and men are incensed. It is proper to destroy and kill in accordance with the basic principle of justice."[30] He turned against the Bakufu and initially expected the anti-Bakufu daimyō to overthrow the Bakufu but he lost hope in them and decided only "men of high purpose from the grass roots" could save the country by establishing a new order. For his anti-Bakufu activities and conspiracy to assassinate a member of the council of elders, he was arrested and executed, making him a martyr for the cause and a hero of the nationalists of the pre-Second World War years.

Shōin's execution did not undermine the *sonnō-jōi* movement. In fact the zealots became even more determined to achieve their objective. They assassinated Ii Naosuke who had led the effort to punish and quash the anti-Bakufu elements. The growing *sonnō-jōi* sentiment resulted in the anti-Bakufu sentiment congealing at a higher level rather than being largely a grass-roots movement. The center of the imperial court, Kyoto became the locus of the *sonnō-jōi* movement. The anti-Bakufu daimyō began to play a critical role in conjunction with ambitious court advisers.

With the departure of the strong-willed Ii Naosuke, the moderates took charge in the Bakufu. Faced with the growing anti-Bakufu sentiment the moderates sought to gain the cooperation of the imperial court and the leading daimyō to neutralize the dissident activists and establish a consensus at the top. The anti-Bakufu elements were also trying to win support from the imperial court for their cause. The most important clan in this circle was Chōshū whose leadership had succumbed to the militant *sonnō-jōi* activists who were Shōin's followers. Some high court officials were also inclined to cooperate with the zealots.

Emperor Kōmei, who had earlier rejected the Bakufu's request to support the policy of concluding a treaty with the United States, came to favor cooperating with the Bakufu. This policy, known as *kōbu-gattai* (union of the court and the military) was symbolized by the marriage of the Shogun Iemochi and the Emperor's younger sister, Kazunomiya, in 1862. This meant that the political role of the imperial court was formally established. This policy of cooperation between the Bakufu and imperial court was supported by Satsuma, a major "outside" clan as well as the collateral house of the Bakufu, Aizu (Fukushima prefecture). The Chōshū clan dominated by the radicals, with the cooperation of like-minded court officials, was determined to pursue a *sonnō-jōi* course, and got Emperor Kōmei to adhere to an anti-Western policy and compelled the Bakufu to agree to adopt a policy of seclusion.

Chōshū set out to implement this policy and fired upon Western vessels passing through the straits off the Chōshū domain. The Western nations retaliated. Suffering defeat Chōshū shifted its position and began to Westernize its military forces. Satsuma, which had not pursued a fanatical anti-Western stance, also experienced the power of Western forces when British warships attacked its home base in retaliation for the killing of an Englishman. This encounter convinced the Satsuma clan leaders of the need for Japan to build a naval force. As a result in the following (Meiji) era Chōshu leaders focused on building a modern army and Satsuma leaders concentrated on naval arms.

The faction in favor of *kōbugattai* decided to drive out the radical Chōshū activists and their court supporters. In mid-August 1863 the Satsuma-Aizu coalition compelled the *sonnō-jōi* activists to leave Kyoto. Thus they prevented the reimposition of the seclusionist policy, banned the *sonnō-jōi* court officials from court and relieved Chōshū of guard duties. In the summer of 1864, persuaded by the radicals, Chōshū sought to reenter Kyoto by force. This led the Bakufu to launch a military campaign against Chōshū with the support of Satsuma and Aizu forces. Chōshū leaders were compelled to punish those who had launched the attack on Kyoto.

The *kōbugattai* coalition began to unravel. Satsuma leaders wanted to establish a government dominated by the major clans but, with Chōshū seemingly out of the way, some Bakufu officials set out to reestablish Bakufu supremacy. This move disturbed the Satsuma clan chief and he began contemplating the possibility of cooperating with Chōshū. There was also a move behind the scenes to establish an alliance between Satsuma and Chōshū. The leaders of this movement were Satsuma's Saigō Takamori (1827–77) and Ōkubo Toshimichi (1830–78). They got Chōshū's Kido Kōin (1833–77) to agree with them and by early 1866 an alliance was formed.

The Bakufu officials decided to get rid of the obstreperous Chōshū clan once and for all and launched a second campaign against it in the summer of 1866. But this campaign failed because this time Satsuma did not participate. In the midst of the campaign Shogun Iemochi died, and his successor, Tokugawa Keiki (1837–1913), called off the campaign.

The coalition of Satsuma and Chōshū posed a serious threat to the Bakufu because Satsuma was the second largest clan and had a large samurai population, a ratio of one samurai to three commoners unlike the national average of one to seventeen. Chōshū, dominated by the radicals, also had a formidable samurai population with a ratio of one samurai to ten commoners. It had been a hotbed of militant nationalists and it had been busily modernizing its military force since its conflict with the Western naval vessels in 1863.

The anti-Bakufu court officials, led by Iwakura Tomomi (1825–83), sought to get the Emperor to remove the imperial advisers who favored cooperating with the Bakufu. Emperor Kōmei refused to do so but he died in December 1866. This strengthened the hands of anti-Bakufu court officials like Iwakura. A fifteen-year-old Emperor Meiji (1852–1912) mounted the throne, and Iwakura and opponents of *kōbugattai* gained ascendancy at the imperial court. Iwakura conspired with the Satsuma leaders to end the policy of *kōbugattai* and restore imperial rule.

Seeing the Bakufu moving to modernize its military force the triumvirate plotting the overthrow of the Bakufu, Saigō, Ōkubo, and Kido, pushed for military action. The Tosa clan leaders were inclined to support the Satsuma-Chōshū group but did not favor recourse to force, so the Tosa clan chief persuaded Shogun Keiki to voluntarily restore political authority to the Emperor. Keiki agreed to do so and at the end of 1867 restored political authority to the Emperor. He did so, he explained, to avoid a national crisis. Evidently he expected to head a new parliamentary government that the Tosa leaders envisioned establishing. He also expected to retain the enormous Tokugawa demesne. Thus the end of Tokugawa rule was effected without a major civil war. A brief skirmish ensued when Keiki was confronted with the anti-Bakufu leaders' plan, in particular Saigō's plan, to deprive him of his holdings. Saigō provoked Keiki to attack the Satsuma-Chōshū forces. Keiki's forces were defeated and he was compelled to surrender the Edo Castle to the imperial forces led by Satsuma and Chōshū. Pockets of resistance continued, for example among the collateral Aizu clan, but these were subdued rather quickly, so 267 years of Tokugawa rule ended. In early 1868 the Emperor established the imperial court in Edo, renamed Tokyo.

The most important event that provoked this was undoubtedly the arrival of the Western powers that brought about a national crisis. The economic difficulties that the Bakufu and the daimyō domains were experiencing toward the end of the Tokugawa era weakened the feudal order and caused growing discontent among the lower-level samurai as well as the commoners. There were increasing numbers of disturbances, including peasant uprisings aiming "to reform the society" but they were not sufficient to weaken Bakufu control. At the same time intellectual developments such as the rise of the school of National Learning fostered the basis for anti-Bakufu, pro-imperial sentiments. The growing crisis led the old feudal clans, the so-called "outside lords" to try to assert their power against their old nemesis the Tokugawa clan. In a way what happened was an old-fashioned feudal power struggle. The faction that won was the Satsuma-Chōshū clan alliance. The difference in the quality of leadership in the two camps may have resulted in the failure of the Bakufu. The opposition camp was led by ambitious, young, lower-level warriors of Satsuma and Chōshū while the Bakufu's leadership consisted of old-establishment leaders. There was little infusion of "men of talent" from the lower ranks to leadership positions.

FOUR

Establishment of the Meiji Regime

With the relinquishment of political authority by Tokugawa Keiki imperial authority was restored. The young Emperor Meiji formally resumed authority over the land. The actual wielders of power, however, were the leaders of the Satsuma-Chōshū clans who manipulated the Emperor as a figurehead to promote their own agenda. So the Meiji Restoration was really the transference of power to a new clique of ambitious political leaders with engrained feudal values. But they had to convince the populace that imperial rule was being restored and instill in them a sense of respect and reverence for the Emperor, for whom the masses had no direct political ties since the Kamakura era because they had been subjected to the political authority of the feudal clan chieftains and the Bakufu. Hence in order to get the populace to accept the new order the new leaders issued a general pronouncement immediately after the Restoration. It declared:

> Our country is known as the land of the gods, and of all the nations in the world, none is superior to our nation in morals and customs ... [People] must be grateful for having been born in the land of the gods, and repay the national obligation ... In antiquity the heavenly descendants opened up the land and established the moral order. Since then the imperial line has remained unchanged. Succeeding generations of the honorable personages profoundly loved the people, and the people reverently served every honorable personage ... All things in this land belong to the Emperor. When a person is born he is bathed in the Emperor's water, when he dies he

is buried in the Emperor's land ... Emperors have prayed day and night for the well-being of the people ... that there would not be famines, or epidemics ... However, during the past 300 years the imperial way had not prevailed ... Corruption was rampant, virtuous persons were punished, evil men enjoyed good fortune ... Now finally imperial rule has been restored, and fairness and justice prevail in all things ... If we repay even a smidgen of the honorable benevolence we will be doing our duty as the subject of the land of the gods.[1]

The underlying principles in this precept were later embodied in the Imperial Rescript on Education issued in 1890 and recited by all school children until the end of the Second World War. This was part of the process of image-making of the "living god" that was undertaken by the Meiji leaders to mold the people's pro-Emperor, nationalistic mind-set.

Aside from indoctrinating the people to be loyal and submissive to the Emperor, in effect to their political system, the people who gained power had to establish a mechanism to enable them to retain their newly gained authority. Hence the reforms and revisions of the old ways and institutions started as soon as Tokugawa rule was replaced by the oligarchy which proclaimed the new era of the Emperor Meiji beginning in 1868.

MEIJI RESTORATION

The new political leaders were confronted with formidable tasks. They had to end the Tokugawa feudal order and establish a tightly controlled centralized government. So aside from the restoration of imperial authority what transpired was the restructuring of the society and its institutions.

Among the first order of business was to prevent the nation from succumbing to the fate that other Asian nations had undergone, namely control by the Western powers. Hence the achievement of *fukoku kyōhei* (rich nation, strong military) was the primary concern. At the outset the leadership consisted of Saigō, Ōkubo, and Kido, the "big three" most responsible for the Meiji Restoration, but a number of able men from Chōshū and Satsuma, as well as a few imperial court aristocrats, were in the circle of the new power elite.

Controlling the anti-Meiji forces was accomplished fairly readily. Tokugawa Keiki meekly relinquished his authority. The major opposition clan, Aizu was subdued as well as some anti-imperial bands of samurai. The peasant uprisings to "remake the society" that started at the end of the Tokugawa era in 1866 continued into 1868. Their objectives were renunciation of debts and dues, and the targets of attack were the local leaders and rich merchants who had infiltrated the villages. To subdue popular discontent the Meiji leaders waved the flag of benevolent rule and aid to the masses but, fearing the spread of public unrest, they executed the leader of a particularly demanding proponent of tax reduction and public aid. The Meiji leaders thus quickly discarded the facade of extending benevolence to the masses and did little for the social and economic well-being of the common people. Politically the Charter Oath of Five Articles issued in April 1868 included articles on deliberative assemblies, and participation of all classes in the administration, but political participation by the masses was not on the agenda of the new oligarchy.

POLITICAL REFORMS

In order to achieve their objectives of *fukoku kyōhei* the oligarchs realized that they had to adopt Western science and technology. One of the components of their anti-Bakufu slogan, *jōi* (repel the barbarians) was quickly abandoned therefore, and Article 5 of the Charter Oath stated "Knowledge shall be sought throughout the world so as to invigorate the foundations of imperial rule." The leaders pursued what Arnold Toynbee refers to as a "Herodian" course. Toynbee explains that when the Herodian man "finds himself in the predicament of being confronted by a more highly skilled and better-armed opponent, he responds with the enemy's own tactics and own weapons."[2] This is the course that the Meiji leaders pursued.

The first order of business was the transformation of the political order. The initial step was the elimination of the existing feudal domains (*han*) where the clan chiefs still retained administrative authority. To initiate the abolition of the *han* system the new leaders persuaded the clan chiefs of Satsuma, Chōshū, Tosa and Hizen (in Kyushu) to voluntarily restore their domains to the Emperor. This was accomplished in March 1869. This compelled the other *han* chiefs (daimyō) to follow suit and by early 1870 all 270 *han* domains were restored to the imperial government. Han chiefs expected their provinces to be preserved under the imperial government and they would retain their authority in their domain with a fixed stipend. But the government decided to abolish the *han* as administrative units. In August 1871 it replaced the more than 270 han with prefectural units. The daimyō were given a generous stipend. In 1888 the prefectures were consolidated into forty-six units. The prefectural governors were appointed by the central government. A number of the former daimyō were appointed governors.

The abolition of the han system meant the loss of employment for the former samurai retainers. They were given a fraction of their former stipends. They also lost feudal privileges such as their social status above the commoners, the right to bear swords, to cut down commoners with impunity, to have distinctive attire and hairstyles. Some joined the new army and navy, or became policemen, teachers or government employees but many had to engage in work that they formerly regarded as being beneath their dignity in agriculture, commerce, and crafts. With the loss of fixed stipends and special status they became a potential source of opposition to the new order.

At national level a council of state with three branches was established, and remained in effect until the cabinet system was introduced in 1885. At the local level towns and village administrative units were established. Political authority extended from the center to the governors and to the local leaders.

As the oligarchs, mainly leaders from the provinces of Satsuma and Chōshū, went about consolidating their control of the power structure they encountered some opposition, primarily from the dispossessed former samurai. The leader who empathized with the disaffected former samurai was Saigō Takamori. Saigō was not in favor of many of the changes being instituted. What he wanted was military rule based on the support of the disaffected lower-class samurai. He was unhappy with the course that the new leaders were pursuing and returned to Satsuma (now Kagoshima prefecture) to build his power base there. In 1873 when the leaders of the new government were abroad on the Iwakura mission to the

United States and Europe to foster closer ties, Saigō returned to Tokyo to get the caretaker officials to launch an invasion of Korea. The ostensible reason was to chastize the Korean government for having made some critical pronouncements about Japanese merchants' activities in Korea. The real motive was to marshal the support of the discontented samurai. This effort was thwarted by the members of the Iwakura mission who returned to block Saigō's plan. Saigō returned to Kagoshima and those who had supported him resigned. Having lost this opportunity to regain their privileged position, a series of anti-government uprisings was staged by the former samurai. Most of these occurred in 1876.

After returning to Kagoshima Saigō started a private school for military training and the indoctrination of the youths with feudalistic concepts. Kagoshima, under Saigō's control, had not implemented many of the Meiji government's reforms and was acting as if it were an autonomous state. For example, samurai stipends were not eliminated and sword-bearing by the former samurai was permitted. The former samurai were organized into local army units. Ōkubo Toshimichi, a former Satsuma warrior but now the leading figure in the Meiji government, sought to bring Kagoshima under government control and dispatched officials to Kagoshima for this purpose.

Urged on by his supporters Saigō decided to rise against the government and in February 1877 he led a march to Tokyo. As he moved north in Kyushu he was joined by thousands of discontented former samurai and his force eventually numbered forty-two thousand. The government sent members of the new army, not samurai but commoners, scoffed at by Saigō men as "dirt farmers," to stop the Saigō forces. The army of peasants forced Saigō's forces to retreat. With the failure of his cause Saigō committed *hara-kiri*. This major conflict involved sixty thousand government troops and forty thousand Saigō warriors. Both sides suffered heavy casualties. Dirt farmers had shown that they could fight and win, and this was the end of armed resistance to the new government. From now on those who were unhappy with the monopolistic control of the Meiji leaders turned to the popular rights movement to challenge the oligarchs.

The popular rights movement had started before the Saigō uprising. The main base was the province of Tosa (current Kōchi prefecture) in Shikoku. Tosa was one of the quartet of provinces (Satsuma, Chōshū, Hizen, and Tosa) that led the opposition against the Tokugawa Bakufu. But the Tosa leaders were essentially left out of the power structure controlled by the Satsuma and Chōshū clique. Among the Tosa leaders was Itagaki Taisuke (1837–1919) who had supported Saigō's Korea project and resigned when it was blocked by Ōkubo and Kido. In 1874 Itagaki and his cohorts submitted a memorial to the government asking for the establishment of a national assembly. The petition was founded on Western liberal principles and frequently cited John Stuart Mill's concepts. The government did not accede to the petitioners' proposal which aroused broad public interest and discussion, and marks the beginning of the popular rights movement.

As the movement was getting extensive support from the press the government introduced a law to curb the press in 1875. The law resulted in fines and imprisonment of journalists critical of the government. The journalists, however, refused to succumb to government pressure and criticism continued.

Itagaki continued his fight for the establishment of a national assembly and the broadening of the power base. As political agitation in favor of the popular rights movement grew the government sought to restrict political gatherings and associations by issuing the law of public meetings in 1880. This did not restrain the fighters for political rights, and Itagaki and his cohorts continued to call for the establishment of a national assembly as well as prefectural assemblies. Of the big three architects of the Meiji Restoration only Ōkubo Toshimichi remained as the actual wielder of power in the mid-1870s because Saigō had rebelled and died, and the more liberally inclined Kido, who had been in and out of the government, died in 1877. In 1878 Ōkubo was assassinated by a follower of Saigō. This resulted in the political leadership falling to Itō Hirobumi (1841–1909), Ōkuma Shigen-obu (1838–1922), and other members of the council of state.

Faced with the growing demand for the establishment of a national assembly in late 1879 Iwakura advised the Emperor to ask council members to submit written opinions on whether or not a constitution should be framed. Most members of the council favored moving gradually toward the formation of a limited constitutional monarchy. In early 1881 Ōkuma submitted his memorial favoring a parliamentary government modeled after the British system and asked that a definite date be fixed for its establishment. This upset Itō and the other conservatives. Ōkuma had violated the traditional practice of adhering to a consensual position; he had acted independently. Itō's antagonism toward Ōkuma exploded when Ōkuma and his colleagues criticized the government for selling its Hokkaido holdings at a bargain price to a member of the ruling group. Itō and his circle succeeded in getting Ōkuma dismissed from government. But to placate the public, in October 1881 the government announced its decision to draft a constitution and establish a national assembly by 1890. Thus it could be said that Ōkuma had compelled Itō to proceed towards the drafting of a constitution despite his earlier decision to move slowly.

This decision delighted the advocates of popular rights. Itagaki then proceeded to organize a political party, the Liberal Party. Among the party leaders were men who admired Rousseau's ideas. The party's statement of principles started with: "Liberty is the natural state of man and the preservation of liberty is man's great duty." A second political party, the Constitutional Reform Party, was organized by the followers of Ōkuma and Fukuzawa Yukichi (1835–1901), an advocate of English liberalism. It was somewhat more conservative than the Liberal Party and took English parliamentary government as the model. It had the backing of the growing business enterprise, the Mitsubishi company. Although ideologically there was no significant difference, the two parties failed to cooperate to combat the oligarchy. The Reform Party leaders regarded the Liberal Party as too radical while the latter saw the former aiming "to please the old and the rich." To seek public support the parties engaged in public-speaking tours.

The government sought to curtail these activities by issuing a law in 1882 banning public lectures and restricting the activities of local political organizations. This only induced the activists to become more vehement in opposing the government, and local disturbances involving the peasantry became more common. In some cases the local authorities resorted to harsh regressive measures. One incident in 1884, in which the activists called for the overthrow of despotism, resulted in the execution of the leaders. These incidents caused dissensions in the Liberal Party. Some members became disillusioned with Itagaki because he had accepted money from Mitsui to travel abroad. Party unity was weak in the Reform Party. This led Ōkuma to leave the party. But the parties still managed to oppose the government on certain instances. When the government was negotiating for treaty revisions with the Western powers some Liberal Party leaders opposed the agreement because it provided for legal cases involving Europeans to be tried by Western judges, and the Western nations were given the right to review the legal codes to be adopted by Japan. Opposition by party leaders led the government to issue the Peace Preservation Law in 1887 and eject all troublemakers from Tokyo.

FRAMING OF THE CONSTITUTION

In the midst of these turbulent activities Itō proceeded with the drafting of a constitution in accordance with his 1881 pronouncement. In preparation of the drafting of the constitution Itō went to Europe in 1882 to gain firsthand knowledge of European constitutions. Those who favored a constitution with a strong monarchy looked to Bismarck's Germany. They were influenced by Hermann Roessler, a German authority on jurisprudence, teaching at Tokyo University. Thus Itō went to Germany and listened to constitutional discourses by the German political scientist Rudolph von Gneist and then he went to Austria to meet Lorenz von Stein. He claimed that he was persuaded to follow the German model, rather than the liberal systems of England, America or France. He remained abroad for over a year during 1882–83. On the way back to Japan he stopped briefly in England.

Upon his return Itō instituted a number of administrative changes to strengthen the Emperor system and the position of the oligarchy. In 1884 he created a system of peerage consisting of the nobility, and high-ranking government officials, and military officers. Itō himself became a count as did Yamagata Aritomo (1838–1922), his Chōshū cohort. The peerage was designed to form the upper house of the pending legislature as the House of Peers. In 1885 Itō replaced the state council with a Western-type cabinet system. At the same time, to retain the autonomy of imperial household affairs, the Ministry of Imperial Household and the office of the Lord Keeper of the Privy Seal were created. In 1888 he created the Privy Council to examine the proposed constitution and also serve as a special advisory body to the Emperor. While the officials were working on drafting a constitution they also proceeded to draft an Imperial House Law limiting imperial succession to male members of the imperial family, in contravention to historical precedents whereby female members were eligible to ascend the throne.

In 1886 Itō and his assistants began drafting the constitution. The draft was presented to the Privy Council for examination in 1888. In the course of the discussion Itō was compelled to argue against those who wanted to uphold the absolute authority of the Emperor. They objected to Article IV which stipulates that the Emperor exercises the rights of sovereignty in accordance with the provisions of the constitution. This, they contended, restricted the rights of the Emperor. Itō maintained that constitutional government entails restrictions on the ruler's sovereign rights. The opponents then argued against Article V which initially stated that the Emperor exercises legislative power with the "approval" of the Diet. Those who favored restricting the rights of the people, including an earlier champion of Westernization, Mori Arinori, objected, and despite Itō's opposition, got the wording changed from "approval" to "assistance." However, when Mori objected to the term "rights of the subject" and proposed changing it to "status of the subject" he failed to reverse the wording. The draft was approved by the Privy Council after six-months' deliberation, and it was promulgated on February 11, 1889.

The constitution vested the rights of sovereignty in the Emperor but he was to exercise it in accordance with provisions of the constitution, so Itō's view prevailed here. The Diet, a bicameral legislature, the House of Peers and House of Representatives, was established. It was designed to "assist" the Emperor in exercising his legislative duties but he could issue imperial ordinances when the Diet was not in session. He also held the power of veto over laws passed by the Diet. He was the supreme commander of the armed forces and had authority to declare war, make peace, and conclude treaties. He appointed cabinet members and other government officials, who were responsible to him, not the Diet. The only real power that the Diet held was fiscal. New taxes and changes in tax rates required legislative approval. Thus the Diet had a voice in budgetary matters but if it failed to approve the budget the previous year's budget went into effect. Because the armed forces were responsible to the Emperor, not the Diet or the cabinet, the concept of "independence of the supreme command" came into being. This enabled military leaders to bypass the cabinet and appeal directly to the Emperor on military affairs. The rights and liberties of the people were granted "within the limits of the law."

The Diet did not become an institution which provided the people with a voice in the government. Members of the House of Peers consisted of members of the imperial family, the peers, and imperial appointees. Members of the House of Representatives were elected but the franchise was limited to male subjects over twenty-five years of age who paid a fixed amount of tax. In the first Diet election of 1890 only 1.14 percent of the population qualified to vote. Thus the constitution did not dislodge the oligarchs from positions of power. As members of the Privy Council, House of Peers, court officials, and cabinet members they functioned as imperial advisers. The leaders among them formed a small clique who controlled the real source of authority. This clique came to be known as the *genrō* (elder statesmen) and Itō, Yamagata and a few others formed this circle of elite power-wielders.

Earlier in 1878 prefectural assemblies were introduced but they had little authority because the governors, appointed by the central government, had control over all bills.

SOCIAL REFORMS

The other aspect of the old feudal order that was transformed was the abolition of the rigid class system. In 1869 the reclassification of the old classes was initiated and finalized in 1872. The court aristocrats and former daimyō were classified as peers, the former upper level samurai as *shizoku* (samurai clan), and the rest as commoners. The outcaste groups were designated "new commoners." The class distinctions were legalized; the class status of each family was registered in the family registers. So class consciousness persisted. But the common people were now allowed to have family names, intermarry with other classes, and change occupations. Thus the peasants were no longer bound to the soil. They were allowed to own land, and in 1872 they were granted the right to buy and sell land. The former samurai's right to cut down commoners with impunity was eliminated, and in 1876 they lost the right to bear swords.

FURTHER INSTITUTIONAL CHANGES

The legal system in Tokugawa society was based on rule-by-status and the enforcement of law was dependent on the Bakufu and the daimyō and their officials. There was no such thing as rule-of-law. It was rule by the will of the ruling class. For the masses the system was arbitrary. They had no rights, only the duty to obey. In order to get the unequal treaties, which included provisions for extraterritorial rights exempting Westerners from the Japanese legal system, revised the Meiji authorities decided to adopt a Western-type legal system. They turned to the French legal system because it was codified and administered by professional judges rather than the Anglo-American common law system with a jury system that allowed ordinary people to determine judicial cases. A court system from higher to lower levels was established but an independent judicial system with a supreme court was not established. The Privy Council, the imperial advisory organ, was given the right to decide on the constitutionality of the laws and administrative actions. A penal code, code of criminal procedure, commercial code, and civil code were adopted during the course of the 1880s and 1890s.

The Meiji government also established a national police system. In Tokugawa society enforcement was in the hands of the Bakufu and daimyō officials. Their function was not to protect the rights of the people but to keep them in line. The Meiji leaders set out to institute a Western-type police system but, in accordance with the traditional concept, the system had as its chief function keeping law and order, not protection of the rights of the people. Initially the police system was under the local governments but in 1874 the Ministry of Home Affairs was put in charge of the system. When the cabinet system was adopted in 1885 the police commissioner, under the Minister of Home Affairs, was given the authority to oversee the nation's police system. The police had the authority to censor the press and control political activities. In effect a "police state" was established. At the local level the police considered themselves to be heirs to the Tokugawa samurai and went about with sabres at their side.

Under the Tokugawa system military duty was the responsibility of the samurai class. Now that the samurai's special status was dissolved, the government had to establish a modern army and navy to accomplish its objectives of *fukoku kyōhei*. Initially there was disagreement as to whether universal conscription should be adopted or whether the former samurai of the major han should constitute the new army. The advocate of universal conscription, Ōmura Masujirō, was assassinated by discontended former samurai, and in 1871 an army consisting of warriors from major han, Satsuma, Chōshū, and Tosa was organized. But in order to build a strong military, universal conscription was deemed necessary. Yamagata Aritomo became the architect of the new army. He instituted universal conscription in 1873. He moved to establish an army modeled after the Prussian army that had just defeated France in the Franco-Prussian War.

The imperial pronouncement on military service stressed universal service with samurai-commoner class distinction eliminated. Initially, however, those with higher education, high taxpayers, and family heads were exempted from service. Consequently younger sons of poorer families were the ones liable for three years of compulsory service. In 1882 the Imperial Precept to the Soldiers and Sailors was issued. The precept stressed loyalty above all. It held that "the protection of the state and the maintenance of its powers depend upon the strength of its arms ... neither be led astray by current opinions nor meddle in politics, but with single heart fulfil your essential duty of loyalty."[3] In other words they were not to think as independent individuals but simply serve. The common soldiers came from the lower classes but the officers, especially generals, came in the main from the shizoku from Satsuma and Chōshū.

The government had to create a new division of the armed forces, a navy. It did not have capacity for the building of naval ships so in 1875 it purchased three ironclad warships from Britain. The navy was modeled after the British navy, and the top positions were occupied by Satsuma men.

ECONOMIC RECONSTRUCTION

In the economic realm the task confronting the Meiji leaders was the transformation of what was basically an agrarian economy of the Tokugawa period into an industrial economy. In the West, since the industrial revolution of the eighteenth century science and technology had been utilized to build plants for mass production. The Meiji leaders were aware that to meet the goal of becoming a "rich nation" required swift industrialization.

The first step taken was the revision of the rigid landholding system. The Meiji government lifted the restrictions that bound the peasants to the land and gave them the right to own land.

The government needed financial resources to build the industrial sector of the economy. The primary source was taxation imposed on the farmers. Owners of farmland were required to pay three percent of the assessed value of the land. This came to about thirty-three percent of the total yield on the land, close to forty percent limit that the Bakufu had placed on its own land in the Tokugawa era. Faced with the demand for lower taxes the government lowered the rate to 2.5% in 1876 but this still meant a heavy burden on the farm population. In the early 1870s ninety percent and between 1875 and 1879 80.5% of the government's tax revenue came from the land tax. The burden on tenant farmers continued to be onerous as landowners generally collected more than sixty percent of the crop produced by them. With payment of miscellaneous dues on top of this the tenants managed to retain only about thirty-two percent of the crop. This contrasts with the thirty nine percent of the yield that Tokugawa tenant farmers were able to retain. In the 1870s about one third of the arable land was farmed by tenant farmers.

With the income derived from the farming community the government developed the nation's industrial capacity. Economists Kazushi Ohkawa and Henry Rosovsky posit several stages in Japan's economic growth from the Meiji period to the present. The years from 1868 to 1885 are seen as the period when the groundwork was laid for modern economic growth. The first phase commenced in 1886 and extended to 1905. The second phase extended from 1906 to 1952. The post-Second World War period of economic growth started in 1953 with Japan emerging as a world class economic power.[4] Economic production in early Meiji consisted primarily in textile and food production. The government took an active part in adopting measures to advance industrial production, especially in the textile industry. It built model plants and provided subsidies to private entrepreneurs. In 1870 the first modern silk filature and new cotton spinning mills equipped with modern imported machinery were constructed. Experimental factories were built in many areas, and the mining industry was developed with the help of foreign technicians.

An important aspect of the move to foster economic growth was the modernization of the transportation and communication systems. The government began constructing railroads. The first railroad to open was the Tokyo-Yokohama line in 1872. In 1889 the line linking Tokyo and Kobe was completed. Eventually an entire network of railroads was completed which was operated by the Ministry of Railroads. Government-run railroads were not privatized until 1987. In 1869 the government also began constructing telegraph lines. These were tied in with the postal system which was established in 1871. In shipping the government helped the Mitsubishi Company develop its merchant fleet.

These projects to build up the economic system were costly. The land tax instituted in 1873 was the main source of revenue. Consumer taxes on sake and tobacco were also introduced but the deficit mounted. The government was compelled to borrow from big merchant houses and foreign nations, and issue nonconvertible paper notes. The situation worsened with inflation. Confronted with this situation the finance minister, Masakata Masayoshi (1835–1924), reduced government spending, introduced additional indirect taxes, issued convertible currency, and strengthened the banking system by establishing the Bank of Japan. By these measures Masakata stabilized the economy.

These measures, however, placed a heavy burden on the peasants whose land tax remained the same while the price of rice dropped. Since taxes had to be paid on the basis of the price of rice the peasants had to pay 32.8% of the rice crop as tax in 1884 in contrast to sixteen percent in 1881. This led to outbreaks of agrarian riots.

A characteristic of the government's economic policy was the close alliance between government and private entrepreneurs which characterized the Japanese politico-economic set-up to the

Second World War and after. From the outset there were close links between the Meiji oligarchs and the rich merchant houses that had emerged in the Tokugawa period. In the conflict between the imperial forces and Bakufu, major houses such as Mitsui and Kōnoike provided funds to the imperial faction. At that same time they also funded the Bakufu so that they would have the goodwill of whichever side won.

When the imperial forces won they granted special favors to the merchant houses that had supported them. They were granted the right to serve as tax collectors. The rice that the peasants paid was converted to money so houses like Mitsui functioned as rice dealers and tax collectors and so gained great financial benefits. They also got government support to enter the banking business. Hence banks like Mitsui and Mitsubishi emerged in the early Meiji years and have remained as major banking firms. The government transferred, at low prices, the many state-owned business enterprises to these houses. These companies also entered mining and Mitsui became a major coal-mining firm. Mitsubishi was not a Tokugawa era merchant house but began as a business enterprise started by a former samurai, Iwasaki Yatarō (1834–85), a member of Tosa clan. With the support of the Tosa clan Iwasaki built up a shipping firm and gained the support of the Meiji government, which sold the ships that it had acquired to Mitsubishi at a low price. It provided government subsidies to enable Mitsubishi to become a major shipping firm to replace the foreign shipping firms active in Japan. Mitsubishi, like Mitsui, began to engage in numerous other economic activities such as banking, foreign trade, and manufacturing. Other business enterprises, like the Sumitomo bank, that emerged in this period also received government support. Thus the gigantic monopolies that came to characterize the pre-Second World War period in Japan, the *zaibatsu*, had their roots in the early Meiji years.

The first phase of modern economic growth (1886–1905) began as industrial factories, business enterprises, and banking began to expand, but agriculture was still the key sector of the economy. In 1898 eighty-two percent of the people lived in villages and small towns. With the increase in cultivated areas, and improved means of farming agricultural production increased. Rice and other food production increased by about forty percent from the mid-1880s to the mid-1910s. Raw silk and tea were the chief export items in the early Meiji years. From 1868 to 1893 raw silk comprised forty-two percent of Japan's total exports.

Beside extensive railroad construction the government played an important role in developing marine transportation. By the Sino-Japanese War of 1894–95 Japanese merchant ships numbered well over five hundred. By 1913 half of overseas trade was carried in Japanese ships.

The industry that developed rapidly from the early Meiji years and remained a key component of the economy was textile manufacture. In 1900 70.7% of the factories were in this field. Sixty-seven percent of the factory workers were employed in textile factories, the vast majority being female workers laboring long hours for subsistence wages. Cotton textile production increased rapidly with extensive use of machinery. In the early Meiji period large amounts of cotton yarn and cloth were imported but government and private plants began employing steam-powered spinning machines. By the end of the century domestic demands were being met and manufacturers began turning to foreign markets. Initially silk filature relied primarily on hand-reeling but machine-reeling increased as larger plants were built. By 1910 seventy percent of the raw silk was produced by machine-reeling, although hand-reeling continued in small shops in the countryside. Japan soon emerged as one of the world's major raw silk producers. In 1897 Japan produced twenty-four percent of the world's raw silk and by 1904 it had become the world's largest producer with a thirty-one percent share. In 1913 cotton and silk textile products amounted to nearly three-fifths of Japan's total exports.

The production of other items such as paper, sugar, cement, and glass also increased but the areas where the government focused were in heavy industry and mining. At the outset the government engaged in mining but by mid-1885 it turned the business over to private companies like Mitsui. Workers labored in coal mines under hazardous, difficult conditions, in some cases they were forced to work like semi-slaves. The demand for coal in the factories and railroads propelled coal mining to increase nearly twenty-three fold from 1874 to 1897. Iron and steel production did not develop much in the nineteenth century, and production only began to rise significantly with the Russo-Japanese War and after. Shipbuilding and manufacturing of machinery did not advance much in this period and most of the vessels and machinery were imported, primarily from England.

EDUCATION

The Meiji leaders focused on education in order to bring Japan into the modern age. The government needed literate soldiers, factory workers, business employees, and government employees to achieve its goal of "rich nation, strong military." Hence in 1872 it established a system of compulsory elementary education. In issuing the education ordinance the government stated that there shall be "no community with an illiterate family, nor a family with an illiterate person."

There was disagreement about the focus of education. Shinto nationalist scholars believed that appreciation of the "imperial way" and respect for the imperial court should be emphasized while the traditional Confucian scholars believed Confucianism should be at the heart of education. However, the proponents of "civilization and enlightenment" like Fukuzawa contended that the object of education is to enable Japan to enter the modern age, and adopt Western knowledge, so they emphasized the importance of practical education. The framers of the educational system turned to the West for models.

The cost of education was to be paid by the tax-payers at the local level and by the payment for tuition. For the common peasant families the tuition cost of 12.5 sen to fifty sen per month was prohibitive because the average income of the common people was only 1.75 yen a month (there are 100 sen in a yen). So few could pay the tuition and attendance remained low. Gradually this improved and in 1872 attendance by school children was twenty-eight percent, but by 1878 it had risen to forty percent. The number of girls attending school remained low until the turn of the century. The framers of the Education Act of 1872 asserted that: "In the way of mankind, there is no distinction between men and women. There is no reason why girls cannot be educated as well as boys. Girls are the mothers of tomorrow, They are to become the educators of children. For this reason the education of girls is of utmost importance."[5] But initially the traditional view that education of girls was not necessary persisted. A prominent writer Higuchi Ichiyō (1872–96) who was of school age in the late 1870s recalled that her mother believed: "It is harmful for a girl to get too much education."[6] In 1876 forty-six percent of the school age boys were in school but only sixteen percent of the girls were in school. By the end of the nineteenth century girl attendance had barely risen to fifty percent, but by the end of the first decade of the twentieth century it had risen to ninety-six percent.

The number of years of required attendance was four at first but it was reduced to three. It was extended to four years again in 1900 and to six years in 1907. It remained six years until after the Second World War period when it was extended to nine years. The curriculum in the elementary schools initially was based largely on Western, especially American, readers with passages written or translated by Westernizers like Fukuzawa. Introduction of scientific knowledge was stressed.

In 1879 the Minister of Education, endeavoring to foster public support, moved to decentralize the educational system and, following the American system, gave local boards control of the schools. This move failed because some local communities did not actively support the schools because they wished to reduce expenditure. As a result centralization was restored with greater authority being granted the prefectural governors. To increase attendance tuition charges were dropped in 1900.

By the 1880s the initial pragmatic, liberal focus on education came under growing criticism from proponents of cultural nationalism. They persuaded the Emperor to issue moralistic, educational precepts to shift the educational focus away from Western concepts. They insisted on injecting traditional moral lessons and national history into the curriculum with emphasis on Shintoistic, and Confucian values such as loyalty to the Emperor, patriotism, duty, filial piety, propriety, and obedience. The textbooks came increasingly under government control. In 1883 a state textbook certification system was introduced with the Ministry of Education delineating guidelines. In 1903 the government took over the publication of all primary school textbooks. The fundamental values to be inculcated in school children were embodied in the Imperial Rescript on Education that was issued in 1890. And the moral textbooks instilled in the young pupils the importance of loyalty to the Emperor. The first lesson in the third grade moral text says, "Because of the profound benevolence of the Emperor, we are able to live each day in peace. We must always keep in mind with deep gratitude the great debt we owe him."[7]

The initial Anglo-American orientation that was represented by the Westernizers was replaced in the 1880s by the educational philosophy that was being propounded in Germany by Johann Friedrich Herbart who stressed the importance of developing the students' moral character. At the higher level of the school system the government began to exert its influence. Military drills were introduced in the middle and higher schools in the 1880s, and even universities came under closer government supervision. Tokyo University was renamed Imperial University of Tokyo and became a part of the state system. Its chief function became the training of future bureaucrats and state officials.

EARLY MEIJI INTELLECTUAL DEVELOPMENTS: CIVILIZATION AND ENLIGHTENMENT

After the country was opened to the West the Bakufu as well as some of the feudal clans sought to gain knowledge from the Western nations and sent a number of students abroad to study. In 1862 the Bakufu sent eight students to study in Holland while in 1863 Chōshū sent five students to Britain. Among them were the future Meiji leaders Itō Hirobumi and Inoue Kaoru (1835–1915). In 1864 Satsuma sent sixteen students to Britain. A number of students went to the West on their own. As early as 1857 the Bakufu established an institute to study Western publications and languages. Some missions were sent abroad by the Bakufu, so exposing Japanese to the West. Among them was Fukuzawa Yukichi who returned convinced that Japan had to adopt Western practices and institutions and he became a leading Westernizer.

With the establishment of the Meiji government pursuit of Western knowledge was launched vigorously. Leaders stated in the Charter Oath of Five Articles the goal of pursuing knowledge throughout the world. Increasing numbers of students went abroad, and a large number of foreign language schools opened, and Western books were translated. Western scholars and specialists were invited to teach in the schools and assist in modernizing the nation. Christian missionaries also began to arrive with the lifting of the ban against Christianity.

Among the leaders laboring to "civilize and enlighten" Japan was Fukuzawa Yukichi who began writing books about the West and propagating Western liberal concepts. His works such as *Conditions in the West, Encouragement of Learning,* and *Outline of Civilization* gained a wide readership and continue to be studied today. He was strongly influenced by English liberalism, and emphasized the importance of practical, scientific education, and the need to develop the spirit of liberal, utilitarian concepts. Works by English liberal thinkers, notably John Stuart Mill's *On Liberty*, and Samuel Smiles' *Self-Help* were translated and widely read. Fukuzawa and his cohorts organized an intellectual society, The Meirokusha (Meiji Six Society) and published a journal to spread their views. For the public at large the objects of desire were products of Western technology. A popular children's song enumerating ten most desirable things included gas lamps, steam engines, horse-drawn carriages, cameras, telegrams, lightning conductors, newspapers, schools, postal mail, and steamboats. All these soon became common.

DEVELOPMENTS IN RELIGION

In the realm of religion the ban against Christianity was lifted in 1873 and the principle of religious freedom was adopted. Since 1858 Christian missionaries had been permitted to work in treaty ports after the Bakufu had signed treaties with the West, now missionaries were able to carry on their work wherever they wished. The Christians who had gone underground since the ban on Christianity in the seventeenth century were able to come out in the open. The number of Christian converts remained small but some intellectuals became converts and espoused liberal, humanistic ideals. Among them was Uchimura Kanzō (1861–1930).

Buddhism had enjoyed a somewhat privileged status during the Tokugawa years. The Bakufu required everyone to register with a Buddhist temple. Thus the temples served as semi-official record keepers. With the establishment of the Meiji government many Shintoists launched attacks on Buddhist temples. These acts of vandalism were curbed by the government but the Shintoists continued to support the idea of shoring up Shinto as a virtual state religion. From the outset of the Meiji era the proponents of state Shinto set out to bring all the Shinto shrines under the supervision of the central government. A hierarchy of Shinto shrines, extending from Shinto shrines that enshrine the Sun Goddess, Emperors, and national heroes to the scattered small village shrines, was brought under government authority. They were classified as national shrines, prefectural shrines, local shrines, village shrines and non-status shrines. Folk shrines dedicated to mountains, rivers, trees, stones, and foxes were all brought under official control. Anyone who questioned the mythological origin of the imperial dynasty got into trouble. A Tokyo University professor held that the Shinto worship of heaven was derived from an ancient practice common in East Asia, and that the Harvest Festival claimed by the Shintoists to be a festival honoring the Sun Goddess was actually a festival to honor heaven. For espousing these views he was fired from his post.

FIVE

Developments in
Later Meiji

THE RISE OF CULTURAL NATIONALISM

The government leaders' support of Shinto was linked to the
resurgence of cultural nationalism in the 1880s and after. It was
a reaction against the move to "civilize and enlighten" the country.
To the traditionalists this meant Westernization at the expense of
the values they held dear. Among the influential defenders of
traditional Confucian values was Motoda Eifu (1818–91) who was
a tutor to the Emperor. He states in his memoirs that in tutoring the
young Emperor he emphasized the sacred nature of the national
polity, the negative aspects of Christianity, the differences in Eastern
and Western ways, and the incompatibility of monarchism and
republicanism. He got the Emperor to issue a directive on education
to Itō Hirobumi stating that when the young people enter school
they must first be imbued with principles of loyalty and filial piety,
and Confucianism must be the basis of moral education. Acquisition of knowledge was to come after this. Children of farmers and
merchants need not be exposed to political and social concepts; they
must be educated in matters relevant to work. He was largely
responsible for turning the elementary school curriculum away from
the liberal, utilitarian orientation. His views were shared by others,
even those who had been affiliated with the Meirokusha. The basis
for moral education and history was to be the doctrine of the sacred
origin and history of the imperial dynasty. The move to proclaim the
official moral doctrine resulted in the drafting and promulgation of
the Imperial Rescript on Education in 1890.

The Rescript was drafted by Motoda and Inoue Kowashi (1844–95), the latter a believer in imperial moral leadership. It asserted that the Imperial Ancestors had founded the Empire, and that the subjects have been united in loyalty and filial piety for generations. "[S]hould emergency arise, offer yourselves to the State; and thus guard and maintain the prosperity of Our Imperial Throne coeval with heaven and earth." The Rescript was issued to all the schools and every morning during school assembly the teachers and students recited it in archaic solemn language which they had memorized. The Rescript together with the imperial photograph were lodged in a sacred pedestal. The minds of the young children were molded to ensure that when the time came they would go to battle shouting, "Imperial Majesty, Banzai!"

The picture of the imperial dynasty presented in the Rescript was a culmination of the image-making of the sacred Emperor. The process started with the establishment of the Meiji government in order to rationalize and reinforce the new political order. The Emperor as political and religious leader was emphasized. In effect he was the wielder of the two swords. The mythical founding of the imperial dynasty by Emperor Jimmu in the year 660 B.C.E. was taught in the schools as authentic history. The 11th of February was designated as a day to celebrate Emperor Jimmu's ascension to the throne and November 3 was celebrated as Emperor Meiji's birthday.

Anyone who dared to refuse to bow reverently to the Rescript or the imperial photograph risked trouble. When the Rescript was received by the school where he was teaching Uchimura Kanzō, a Christian educator, refused to bow to it and was dismissed. This confirmed the nationalistic thinkers' belief that Christianity and Japanism were incompatible and they intensified their criticism of Christianity.

In addition to the official measures to foster state nationalism, non-governmental movements to revive cultural pride emerged in reaction to the enthusiasm for things Western. Among the early proponents calling on the Japanese not to forsake but preserve their traditional culture was Ernest F. Fenollosa, an American who arrived in Japan in 1878 to teach philosophy at the University of Tokyo. He became interested in Japanese paintings and woodblock prints. He was perturbed that the Japanese were turning away from their artistic heritage, and was appalled at the neglect of traditional art work. Woodblock prints were being used as wrapping papers, and many Buddhist artifacts had been damaged or destroyed in the anti-Buddhist outbursts earlier. In order to foster Japanese appreciation of their culture he encouraged the Japanese to educate the public about their culture. Among the students Fenollosa influenced was Okakura Kakuzō (1862–1913) who became a prominent teacher of Japanese art. He and Fenollosa worked to establish the Tokyo School of Art.

Others influenced by Fenollosa became proponents of cultural nationalism, but they were not avidly anti-Western nationalists. They favored adopting the best from the West but preserving the essence of Japanese life and culture. In 1888 they began publishing a journal entitled *Nihonjin* (Japanese). They explained that their wish to preserve the national essence did not simply mean the preservation of "old things inherited from our ancestors." They were not advocating resistance to Western things and closing the door to innovation and progress. They wished to adopt the best from the West in "truth, virtue and beauty." They did not favor xenophobic nationalism but believed that working for the good of the country would advance the good of the world. Early advocates of Westernization like Fukuzawa also began to say that he opposed indiscriminate worship of things Western. The spirit of skepticism, evident in his early writings, must be applied in examining Western civilization.

Some of the early liberal Westernizers did become avid nationalists. Among the most influential of these was Tokutomi Sohō (1863–1957). He started out as a student of Christian humanism and English liberalism. He was critical of the emerging political nationalism and published works insisting that "New Japan" must pursue the course of peace and democracy. The event that turned him into a militant nationalist was the outbreak of the Sino-Japanese War of 1894–95 and the Triple Intervention that forced Japan to retract some of the concessions it had gained from China. Since then he became an ardent advocate of imperialism and militarism, writing voluminous nationalistic essays and histories.

WESTERN INFLUENCE ON LITERATURE

The influence of Western culture can be seen in the literary field. In the early Meiji years translations of Western tales and novels began to appear. Among them were Defoe's *Robinson Crusoe*, Bulwer-Lytton's *Ernest Maltravers,* and Hans Christian Andersen's *Improvisatoren*. After a couple of decades some Japanese writers began writing political novels. They were inspired by the translation of Benjamin Disraeli's *Coningsby*. If the Prime Minister of a great nation like England can engage in writing fiction it was clearly not a trivial activity.[1] Among the early political novels is Yano Fumio's (1850–1931) *Keikoku Bidan* (Inspiring Instances of Statesmanship) based on Plutarch's *Epaminondas*. Yano was a follower of Fukuzawa and had a liberal perspective.

The definitive work that set the literary standard for modern Japanese literature is Tsubouchi Shōyō's (1859–1935) *The Essence of the Novel* (*Shōsetsu Shinzui*) that appeared in 1885. Tsubouchi rejected the traditional didactic novels and believed that the primary task of the novelist should be the realistic depiction of life and human emotions. The writer who realized Tsubouchi's literary ideal was his friend and follower Futabatei Shimei (1864–1909). Futabatei was well-versed in Russian literature. He translated many Russian novels. His first major work, *Drifting Clouds* (*Ukigumo*), reflects influences by Turgenev and Goncharov. The characters in this novel are portrayed as believable, real human beings. The hero lacks will power and decisiveness, too shy to assert himself in his relationship with the girl he loves. Another significant characteristic of *Drifting Clouds* is its colloquial style in contrast to the more formal literary style that was prevalent. Thus Futabatei paved the way for the average reader to feel at home with the modern novels whose heroes are depicted in a manner to which they could relate.

A number of prominent writers followed these pioneer Western-style writers. Not all of them embraced the Western literary trend and some turned to more traditional themes. Mori Ōgai (1862-1922) was widely read in German writers such as Goethe and Schiller and translated their works. But he did not favor simply embracing Western naturalism. He turned increasingly to traditional subject matters, and held that traditional forms and conventions were important. He asserted: "If tea ceremonies were empty forms, the august ceremonials of the state together with ancestor-worship rituals will be empty forms also."[2] Stressing the importance of history he contended: "Civilization rests on history ... One should never forget that ethics and customs which have been verified over many centuries have a good core."[3] Others, however, pursued the naturalist course. Among them was Shimazaki Tōson (1872–1943) who depicted the plight of a member of an outcaste in his *The Broken Commandment* (Hakai). In his other works he continued to focus critically on traditional as well as contemporary attitudes and ways.

Perhaps the most renowned writer of this period of modern literary ascendancy was Natsume Sōseki (1867–1916). Undoubtedly he became a writer best known to the average Japanese because one of his stories *I am a Cat* was included in the public school reader. The cat casts a satirical eye on the foibles of the people around him. Natsume had studied in England and taught English literature. He wrote dispassionately with a light humorous and satirical look at the mundane human interactions, particularly at the family level. His outlook became increasingly somber as he began to be concerned about the inability of the Japanese to deal with the effects of Western civilization. If a person is affected more than superficially by Western civilization, Natsume held, he will have a nervous breakdown. In one of his novels a person asks, "But wouldn't Japan develop more and more from now on?" Another character answers, "It will perish."[4] Higuchi Ichiyō was the first prominent female writer to emerge in the modern period, symbolizing the re-emergence of women writers for the first time since the golden age of women writers in the Heian era. Her novel *Growing Up* (Takekurabe) was praised by Mori Ōgai, calling her writing poetic and her depiction of the characters in the novel as "human beings with whom we can laugh and cry together."[5]

Literature flourished into the twentieth century with eminent writers crowding the scene. In poetry also creative figures emerged producing poems in long stanzas rather than the short haiku and waka. The topics were no longer confined to love or natural beauty but dealt with life and the human condition. A poet of this new age, Ishikawa Takuboku (1885–1912), believed that: "We must rigorously reject all fantasies and concern ourselves with the only truth that remains – necessity!"[6] The poet who continued to compose in haiku style was Masaoka Shiki (1867–1902). He believed in the need to preserve the best in traditional culture. He told his disciples to focus on natural objects, and not to seek to inject logic or reasoning in their poems. He composed haiku poems like: "Cold Moon / shadow of a tombstone / shadow of a pine."[7]

SOCIAL DEVELOPMENTS

The peasantry

The economic policies pursued by the government placed heavy burdens on the peasantry. At the end of Tokugawa rule peasant uprisings demanding reduction of economic burdens broke out. These uprisings continued even after the Meiji government was established. Peasants demanded the elimination of the surviving feudal obligations. Some of the uprisings involved large numbers. The 1870 uprising in present-day Nagano Prefecture involved seventy thousand people. Another uprising in Fukuoka in Kyushu involved three hundred thousand peasants who destroyed 4,590 buildings. In order to deal with peasant discontent the government reduced the land tax in 1876 but the deflationary policy adopted by Finance Minister Matsukata resulted in a drop in farm income and increase in peasant debts. In 1885 more than one hundred thousand families went bankrupt.

As a result of the economic difficulties peasant uprisings continued into the early 1880s, culminating in the Chichibu uprising of 1884. A Hardship Party was organized in Chichibu (in the Kantō region) demanding reduction in taxes and a moratorium on debt repayment. When these demands were not met five thousand protesters marched toward the city of Chichibu. The government sent troops in and crushed the movement. The leaders were executed or imprisoned. One leader fled to Hokkaido and remained in hiding for thirty-five years.

Faced with starvation some peasants resorted to infanticide. One account tells of a father, in the late 1880s, who unable to bear the agonies of his starving children, decapitated them to relieve them of their miseries. The infanticide rate rose as families kept only one boy and one girl and killed others at birth.

Most of the peasants lived a strenuous life of poverty and long hours of torturous work with little financial return. There was nothing idyllic or romantic about farming. Noting that farm work was more strenuous for girls than working in the textile mills a villager remarked: "They cut trees in the mountains and remove stones to make untilable plots for growing millet and barnyard grass ... They climb steep hills with firewood on their backs, burn charcoal in the snow, dig bracken roots, work all night to make bracken-root powder... They continue working from before dawn until ten and eleven at night."[8] The farm workers struggled in the villages with little relief almost to the present-day.

The villages enjoyed few of the modern facilities and amenities that were beginning to appear in the towns and cities. Life for the peasants remained as primitive and difficult as it was in the Tokugawa years. One young city dweller observed, "There is no one as miserable as a peasant ... The peasants (in northern Japan) wear rags, eat coarse cereals, and have many children. They are as black as their dirt walls and lead grubby, joyless lives that can be compared to those of insects that crawl along the ground and stay alive by licking the dirt."[9]

Confronted with poverty and financial needs many peasants were compelled to send their daughters at near slave wages to the emerging textile plants in the cities or dispatch them to the public brothels in the cities.

Faced with economic difficulties tenancy rose among the peasantry. In the early Meiji years the rate of tenancy was twenty percent of the cultivated land. This rose to forty percent in the late 1880s, and forty-five percent in 1910. The rental charges were forty-five to sixty percent of the crop on rice fields; in extreme cases it was as high as eighty percent. An indication of the growing poverty of the population was the decline in the number of voters. Voters, restricted to males, had to pay a tax of five yen or more to be eligible to vote. Taking 1881 as index 100, the figure dropped to eighty-four in 1886, sixty-four in 1891 and fifty-nine in 1894. Neither the government nor the emerging opposition parties lifted a hand to help the impoverished peasants.

Military conscription was an additional burden for the peasants who constituted a large percentage of the population. At the end of its regime the Bakufu was moving to enlist peasants into its forces to shore up its defense against the opposition. In 1864 it enlisted as many as fifteen hundred peasants to combat the anti-Bakufu insurgency in Mito-han. It continued to enlist peasants into its forces and armed them with rifles but this did little to help it crush the opposition. Anti-Bakufu clans like Chōshū enlisted peasants into its "shock troop" unit. When the Meiji government introduced universal military conscription the peasants were not gratified in being asked to perform the task formerly reserved to the samurai. They were suspicious and fearful of the system. It was often referred to as *ketsuzei* (blood tax). Many peasants believed that blood was to be taken from them. Rumors spread that "they will draft young men, hang them upside down, and draw out their blood so that Westerners can drink it."[10] Riots against military conscription broke out in different areas. The rich could pay their way out of having their sons serve in the army but the fee was too high for the common peasants. Also family heads and eldest sons were exempt so only younger sons were subject to the draft. The government did its best to convince the peasants of the importance of serving, and the Sino-Japanese War of 1894–95 fired up militarism throughout the land. The young peasants remained gun-fire fodder until the end of the Second World War.

Factory workers

As Japan industrialized workers in the industrial plants steadily increased in number. Working conditions and relations with employers were unlike those in the small shops where a close personal master-follower relationship prevailed. In theory the master was supposed to care for the well-being of the workers like a father. The employer-employee relationship of the new industrial plants was much more impersonal. The object of the employer was to increase productivity and financial gain. The result was unrestrained exploitation of the workers who were expected to behave in the traditional mode of hardwork, obedience, loyalty to the employer. Thus long hours, low wages, unsafe working conditions were common.

The majority of the workers in the textile plants were young workers. Young farm girls were sent into the weaving sheds, cotton spinning mills, and silk filatures. The peasant families were impoverished and the income received by sending their young daughters to the silk and cotton plants was essential for their survival. The families received a fixed sum of money to have their daughters work in the plants for a certain number of years as virtually indentured servants. In the late nineteenth century eighty to ninety percent of the workers in these factories were women; forty-nine percent of the workers were under twenty and thirteen percent were younger than fourteen. They were commonly housed in factory dormitories where they were closely guarded. They usually worked twelve hours a day with only one short period for lunch. During busy periods they were put to work as much as nineteen hours a day. In small weaving shops and silk filatures the workers were required to produce a fixed quota. Those who failed to do so were regarded as slackers and were punished by reduction in food. They were even punished physically. The hardships and crowded unsanitary conditions resulted in many contracting tuberculosis, and the death rate from tuberculosis was high among the textile plant workers. Those who contracted tuberculosis either died at work or were sent home. A 1913 government survey indicated that forty percent of those working in these plants died of tuberculosis and seventy percent of those who died after returning to their village died of the disease. The spread of tuberculosis in the countryside has been ascribed to the afflicted workers who returned to the villages, and tuberculosis became a major killer in prewar Japan. Long hours and pressure to work at a fast pace resulted in high incidence of accidents. The employers attributed this to carelessness by the workers and the Factory Act of 1911 contained no provisions to ensure the safety of workers.

The wages of the textile workers were lower than the pay the workers in India received, a land where the standard of living was assumed to be lower than that of Japan. In 1891 the labor cost to produce one hundred pounds of cotton yarn in Japan was 135.5 sen. In India it was 151.9 sen. The Japanese textile workers were paid one tenth the wages of British workers in 1893. The male workers received higher wages than women. In 1898 men in ten cotton-spinning plants were paid 24.5 sen a day compared to 13.9 sen for women. Workers in heavy industry were paid more but still earned barely enough to support their families. The employers argued that cheap labor was necessary to enable Japanese manufacturers to compete in the international market. The entrepreneurs, however, accumulated huge profits and by the twentieth century many super-wealthy tycoons emerged.

The area where the workers were exploited most harshly was in coal mining. Although some prisoners were used in state enterprises in the early Meiji years, it was in mining where prisoners were utilized in larger numbers and over a longer period. The practice prevailed from 1873 to 1931 though the percentage of prisoners employed in mining gradually declined. In addition to prisoners the miners came from the impoverished peasantry, the outcaste community, and after the colonization of Korea, Koreans. One of the largest coal mining enterprises was the Miike coal mines in northern Kyushu run by the Mitsui company. In 1896 seventy-five percent of the miners were convicts. Even though the percentage of convicts used in mining declined in Miike by the turn of the century, an increasing number of prisoners were sent to the mines in Hokkaido. They were made to work long hours and in many mines they were housed in "octopus rooms," in effect prison cells. Treatment of miners was brutal in most mines. When miners rioted in the 1880s, protesting onerous working conditions and treatment at the Takashima mines managed by the Mitsubishi company, a reporter went to investigate the working conditions. He found that miners were working deep underground in high temperatures, and were beaten if the crew boss thought they were slackening the pace of work. If they tried to escape they were trussed up and clubbed. He reported that when a cholera epidemic broke out in 1884 half of the three thousand mine-workers contracted the disease and died. The day after a person caught the disease he was taken out and burned, whether he was dead or alive.

After Korea was annexed a large number of Koreans were dragooned into the work force and sent to the Kyushu and Hokkaido mines. The number of Koreans sent to the mines increased drastically during the Second World War. In 1944 over 128,000 Koreans were in the mines, 31.9% of all miners. The Korean workers were treated much more brutally than Japanese workers. One woman miner noted that the Korean miners were "beaten up all the time by the guards. They would beat Japanese too, but they beat up Koreans much more severely."[11] One Korean miner, who had been forced into the mines in 1942, tried to escape.

He was captured and, "I was tied up with a rope and beaten. I fainted but was revived with a bucket of water. They then placed two iron rods on the stove, heated them up and applied them on my back. I smelled my burning flesh ... I passed out." He tried escaping again, was caught, tortured and sent to another mine where the same brutal treatment prevailed and many miners died. One of his fellow miners was tortured and went mad.[12]

Women and children were also sent down the mines. The ban on using women in the mines did not take effect until 1928. The ban was revoked in 1938 because of increasing labor shortage during Japan's war against China. In 1946 under U.S. occupation a total ban on employing women in the mines was imposed.

The government did little to ensure the safety and well-being of the workers. In fact it stood behind the entrepreneurs. The Civil Code of 1890 upheld the concept of "freedom of contract" and prevented the workers from engaging in strikes. The Police Regulation of 1900 prohibited the organization of workers to stage strikes. Some acts were passed to regulate conditions in the mines and factories. In 1905 a mine act and in 1911 a factory act were passed but because of opposition by the industrialists they did not come into effect until 1916. The provisions were modest. The acts limited the workday for women and children under fifteen to twelve hours a day. The minimum age of employment was fixed at twelve. For light work it was ten years of age. No restrictions on night work were imposed. Even these modest provisions were violated. During the First World War children under eight years of age were employed in match factories.

The movement by the workers to gain better pay and working conditions did emerge but only on a limited scale. The first strike was staged by women cotton-mill workers in 1884 but they failed to gain concessions. Other strikes were staged after the Sino-Japanese War but they were ineffective in winning better wages and conditions. But around this time movements to organize unions began to emerge. The first serious effort was made in 1897 with the establishment of the Society for the Protection of Trade Unions under the leadership of Takano Fusataro (1868–1904), an admirer of Samuel Gompers, and Katayama Sen (1859–1933), a believer in Christian socialism and international communism. Led by this group organizations of ironworkers, railroad workers, and printers emerged but they emphasized reforms and did not focus on strikes to gain concessions. In 1912 Suzuki Bunji (1885–1946), a Christian social worker, organized the *Yūaikai* (Fraternal Organization) to foster harmony between labor and capital. But by 1915 Suzuki began to support the workers' right to organize and strike. So the *Yūaikai* began to take on the characteristic of a labor union, and the government began to harass it. Around this time strikes broke out with greater frequency even though they remained illegal. In 1914 there were fifty strikes involving a modest number of workers, 7,900. In 1919 the strikes had increased to 497 with sixty-three thousand workers participating. The number of union members increased in the 1920s. In 1921 there were 103,400 members and in 1926 about 385,000. Still this constituted only six to seven percent of industrial workers.

In 1919 the *Yūaikai* moved toward establishing itself as a labor union and changed its name to *DaiNihon Rōdō Sōdōmei Yūaikai* (Yuaikai of All Japan Federation of Labor). It declared its objective to be the freedom to organize labor unions, elimination of child labor, and a minimum wage. It also called for universal suffrage, revision of the Police Regulation Law, and democratic reforms in the educational system. The movement began to gain some concessions. For example in 1919 the Kawasaki shipyard workers in Kobe won an eight-hour workday agreement. This was followed by similar agreements in other heavy industrial plants. Concessions were not granted to female textile mill workers, however. They continued to work eleven to twelve hours a day.

The *Yūaikai* leadership did not favor militant action by the workers but the mine-workers tended to be more active in protesting the working conditions. Christian reformers and socialists encouraged the miners to organize unions. The first organization was formed in 1902 in Hokkaido to encourage self-help but the leaders also called for "equal rights and freedom in our relationship with the capitalist employers." The strike staged in 1907 in Hokkaido led to violence and destruction of property by the strikers. The government sent in troops to quell the strikers. In 1918 when protest against rice prices took place the miners also protested about high rice prices. They demanded higher wages, and engaged in destruction of property. Again the army was sent to disperse the demonstrators. In subsequent strikes the leaders endeavored to curb unruly actions by the strikers to prevent the employers from calling on the government to send in troops. So there was no violence in the strikes of 1924 and 1927 but strikers gained little from their activities.

A split emerged in the Rōdō Sōdōmei Yūaikai leadership as the more radical elements began advocating the overthrow of the capitalists and taking over the means of production. Clearly the impact of the Bolshevik Revolution was influential among the radical leadership. Syndicalists led by Arahata Kanson (1887–1981) advocated engaging in militant action while the more moderate group favored gaining concessions through peaceful means. The militants' position was enhanced when the workers staged a strike at the Mitsubishi and Kawasaki shipyards in Kobe because the employers locked out the workers and the governor called in army troops against the strikers. But the moderates still remained influential in the *Sōdōmei* so the Communist-led unions broke with the *Sodomei* and formed the Labor Council (Rōdō Hyōgikai) in 1925.

The government began to make some concessions during the 1920s, a decade of rising democratic demands. In 1925 the Police Regulation Law was revised, eliminating restrictions on labor activities. But it restricted strikes in public enterprises and defense industries. Violence in labor disputes was to be controlled. The Great Depression of 1929 and subsequent Japanese military activities on the continent had a restraining effect on the labor movement. Workers did not want to be viewed as being unpatriotic when Japan was launching a "righteous" war. In 1933 the Industrial Labor Club was organized, emphasizing "industrial patriotism." In 1938 the Patriotic Industrial Association was established and in 1940 all independent labor unions disbanded and joined the Patriotic Industrial Association.

Women in the new age

The new age did not result in any rise in the status of women. Legally, politically, and socially they continued to be treated as they were in the feudalistic Tokugawa society. The philosophy of Kaibara Ekken still governed the male-dominated society. At the outset, during the period when the movement for "civilization and enlightenment" was vibrant some advocates championed the cause of women. Among them was Fukuzawa Yukichi who called for equality between men and women. He asserted: "Men are human beings, so are women." The family system should be built on the relationship between husband and wife, not on father and son as taught by the Confucians. "The great foundation of human relations consists of husband and wife. The relationship between husband and wife emerged before that of parents and children or brothers and sisters," he contended. He continued: "Marriage being a partnership of equals, women should have the same rights as men to run the household, own property, get a divorce, remarry, and so on." He also pointed out that women are just as intelligent as men; girls should be given the same upbringing and education as boys.[13] Others of his circle shared Fukuzawa's views. Mori Arinori condemned the unequal husband-wife relationship that prevailed in Japan and argued that upon marriage marital contracts should be signed defining the rights and obligations of both parties.

Some women participated in the people's rights movement that emerged in the 1870s. But granting rights to women was the farthest from the minds of the Meiji leaders. In 1882 the government prohibited women from making political speeches, and in 1890 it banned women from taking part in any political activities. They were even forbidden to listen to political speeches. The Police Security Regulations of 1900 prohibited women from forming any political organization. The Meiji Civil Code of 1898 gave the head of the extended family virtually absolute authority over the members of the family. Some of the more liberal practices that prevailed among Tokugawa townspeople were eliminated. Primogeniture was mandated for all classes. The extended family head was given the right to control the family property, determine the place of residence of all family members, and approve or disapprove marriages and divorces. The wife was placed under the absolute authority of the family head and husband. She had no legal rights. One of the provisions stated, "cripples and disabled persons, and wives cannot undertake any legal action."

The Christian leaders set out to try to eliminate polygamy and public brothels. The legal code of 1870 provided for legal recognition of concubines. In 1882 the practice of registering concubines in the family register was ended. Women committing adultery were punished severely but men could do so with impunity. Brothel districts continued to exist in most cities. Those serving in the brothels were young girls and women who were sold into the brothels by impoverished families, mostly poor peasant families. As the urban population grew so did the patrons of brothels. As a result the number of brothel inmates steadily increased. In 1904 there 43,134 servers in the public brothels. By 1924 the number had risen to 52,325. This inhumane system prevailed until the end of the Second World War.

Among those who sought to close brothels was a Christian educator, Yajima Kajiko (1833–1925). The only place she and the reformers were successful in getting public brothels banned was in Gumma prefecture, near Tokyo. In 1882 the prefectural assembly banned public brothels in that prefecture. The leader of the Salvation Army, Yamamuro Gumpei (1872–1940), was another fighter against the institution but his attempts were not successful although he succeeded in freeing some indentured girls and women. The efforts to ban the system were circumvented whenever there was a famine that compelled starving peasants to send their daughters into the brothels. They were sent not only to brothels in Japan but many were sent to overseas brothels in the Asian continent as well as in South-East Asia. It is estimated that in 1910 there were anywhere from three thousand five hundred to five thousand Japanese women in Singapore brothels.

Although the education act called for the education of both boys and girls, as noted earlier, attendance by girls was low until the turn of the century. Education of girls was limited largely to the elementary school level. Above the elementary school level the government decreed in 1879 that boys and girls must attend separate schools. In 1895 there were only thirty-seven schools for girls above the elementary level. These were operated primarily by missionaries. The first college for women was established only in 1911. In 1899 the Ministry of Education stated the goal of high school education for girls was to educate them to become "good wives and wise mothers." It held that "elegant and refined manners, and docility and modesty are qualities that must be fostered." Hence the domestic arts were stressed and few courses in mathematics, science or foreign languages were included in the curriculum. This attitude prevailed also among family members.

Ishimoto Shidzue (1897–) recalled in the 1930s, "Consciously or unconsciously, my mother taught her daughter to crush her desires and ambitions, and trained her to be ready to submerge her individuality in her husband's personality and his family's united temper."[14] As noted above a large percentage of girls labored on family farm plots or in textile mills. The one area that became open to women was teaching in the elementary schools. Here too they were usually assigned to the lower grade classes but at least teaching was open to them. The number of women in college remained small until the end of the Second World War but it was also an avenue not open to most males from farm and working families. The one area that opened up for Japanese women earlier than American women was medicine. The pioneer woman who fought for the right to become a medical doctor was Takahashi Mizuko (1852–1927). The government did not grant medical licenses to women so Takahashi, with a few other women, petitioned the government to change its policy which it did in 1884. In order to become a doctor Takahashi applied to a medical school but was denied admission. She then staged a sit-in for three days and three nights at the front gate of another school to compel it to admit her which it finally did. In 1887 she became the first woman doctor in Japan. Another woman who fought for women's right to become doctors was Yoshioka Yayoi (1871–1959). In 1900 she established a preparatory medical school for women. The graduates of her school, however, could not practice medicine until 1912 because the government refused to certify the school and did not allow its graduates to take the national medical examination. After 1912 the enrollment in Yoshioka's medical school increased and by 1928 over eight hundred students had received medical education in Yoshioka's medical college.

Women's struggle to gain social and political equality did not really gain momentum until the socialist-communist movements after the turn of the century.

TURN OF THE CENTURY POLITICAL DEVELOPMENTS

The adoption of the constitution and the establishment of the Diet should have provided a chance for those excluded from the inner power circle to break the monopolistic control of the oligarchs.

But the oligarchs retained the means of control within and without the framework of the constitution. They still had personal links to the Emperor who retained sovereign power under the constitution. He remained "sacred and inviolable." The cabinet was appointed by the Emperor and was responsible to him, not the Diet. The oligarchs were members of the Privy Council, and the House of Peers. They monopolized the premiership. Itō was the leader who held that position most often. The armed forces were not subject to Dietary control except on budgetary matters. The military was virtually the personal bailiwick of Yamagata Aritomo who, on various occasions, served as general chief of staff, minister of war and Prime Minister. The practice of the small clique of power-wielders arriving at consensual decisions made the whole system function outside the constitutional framework. The wielders of power were most often not persons holding key positions but those who operated from behind the scenes.

The first Diet elections were held in July 1890. The franchise was highly restricted. The two opposition parties were the revived Liberal Party under Itagaki and the Progressive Party (former Reform Party) now bereft of Ōkuma's leadership for he had left the party in 1884. The former won 130 seats and the later forty-one. The pro-government party won seventy-nine seats.

The political parties were organized primarily on the basis of personal and regional ties rather than on definitive principles and objectives. They failed to work together to challenge the government leaders and devoted as much time and energy on interparty and intraparty disputes. The government leaders assumed the stance of "standing above parties" and did not bring party leaders into the cabinet.

Yamagata, who was Prime Minister when the first Diet convened, took an especially hard line toward the political parties. Itō, on the other hand, was more willing to adopt a moderate stance. Thus a breach began to develop between the two leaders. Yamagata became the leader of the "military" faction and Itō the "civil" faction.

The constitutional provision that gave the Diet the authority to challenge the government was taxation and the budget. Confronted with adamant opposition in the Diet over the budget the government leaders quite often dissolved the Diet, held a new election and sought to influence the vote by bribery, intimidation and even violence. In 1892 when the Diet sought to reduce the naval budget the government, headed by Itō, invoked article 67 of the constitution which stipulated that fixed expenditure based upon the supreme powers of the Emperor could not be rejected or reduced by the Diet, and got the Emperor to issue an edict asking the Diet to accept the budget which was essential to national defense. In other words, the Emperor was a tool of the power elite, the so-called "genro." This undermined the Diet's only legal basis to challenge the government.

In the midst of the political squabbles between the government and the political parties a foreign policy crisis developed that compelled the two sides to put aside their differences and join hands in face of a national crisis. This was the confrontation with China.

CONFRONTATION WITH CHINA OVER KOREA

From early in the Meiji era some Japanese leaders harbored imperialistic designs on Korea. This was revealed in Saigō's plan to launch a campaign against Korea. In 1876 Japan persuaded Korea to establish diplomatic relations and accept an unequal treaty providing special rights to Japanese in Korea. In Korea there was disagreement between those who opposed opening the country to the outside world and those who favored modernizing the country by following the course adopted by Japan. The anti-Japan conservative faction staged an uprising in 1882. The Queen asked the Chinese government to intervene. In Japan the war faction led by Yamagata, used the attack on the Japanese legation as a pretext to send troops into Korea. The rebels were defeated by Chinese forces but the Japanese war faction used the turmoil in Korea and the extension of Chinese forces there as an excuse to expand its military and naval forces. Itō, on the other hand, felt that Japan was not ready for a military confrontation with China, and in 1885 negotiated an agreement with the Chinese leader, Li Hung-zhang. The Li–Itō Convention provided for the withdrawal of Chinese and Japanese forces from Korea. Both nations agreed to notify the other nation before they dispatched troops into Korea.

Unrest in Korea continued as economic hardship beset the people. In this situation a religious cult, the Tong Hak Society, emerged pledging to save Korea from foreign encroachments, and to aid and enrich the poor. In 1894 the society staged an uprising. The Korean government asked the Chinese government for help to subdue the rebels. Thereupon the Japanese leaders went on wartime footing and dispatched troops to Korea even before they were notified of China's decision to send in troops. Japanese intervention led to clashes with Chinese forces and Japan declared war on China in August. So started Sino-Japanese War.

The Japanese army and navy had been modernized and were better prepared for warfare than the Chinese. China had been beset by the intervention of Western powers since the Opium War with Britain (1839–1842) as well as by domestic uprisings. The Japanese forces moved north, and crossed the Yalu River into Chinese territory. The Japanese navy defeated the Chinese fleet on the Yellow Sea and gained naval supremacy. They then dispatched troops into Liaodung Peninsula and captured Port Arthur. China accepted Japanese military supremacy and decided to negotiate an end to the war. Itō did not favor inflicting a crushing blow on China because he believed it would disrupt the political order in China and could result in further Western encroachments in that country. In March 1895 Li Hungzhang arrived in Shimonoseki and negotiated a peace treaty. The terms of the settlement entailed Chinese recognition of Korean independence, cession of the Liaodung Peninsula, Formosa, and the Pescadores to Japan, payment of an indemnity, conclusion of a commercial treaty with Japan, and extension of certain navigational, and manufacturing rights to the Japanese.

The war aroused war fervor and nationalistic sentiments among the Japanese. Even intellectual liberals like Fukuzawa Yukichi became chauvinistic proponents of total defeat of China. Christian leaders like Uchimura Kanzō also saw the war as a just war. In a way this conflict can be seen as an epochal event that aroused and fostered Japanese militarism and imperialism. Henceforth Japanese foreign policy would take a much more aggressive, chauvinistic turn.

The Japanese victory, however, gave rise to new problems in international power politics. Russia also hoped to extend its influence into Manchuria and Korea so it objected to the Shimonoseki settlement that gave Japan control over the Liaodung Peninsula. She persuaded France and Germany to join in a protest over Japanese acquisition of the peninsula. Faced with the triple intervention the Japanese government was compelled to relinquish its control over the peninsula in return for additional indemnities. This affair aroused the Japanese public and triggered anti-Russian sentiments. Faced with the confrontation with Russia the government began to increase the size of the army and navy.

Japanese acquisition of Formosa was resisted by the residents of the island but the Japanese quelled the resistance and began implementing a colonial policy that was relatively liberal. The governor-general adopted a policy of promoting the welfare of the indigenous population and introduced measures to enhance health and sanitary conditions, improve the infrastructure, and increase agricultural production. As a result Japanese colonial policy in Formosa proved to be fairly enlightened.

Japanese efforts to extend its influence into Korea encountered more obstacles. In Korea the struggle between the pro-Japanese faction and the group that sought to resist Japanese incursions led to a faction, headed by Queen Min, to turn to Russia for support. One result was that Japanese officials played a part in assassinating Queen Min. This resulted in the resurgence of anti-Japanese sentiments in Korea and a renewed turn to Russia for aid. This rivalry between Japan and Russia in Korea contributed to the outbreak of the Russo-Japanese War.

Following the Sino-Japanese War Japan increased its economic activities in Korea, exporting cotton products to Korea and importing Korean rice. It also engaged in railroad construction and began to move toward the Yalu River to develop the timber industry in that region. This clashed with Russian interests. Russia had agreed in the Nish-Rosen Agreement of 1898 not to hinder Japan's commercial and industrial relations with Korea but the Japanese move into the Yalu River region clashed with Russia's hope of developing the timber industry there.

Russia's primary interest, however, was in extending its interests in Manchuria and also acquiring an ice-free port in East Asia. In 1896 Russia got China to agree to the construction of a railroad across northern Manchuria to connect the Trans-Siberian Railroad to Vladivostok. Thus the Chinese Eastern Railroad came to be constructed. Following the *Triple Intervention* Russia got China to agree to lease the Liaodung Peninsula and Port Arthur for twenty years. Thus Russia acquired what she had forced Japan to relinquish. Russia also got the right to build the South Manchurian Railroad to link the Chinese Eastern Railroad to Port Arthur. In order to establish a direct link between Vladivostok and Port Arthur Russia wished to gain access through Korea and so opposed Japan's move to extend her dominion into Korea.

Japan was concerned about Russian designs on Korea as well as the presence of Russian troops in Manchuria which had been dispatched there during the Chinese Boxer Rebellion of 1900. The troops were to have been withdrawn after the end of the Boxer Rebellion but Russia delayed the withdrawal. In preparation for a possible conflict with Russia Japan concluded the Anglo-Japanese Alliance in 1902. Britain and Japan agreed to maintain the *status quo* and general peace in East Asia, and in case one of the parties got involved in a war the other party would remain neutral unless Japan or Britain themselves were attacked by more than one power. Japanese officials initiated discussions with Russia with the aim of getting Russia to acknowledge Japan's special interests in Korea. In return Japan would recognize Russian interests in Manchuria. Neither side was willing to grant the other a free hand in Korea or Manchuria. Negotiations broke down and Japanese officials decided on war in February 1904.

After naval skirmishes off the coast of Inchon, the Japanese fleet under Admiral Tōgō attacked the Russian Pacific fleet stationed in Port Arthur on February 9. Then it declared war on Russia on the 10th. Japan was in a more favorable position to fight because it had a well-trained army close to the battle zone while Russia had to transport its troops over five thousand miles from Moscow to Port Arthur. Japanese troops crossed the Yalu into Manchuria and defeated the Russian forces in the Liaodung Peninsula. The Russian fleet at Port Arthur had been crippled but the fortress at Port Arthur presented a more formidable target for the Japanese forces. General Nogi led the campaign from May to December 1904. He launched charge after charge against the fort, paying no heed to the casualties incurred. After 240 days of fighting and a 156 day siege the Russian commander, General Stessel, decided to surrender. At the end of this campaign the toll of dead and wounded Japanese troops came to 57,780. Russian casualties numbered about half that figure. Despite this General Nogi gained the reputation as a great military leader and was lionized by the officials and the people.

The major land battle of the war was fought at Mukden in March 1905. There three hundred thousand Japanese and 310,000 Russian troops engaged in battle. After a ten-day battle the Russian forces were compelled to retreat north. The Russian war planners awaited the arrival of the Baltic fleet that was sent to the battle zone in October 1904. After an eighteen thousand mile trouble-laden journey the fleet arrived at the East China Sea. As it sought to pass through the Tsushima Straits between Korea and Japan it was met by the Japanese fleet commanded by Admiral Tōgō and was decimated in a twenty-four hour battle.

This loss persuaded the Russian government to accept the offer of President Theodore Roosevelt to mediate an end to the war. The delegates from the two nations met at Portsmouth, Maine in early August 1905 and signed the Portsmouth Treaty. Russia did not relinquish much in the Far East. Japan acquired the southern half of Sakhalin Island, the Russian Liaodung leasehold, and the South Manchurian Railroad. Russia also recognized Japan's paramount interests in Korea.

The Japanese gains under the treaty fell far short of what the public had expected. This led to protests by ultra-nationalists and violent clashes with the authorities. The war had aroused Japanese nationalism but not everyone had glorified the war. Budding socialist leaders like Kōtoku Shūsui (1871–1911) and others had expressed concern about the increasing hostility between Russia and Japan even before the outbreak of the war. Continued opposition to the war resulted in their imprisonment. Some writers also opposed the war. The poet Yosano Akiko (1878–1942) wrote a poem calling on her brother not to partake in the war. "Whether the fortress of Port Arthur falls / or does not fall, / is it any concern of yours."[15]

The victory over Russia made Japan a major player in the Far East. It led to the extension of Japanese interests in Manchuria and a more aggressive move in Korea. Beside Russia's recognition of Japan's paramount interests in Korea, the United States recognized Japan's special interests in Korea in the Taft-Katsura memorandum of July 1905. In return Japan agreed not to attempt to extend its influence into the Philippines. In renewing the Anglo-Japanese Treaty in 1905 Britain also recognized Japan's paramount interests in Korea.

This enabled Japan to move toward turning Korea into a protectorate and eventually a colony. In early 1906 Itō became the

Resident-General in Korea and began intervening in Korean foreign as well as domestic affairs. This triggered Korean opposition and violent conflicts. During 1906 and 1907 fifty to seventy thousand Koreans sought to combat Japanese incursion in Korean affairs. Itō brought in twenty thousand Japanese troops to crush the resisters and close to twelve thousand Korean fighters were killed between 1907 and 1908. In the fall of 1909 a Korean patriot killed Itō in Harbin, Manchuria where he had gone to confer with the Russian Finance Minister. This provided the hardliners like Yamagata with an excuse to push for the annexation of Korea, which took place in August 1910. The Koreans were compelled to endure Japanese rule until the end of the Second World War.

DOMESTIC DEVELOPMENTS AT THE END OF THE MEIJI ERA

The political parties cooperated and supported the government during the Sino-Japanese War approving the government's request for increasing military defense funds. But they failed to gain access to the government. The interparty rivalry made it possible for the oligarchic clique to take advantage of this by playing one party off against the other. Recognizing this situation the party leaders decided to form a united party, and in June 1898 dissolved the two parties and formed a new united party, the Constitutional Party.

Faced with this situation Itō considered establishing his own political party to parry the party leaders' opposition to his policies. But he failed to get the oligarchs' support for this plan. Yamagata, the conservative, authoritarian leader of the oligarchy, was adamant in his opposition.

Itō and Yamagata had cooperated in running the government since the departure of the three leaders of the Meiji Restoration, Saigō, Kido, and Ōkubo. Itō was more moderate, liberal, and flexible than Yamagata who was a more formidable defender of oligarchic control. Itō was the leader of the civilian and Yamagata the leader of the military faction. Yamagata had a strong power base in the army and the bureaucracy. He opposed Itō's plan to organize a political party asserting that it would bring about party government and democracy, and clash with the national polity. Faced with opposition from the ruling clique Itō, who was then Prime Minister, resigned and asked the Emperor to request Itagaki and Ōkuma to form a new cabinet. Thus the first party government came about in June 1898. Yamagata lamented this development as the end to the Meiji government.

Ōkuma became Prime Minister and Itagaki the Minister of Home Affairs. Even though the two parties had been merged into a united party, factionalism continued with squabbles over cabinet positions dividing the party. This resulted in a split between the two factions with Itagaki and his group leaving the cabinet. Ōkuma's attempt to carry on without the support of the former Liberal Party failed, and he had to resign. The party government had lasted only four months. The Constitutional Party then split into two separate parties.

Yamagata became the next Prime Minister and with the cooperation of the reconstituted Constitutional Party and by bribing Diet members he was able to raise taxes. Among the measures that he introduced were lower property qualifications for the franchise, an increase in the number of Diet members (from 300 to 369), and the introduction of the secret ballot. In order to end the spoils system he removed most bureaucratic positions from the appointment system and brought them under the examination system. He made the bureaucracy semi-autonomous, laying the basis for the system that came to function as a bulwark of entrenched conservatism to the present. He also revised the army and navy regulations making only active army and navy officers of the two top ranks eligible to serve as war and navy ministers. He introduced the Police Regulation Act of 1900 designed to curb the labor union organizers.

Itō continued his plan to organize a political party. The members of the Constitutional Party joined Itō in forming the *Rikken Seiyūkai* (Friends of Constitutional Government Association) in 1900. Itō formed a cabinet with the support of the *Seiyūkai* but he encountered opposition from the House of Peers, many of whom had been appointed by Yamagata. Faced with the opposition from the House of Peers and high-ranking bureaucrats as well as friction within the cabinet, Itō resigned, thus ending his effort at party government.

Itō was the last Prime Minister from the genrō clique. The government leadership passed on to Katsura Tarō (1847–1913), a disciple of Yamagata, and Saionji Kimmochi (1849–1940), a descendant of the Heian aristocracy. Saionji was liberally inclined, and was drawn to Rousseau's political concepts in his youth. In the background, of course, were the genrō, Itō and Yamagata. The latter turned out to be the chief power behind the bamboo screen. Katsura who had become Prime Minister found Itō's dual role as genrō and party chief frustrating and got Yamagata to ask the Emperor to have Itō cut his ties to the political party. Itō had to comply and in effect he retired from active politics in 1903. Itō's place as head of the *Seiyūkai* was taken by Saionji.

Katsura was Prime Minister during the Russo-Japanese War. He was succeeded by Saionji in 1906. The two men headed the cabinet alternately for the next twelve years. Yamagata became critical of Saionji, concerned that his ties with the *Seiyūkai* would undermine his power base. So he criticized Saionji as being soft on the socialists who were advocating political and social reforms.

Among the early socialists was Sakai Toshihiko (1870–1933). Some socialists were inclined to favor anarcho-syndicalism. Kōtoku Shūsui was a leading figure among them. There were also Christian reformers like Uchimura Kanzō. Among the early female activists in this circle was Kanno Sugako (1881–1911). The socialists organized the Commoners' Society (*Heiminsha*) in 1903 and began publishing a newspaper the *Heimin Shimbun*. When the Russo-Japanese War broke out they opposed the war. Sakai and Kōtoku were jailed and the *Heimin Shimbun* was suspended. After the war in 1906 the more moderate elements set out to organize the Socialist Party and received Saionji's approval. Among the leaders of this moderate faction was Katayama Sen who was active earlier in seeking to organize workers' unions. In order to carry on the struggle he and his cohorts organized the Social Democratic Party in 1901 but the government immediately disbanded the party.

Among the more radical elements was Kōtoku Shūsui who had gone to the United States after his release from prison in 1905. He remained in the United States until 1906 and established contacts with anarchists. Upon his return to Japan he became the informal leader of those who shared his philosophy. Among them was Kanno Sugako. She became the key figure in a plot to assassinate the Emperor. The plot was uncovered, and though Kōtoku was not directly involved he was charged, with a dozen others, with high treason.

Kanno had become involved in the radical reformist movement in order to fight for the improvement of women's plight. She became active in a movement to end the legalization of brothels, a movement led by Yajima Kajiko. Then she joined the *Heiminsha* circle and opposed the Russo-Japanese War. In her writings she protested the treatment of women in Japan. She wrote. "In accordance with long-standing customs, we have been seen as a form of material property. Women in Japan are in a state of slavery. Japan has become an advanced, civilized nation, but we women are still denied our freedom by an invisible iron fence ... Our ideal is socialism, which aims at the equality of all classes."[16] She became the key figure in the plot to assassinate the Emperor though the government charged Kōtoku with being the chief culprit. The plot, known as the Great Treason Incident, was uncovered in 1910 and twenty-six people were arrested. Of these twelve were executed, including Kanno and Kōtoku. During her interrogation Kanno remained adamant about sticking to her convictions. She asserted she had no regrets and though she felt sorry for the Emperor, "he is, as Emperor, the chief person responsible for the exploitation of the people economically. Politically he is at the root of all the crimes being committed, and intellectually he is the fundamental cause of superstitious beliefs." Facing imminent execution Kanno sought desperately to learn English. She notes, "the time had come for me to learn to read at least some simple English selections. I had to do so before I died ... I probably don't have much time left, so I guess I won't be able to master the language. I regret this very much."[17]

The execution of the twelve accused was lamented by a writer, Tokutomi Roka (1868–1927). He asserted: "The government officials who killed the twelve conspirators in the name of loyalty to the Throne are in fact the ones who are truly disloyal and unrightous subjects ... We must not fear rebellions. We must not be afraid to be rebels ourselves. What is new is always revolutionary."[18]

This incident put a temporary damper on the socialist movement and the government under Katsura set out to repress all socialists and totally eradicate any sign of socialist thinking. The government even banned a book entitled *Society of Insects* because of the word 'society.'

Soon after this incident, in August 1911, Emperor Meiji died, thus ending a remarkable era which saw the transformation of Japan from a closed feudalistic society to a "modern" state with political, economic, social, cultural, and intellectual changes. A constitutional government, however flawed, had been established. The rigid feudal social order was abolished and, although the class system still remained, there was greater social flexibility which enabled some lower class members to achieve social mobility. A modern educational system was introduced and education was available to all boys and girls. Industrial and commercial sectors saw significant growth. According to economists Ohkawa and Rosovsky the ground work for economic growth was laid during 1868–85, and the years 1886–1905 constituted the initial phase of modern economic growth. By the end of the Meiji era Japan had entered the second phase which extended to 1952. A modern army and navy had been established and Japan had become a major political and military power in East Asia with victories in the Sino-Japanese and Russo-Japanese wars.

Yet the mores and ways of Old Japan remained entrenched. An authority on Japanese art and a disciple of Fenollosa, Okakura Kakuzo observed: "One who looks beneath the surface of things can see, in spite of her modern garb, that the heart of Old Japan is still beating strongly."[19] A Western scholar saw the persistence of "the ideal of feudal loyalty, the patriarchal system, the attitude toward women, the exaltation of martial virtues."[20] Lafcadio Hearn, who immersed himself in Japanese life and culture, noted that: "In theory the individual is free; in practice he is scarcely more free than were his forefathers ... in every direction, the individual finds himself confronted by the despotism of collective opinion."[21] Emperor Meiji symbolized the persistence of the old order as the sacrosanct ruler. The concept of loyalty to the Emperor was instilled in the young people the instant they entered the public schools. Thus their minds were molded and some would die in battle shouting, "Emperor, Banzai, – hurrah for the Emperor." The Meiji oligarchs encircled the Emperor and exercised power in his name. Anyone who challenged the existing order was condemned as a disloyal traitor. As Kanno stated, the Emperor was the lynchpin that held up the established order.

SIX

The Taishō Years:
the Road to Democracy

FOREIGN RELATIONS

Emperor Taishō who succeeded Emperor Meiji was in poor health. He was on the throne from 1912 to 1926 but in 1921 he had to turn over the imperial duties to his son, Hirohito, who served as regent. At the governmental level Katsura and Saionji served as Prime Minister alternately from 1901 to 1913. The major problems confronting them were fiscal with demands for high funding by the army and navy. In 1914 Ōkuma who had been out of active politics became Prime Minister but before he could turn his attention to domestic policies, he was confronted with the outbreak of the First World War. Japan immediately entered the war on the side of the Allied powers. The Anglo-Japanese Alliance provided them with the excuse to enter the war but the real motivation was to take over the German concessions in China. Japan quickly gained possession of the German holdings in Shandung Peninsula and some Pacific islands.

In 1915 the Japanese government presented China with the Twenty-one Demands. Aside from the transference of the German concessions to Japan, various provisions recognizing Japanese special interests in certain regions, such as south Manchuria were included. The provisions that aroused U.S. concerns dealt with Japanese incursions into China's political, financial, military, and police affairs. Japan eventually deleted the latter conditions and China signed the agreement.

U.S.-Japanese relations had been fairly smooth during most of the Meiji period. The U.S. was supportive of Japan in the Russo-Japanese War and accepted Japanese control of Korea. The issue that began to ruffle feathers was the question of Japanese immigrants in the United States. In the 1890s Japanese immigration to Hawaii and California increased steadily and by 1900 there were sixty-one thousand immigrants in Hawaii, and twenty-four thousand in California. By 1907 in the mainland there were 39,531 Japanese immigrants who arrived directly from Japan and 32,855 who had come from Hawaii. This led to the outburst of fervid anti-Japanese sentiments, especially in California. The press played up the menace of the Yellow Peril and the Asiatic Exclusion League agitated to exclude Asian immigrants. In 1906 the San Francisco school board adopted a plan to segregate Oriental children in the public schools. This was directed mainly against Japanese children because Chinese children were already segregated. The school board said this move was necessary "to save White children from being affected by association with pupils of the Mongolian race."[1] In 1908 President Theodore Roosevelt got the Japanese government to agree to a "Gentlemen's Agreement" to limit the inflow of Japanese immigrants to the U.S. Agitation against the Japanese continued and anti-Japanese riots broke out in San Francisco. In 1913 California passed the Alien Land Act preventing aliens from owning land. In 1922 the Supreme Court held that Japanese were ineligible for citizenship, and 1924 Congress passed an immigration act that prevented people ineligible for citizenship from entering the country.

At the governmental level the two governments began to encounter conflict of interests in China. Japan wanted the United States to recognize Japan's "paramount interests in China" but the only agreement that Japan acquired was the Lansing-Ishii agreement of 1917 in which the U.S. recognized Japan's special interests in China while reaffirming China's territorial integrity and the "Open Door Policy" in China that prohibited the establishment of special spheres of interest.

The other development that aroused United States concern was Japanese presence in Siberia following the Bolshevik Revolution in Russia. In response to French and British appeals the United States sent troops into Siberia to aid the Czech troops that were clashing with Bolshevik forces. The Czech troops were moving across Siberia to return to Europe. Japan readily responded to the request to aid the Czech troops and dispatched seventy-two thousand troops to Siberia. The United States sent a smaller force of seven thousand men. After the Czech troops were repatriated the U.S. withdrew its troops in early 1920 but Japanese forces had advanced as far as Irkutsk, and the Japanese government did not withdraw them until the latter part of 1922 when the Soviet government was consolidating its authority over all of Russia. Japan soon reconciled itself to the presence of the new Russian authority in East Asia and recognized the Soviet government in 1925.

The 1919 Paris peace conference approved Japanese control of the German holdings in Shandung Peninsula and the Pacific islands. It failed, however, to get a clause on racial equality in the covenant of the League of Nations. Following the conference Japanese relations with the major powers remained relatively tranquil. Foreign policy makers like Shidehara Kijūrō (1872–1951) generally pursued a course of international cooperation. In 1921–22 Japan participated in the Washington Conference. The conference resulted in the conclusion of the Four Power Pacific Treaty and the Five Power Naval Treaty.

In the former treaty the United States, Great Britain, France and Japan agreed to respect the signatories' rights in the Pacific Ocean region, and to settle all disagreements by a conference of the four powers. The signatories to the latter were the United States, Great Britain, France, Italy, and Japan. The agreement provided for a ratio of 5:5:3:1.75:1.75 for the naval capital ship tonnage for the United States, Great Britain, Japan, France, and Italy respectively. It also provided for the maintenance of the *status quo* in fortifications and naval bases in the Pacific.

The conference also concluded the Nine Power Treaty. The signatories included the above five powers plus China, Belgium, the Netherlands, and Portugal. The signatories pledged to respect "the sovereignty, independence and territorial and administrative integrity of China." They also affirmed the Open Door Policy to ensure equal commercial opportunities in China for all powers. The policy of international cooperation continued to the end of the 1920s and the rightist government under General Tanaka Giichi (1882–1962) signed the Kellogg-Briand Pact of 1928 which outlawed war.

The Paris conference's decision to grant German concessions to Japan triggered the May Fourth Movement in China. Wide public protests against Japanese imperialism erupted. At the Washington conference a settlement between China and Japan was reached. Japan agreed to return the German holdings in Shandung Peninsula but it got China to agree to allow Japan to retain the railroad on the peninsula for fifteen years. Sino-Japanese relations grew increasingly strained, however, as Japanese authorities intervened in Chinese political affairs during the 1920s when a power struggle among different warlord factions was taking place. Japan had gained control of the South Manchurian Railway from Russia at the end of the Russo-Japanese War, and was attempting to penetrate further into Manchuria and North China. In addition a strike against Japanese textile manufacturers in Shanghai resulted in bloodshed, further arousing anti-Japanese sentiments.

The Japanese annexation of Korea resulted in the establishment of military rule in that country and in economic exploitation with expropriation of farm land and domination of the commercial and industrial market. About fifty percent of the Korean rice crop was shipped back to Japan. Korean rice consumption dropped by half and Koreans were compelled to consume millet imported from Manchuria. Korean protesters against Japanese occupation were curbed forcefully by the Japanese authorities. One protest demonstration in 1919 resulted in close to two thousand casualties and mass arrests.

DOMESTIC POLITICAL DEVELOPMENTS

By the end of the Meiji era the older oligarchs were no longer directly involved in managing the affairs of state. Of the two dominant Meiji leaders, Itō had passed away in 1909 and Yamagata remained in the background as the actual wielder of power. In most instances he decided who should head the government. The political parties had become an integral part of the political process but the leadership was no longer driven by the earlier zeal to fight for "people's rights." They had become part of the establishment. Members of the two major parties, the *Seiyūkai* and the *Kenseitō* (successors to the Liberal Party and the Progressive Party) now consisted primarily of bureaucrats, journalists and businessmen. The parties were linked closely to, and backed by, the two major industrial-financial monopolistic conglomerates, Mitsui and Mitsubishi. By 1918 the political parties had established themselves firmly enough that even Yamagata had to accede to the formation of a party government by Hara Takashi (1856–1921), the head of the Seiyūkai.

Hara was basically conservative and adhered to the policy of "enriching and strengthening" the nation. His primary objective was not advancement of democracy so he resisted the move for universal male suffrage. He did, however, agree to lower the tax payment to qualify for the franchise from ten to three yen. Thus the number of voters increased from 2.6% of the population to double that figure. He refused to heed the labor leaders' plea to revise the Police Regulation Law that restricted union actions. He also moved to curb left-wing groups like the Socialist League. It was Hara who dispatched Japanese military forces to Siberia. In November 1921 Hara was assassinated by a young fanatic who said he did so to gain fame and to bring about revolutionary changes. Thus Hara became the first, but not the last, Prime Minister to be assassinated.

Following Hara's death a series of non-party governments were formed. The task of selecting the Prime Minister was inherited by Prince Saionji following Yamagata's death in 1922. Saionji now became the sole *genrō*, the chief adviser to the Emperor.

The catastrophe that beset the nation in 1923 was not political. It was the great earthquake that struck the Kantō region on September 1. It turned Tokyo into an inferno. The fire ravaged the entire city and over one hundred thousand people died and over half a million were injured. Close to seven hundred thousand houses were destroyed. The most pernicious aspect of the disaster was the vicious rumor that spread accusing the resident Koreans of starting the fire and committing all sorts of crimes. Mob hysteria resulted in attacks on the Koreans with hundreds being killed. An unofficial estimate counted 2,613 killed. Also over 160 Chinese were also attacked and killed. The authorities arrested or summarily executed socialists and labor leaders. Among them was a prominent anarchist Ōsugi Sakae (see p. 122).

The unwarranted attacks on these people aroused a young man, Namba Taisuke, who was influenced by syndicalism and anarchism, to attempt to assassinate the imperial regent, Hirohito. He fired a pistol at him but missed. He was arrested and executed. This incident heightened the vigilance against "dangerous thought" and reinforced right-wing nationalist sentiments. The Minister of Justice and future Prime Minister, Hiranuma Kiichi (1867–1952) organized the *Kokuhonsha* (National Foundation Society) to strengthen the national spirit.

The political parties had continued their propensity to squabble among themselves but in 1924 the contending parties gained a majority in the Diet and cooperated with the head of the Kenseikai, Katō Kōmei (1860–1926), when he was asked by Saionji to form a cabinet. This was the first real party government. The practice of having one of the two major parties form the government began and prevailed until 1932. The move toward democracy was strengthened further under Katō when in March 1925 universal manhood suffrage was adopted. All male subjects aged twenty-five and not indigent, were granted the right to vote.

As a counterpart to the adoption of universal manhood suffrage was the enactment of the Peace Preservation Law to curb "dangerous thought." Specifically it was designed to combat communists and anarchists and other advocates of revolutionary actions. The government's plan to enact a law to protect the right of the workers to organize unions and stage strikes was blocked by the powerful business interests. But the article in the Police Regulation Law that prohibited labor union activities was eliminated.

In 1927 the head of the Seiyūkai, General Tanaka Giichi (1864–1929), became the Prime Minister. Even though Tanaka was the head of a party government his basic beliefs and policies were in tune with the right-wing militant nationalists who were beginning to gain ascendancy. Party government nominally continued until 1932 but the Tanaka government signifies the beginning of Shōwa "fascism" rather than the continuation of "Taishō democracy." As noted in the next chapter, Tanaka adopted a bellicose policy toward China and also took a hardline in suppressing "dangerous thought."

SOCIALIST–COMMUNIST MOVEMENTS

As noted earlier, the Great Treason affair set back the leftist political movement but the Bolshevik Revolution of 1917 provided an impetus to the socialist-communist circle in Japan. The government set out to curb any overt Red Wing activities. Women who had formed the Red Wave Society and marched on May Day were arrested. The communists organized a party covertly in 1922 but the government arrested the leaders in 1923 and the party was dissolved in 1924.

The anarchist movement had weakened after the execution of Kōtoku Shūsui and Kanno Sugako. Among the surviving activist anarchists was Ōsugi Sakae (1885–1923). Ōsugi was an anarchist, socialist and Christian. He was opposed to organized movements and held that: "What I like above all is the blind actions of men, the natural explosion of the spirit. There must be freedom of thought, freedom of action, and freedom of impulses."[2] He continued to seek to propagate anarchist views with Itō Noe (1895–1923), a radical feminist. The authorities had targeted him as harborer of "dangerous thought" and during the Great Earthquake of 1923 the military police arrested him and Itō and murdered them together with Ōsugi's six-years-old nephew.

The socialists first organized their political party in 1906 but the government banned it the following year. In 1920 they organized the Japan Socialist League. Again the government banned it. The socialists began to split into pro-communist and right-wing socialists. In 1925 they organized the Social Populace Party (*Shakai Minshu-tō*). The party established ties with the All Japan Federation of Labor (*Sōdōmei*). In 1932 it evolved into the Social Mass Party (*Shakai-Taishū-tō*) and cooperated with the government that was turning toward militarism and imperialism.

The Japanese communists were unwilling to support the bourgeois parliamentary system and did not back the movement for universal suffrage because they believed it would merely fortify capitalism. The Comintern under Bukharin's leadership directed the Japanese communists to support the movement for universal suffrage and strive for a democratic revolution to overthrow the Emperor system. In 1926 the younger communists attempted to revive the party which had been dissolved two years earlier. The group was initially led by Fukumoto Kazuō (1894–1983). Fukumoto believed it was necessary to purge the party of socialists and fellow travellers and limit the membership to pure Marxist thinkers. The Soviet Comintern condemned Fukumoto for his stress on the intelligentsia and lack of involvement with the peasants and workers.

Even though the communists lacked unity and did not have a broad base of support, the Tanaka government launched a campaign against them. In March 1928 midnight raids were launched throughout the nation and over twelve hundred persons were arrested. The following year a second mass arrest was conducted, and more than seven hundred communists or communist sympathizers were arrested. The victims were treated brutally. They were beaten, stabbed, hanged upside down or choked. Among the victims was Kobayashi Takiji (1903–1933), a novelist who had written novels critical of the exploitation of workers. Among his works are *Absentee Landlord* and *Cannery Boat*. In the latter he describes the terrible conditions in fishing and canning boats where the crews had to work. He was arrested and released but was arrested again in 1933 for joining the communist party. After his arrest he was subjected to torturous questioning and died.

The persecution of communists continued into the 1930s and the communist movement was quashed until after the Second World War. Many communists were jailed and were coerced to renounce the movement. A few, like Tokuda Kyūichi (1894–1953), refused to renounce communism and remained in prison until the end of Second World War. One of the leaders, Nozaka Sanzō (1892–1993), fled to China and worked with the Chinese communists during the thirties and the war years. Marxism had adherents in the academic community. Many professors and students had become interested in Marxist ideology. The purge of "dangerous thinkers" extended into the academic community, many students were arrested and a number of prominent professors were dismissed from their positions.

Christian humanists were prominent proponents of social reforms. They advocated humane reforms but not social or political revolution. Among the early Christian reformers was Uchimura Kanzō. He had studied at the Harvard theological seminary. As an instructor at First Higher School in Tokyo he refused to bow to the

Imperial Rescript on Education and was dismissed. He continued to propagate Christian concepts through his writings. He supported the Sino-Japanese War as a "righteous war" but he opposed the Russo-Japanese War. He was also active in fighting the Ashio Copper Mining company for causing pollution of the rivers and fields in 1901. Kagawa Toyohiko (1888–1960) was another Christian reformer. He fought for industrial and agrarian reforms and spent a great deal of time working to aid slum dwellers. As a dedicated Christian reformer he was compared to St. Francis of Assisi by the founder of the Japanese Salvation Army, Yamamuro Gumpei. Others ranked him with Albert Schweitzer.

The reform movements that emerged in the Taishō years included those of social groups who were, in essence, treated as outcastes, the *burakumin*. The Tokugawa classification of these people as "unclean" (*eta*) and "non-humans" was legally ended but under the Meiji legal system they were classified as "new commoners" and legal, social, political, and economic discrimination continued. Their dwellings were confined to ghettoes and even here the government intervened and violated their rights. In 1919 the government forced the entire *burakumin* community to move because it overlooked an area where the mythical Emperor Jimmu's tomb was presumed to be located. In 1922 the authorities burned down a *burakumin* hamlet, claiming it was a nest of criminals, but the real reason was its location which was near the railroad where the train transporting imperial family members was scheduled to pass. As in the feudal years *burakumin* were treated in a humiliating and degrading fashion. They were denied access to decent jobs and restricted to menial work. Thus they remained impoverished as a class well into the twentieth century. Intercaste marriages were virtually non-existent. They were discriminated against by curators of Shinto shrines and Buddhist temples. In 1859 when a young *burakumin* tried to enter a Shinto shrine he was beaten to death. They were subject to the military draft but they could never rise above the rank of private.

Children were influenced by their parents' biased views so *burakumin* school children consistently faced discrimination from school mates. One woman recalled, "I cannot forget the discrimination I underwent in school. Often other children would tell me, 'Go away, you stink,' or they would say, 'That girl is from *that* village,' and would not include me in whatever they were doing." Another woman related, "When I went to school I was forced to sit in the last row of the classroom all by myself ... On the first day, on the way home, a boy ran after me and told me, 'Hey there, starting tomorrow you can't come to school ... If you come to school, the school will get polluted.' Then he threw rocks at me. This happened many times."[3]

WOMEN ACTIVISTS

The movements for "civilization and enlightenment" and the people's rights did not result in the improvement of women's status. Some women were active in the populist movement from the outset. Among them was Fukuda Hideko (1867–1920) who participated in the people's rights movement and the fight for women's rights. She became disillusioned with the liberal political party members and joined the emerging socialist movement. She fought for her beliefs, writing for liberal and socialist journals. Her articles called for improvement in the working conditions in the textile factories, justice in the family system, and women's rights in general. She opposed the Russo-Japanese War and fought the Ashio Copper Mine for polluting the river vital for farmers downstream. With the failure of the movement to gain in strength Fukuda's life ended in disappointment and poverty. She became disillusioned with the many men she worked with. She remarked, "Men are worthless. They are easily bought off by titles of nobility and medals. In this respect women are more reliable. Among women there are no fools who go about proudly dangling medals around their neck."[4]

There were a few more active women fighters among socialists and anarchists. Most notable among them was Kanno Sugako discussed above (pp. 113–14). The execution of Kanno and her cohort dampened the radical movement briefly but the fight for women's rights continued. In 1911 Hiratsuka Raichō (1886–1971) organized the *Seitōsha* (Blue Stocking Society) to offer publication opportunities for women writers but the advancement of women's rights was the chief objective. Hiratsuka stated: "The *Seitōsha* will be an instrument for women's thought, literature and moral perfection." She declared her stand as a "new woman." "I am a

New Woman, I yearn each day to become a truly New Woman, Each day I work to become a New Woman, The sun is truly and forever new. I am the sun." The first issue of the journal included a poem by Yosano Akiko. She wrote, "The day when the mountain will move is coming ... The mountains have been asleep only temporarily. In antiquity, mountains, all aflame, moved about ... All the women who had been asleep, Have now awakened and are on the move."[5]

The articles in the journal became more radical. Hiratsuka was not inclined toward political and social radicalism and so in 1915 she turned over the journal's editorship to a young radical, Itō Noe, who was barely twenty. Itō had started writing for the Seitō journal when she was seventeen and had been advocating feminist ideals that ran contrary to the conventional emphasis on propriety, restraint, self-effacement, and conformity. In taking charge of the journal she stated her policy would be "no rules, no fixed policies, no principles, no advocacy of any cause." She was against the Japanese convention that taught women to conform and accept their plight. She protested, "There is nobody as hateful as the narrow-minded, obstinate women educators of Japan. With their narrow outlook, opinionated views, ignorance, and superficiality, how could they expect to undertake true education?"[6] She admired Emma Goldman and asserted her individuality and believed that the existing order must be challenged if justice was to be achieved. Thus she criticized other feminists who were seeking to reform things through the existing systems. She joined the anarchist radical Ōsugi Sakae and worked with him advocating radical concepts and working with union organizers in the industrial sections of Tokyo. Then in 1923, as noted earlier (p. 120), they were murdered by the gendarmes.

Another independent-minded woman radical was Kaneko Fumiko (1903–1926) who spent her childhood in Korea and, after her return to Japan, became involved with a Korean anarchist, Pak Yeol (1902–74). In the aftermath of the Great Earthquake when anti-Korean hysteria was at its height they were arrested accused of conspiring to assassinate the Emperor. In fact they had not conspired to do so but during her interrogation Itō was unafraid to state her belief that the Emperor system was a useless entity and that the Emperor was no better than any other person. She believed that the system should be overthrown. She asserted, "the reason I deny the necessity of the Emperor system rises from my belief that human beings are equal."[7] They had made no specific plan to overthrow the Emperor but they were condemned to death. At the last minute the authorities said due to the benevolence of the Emperor her sentence was changed to life imprisonment. She refused to accept the reprieve, tore up the certificate and later hanged herself.

A number of socialist study groups were formed in the Taishō years. In 1920 the Japanese Socialist Federation (*Nihon Sha-kaishugi Dōmei*) was formed but women could not participate in this organization because the Police Security Regulations forbade women from taking part in political organizations. As a result a group of women formed a women's socialist organization, the Red Wave Society (*Sekirankai*) in 1921. The society's manifesto stated: "The *Sekirankai* is a women's organization that plans to participate in the enterprise to destroy the capitalist society and build a socialist society. The capitalist society turns us into slaves at home and oppresses us as wage slaves outside the home. It turns many of our sisters into prostitutes. It turns our [fathers, children, brothers] into cannon fodder ... Sisters who love justice and morality, join the socialist movement."[8] In 1921 they marched on May Day and many were arrested. Because of political oppression and growing disillusionment the society soon disbanded and only a few of the members continued to work for the cause. In the 1930s as Japan began its militaristic expansion on the continent opponents of the establishment were silenced by the nationalistic fervor.

Urban women were inclined to be more active than rural women in the reform movements. But there were a series of tenant disputes during the Taishō years. The most bitterly fought tenant dispute took place in a village in Niigata prefecture in 1922. A tenant union was organized and they asked for a twenty percent reduction in rent. A major landlord brought in the police and drove out the tenants. The protesting tenants were arrested. One woman whose husband was arrested recalled: "The police sprayed red ink on people they suspected and arrested them. Some of those arrested were tied to trees ... I heard that my husband was taken to the Katsuzuka station. I went there, but they refused to let me see him. I can't describe the hard time I had after his arrest. [After her husband was released in 1927] Next year he was arrested in the mass arrests of March 15. After that, the villagers became wary of associating with us, and nobody would come near our house."[9]

Some early fighters for women's rights, especially political rights, did not join the radicals but sought to gain concessions by cooperating with the established authorities. In 1924 when the movement for universal suffrage was gaining support they organized the League for the Attainment of Women's Political Rights but they failed in their efforts when suffrage was granted only to men in 1925. As Japan turned to militarism and imperialism, pressure was brought to bear on women's organizations. They were joined together in the Greater Japan Women's Organization in 1941, and many women leaders cooperated with the government's nationalistic ventures.

INTELLECTUAL AND CULTURAL LIFE

The Taishō years show a turn toward "modernism" in the urban areas. There was a strong interest in Western popular culture and customs. Western movies, music, apparels, food, drink, dancing, sports (such as baseball, tennis, rugby) were embraced gleefully by the modern young men and women, known as *mo-bo, mo-ga* (modern boys, modern girls). They were at the cutting edge of the jazz culture. Modern technologies were beginning to transform the urban centers with electric trams, motor vehicles, neon lights, radios, telephones.

While the urban dwellers were being inundated with things modern and the new age outlook was strong among the young, the way of life of the rural villages remained less affected and traditional ways persisted. Thus the gap between urban and rural Japan continued to widen. For the "city slicker" the "backward" peasants were miserable creatures. One aspiring writer going to a northern village remarked, "There is no one as miserable as a peasant ... They are as black as their dirt walls and lead grubby, joyless lives that can be compared to the life of insects that crawl along the ground and stay alive by licking the dirt ... One can see the kind of people they are by simply looking at their faces ... One can easily recognize a peasant. He can be identified by his ignoble face."[10] The urbanites' contempt for the lowly peasants was reciprocated by the politically aware peasants. One such farmer, Shibuya Teisuke, noted in his diary in 1926, "Ah, Tokyo, you are a murderous machine that sucks out the blood of the peasants in the name of capitalistic, urban civilization ... The people of culture enjoy the glory of life while the producers of essential goods for human life have to live [in misery]."[11]

While the peasants had to work long hours laboring the urbanites were able to enjoy the fruits of culture and literature, for the Taisho era experienced the proliferation of books, magazines, newspapers, and cultural artifacts. The urbanites tended to be better educated than the peasants. The latter could only complete six years of compulsory elementary education at best while many urban young people attended secondary schools and some even went on to college. The number of higher level schools had increased substantially by 1925. There were thirty-four universities, twenty-nine higher schools, and eighty-four professional schools. The number of secondary schools (known as middle schools but comparable to American high schools) increased substantially from the beginning of the century. In 1924 there were 491 boys middle schools and 576 girls' middle schools. With universal primary education the literacy rate of the country was high. This meant that there was a large readership eager to delve into newspapers, magazines, and books.

Circulation of the major newspapers surpassed the million mark while popular and serious journals gained a wide readership. Weekly and monthly magazines filled the news-stands and bookstores. Among the magazine publishers Noma Seiji (1878–1938) emerged as the dominant figure catering to all segments and age groups of society. Entertaining as well as didactic articles and stories were published in his nine magazines. In 1930 the total circulation of his magazines was six million copies. He attributed his success to the fact that he published articles "always a step behind the times." In other words, he did not lead the public but aroused the latent sentiments stirring in the people. Thus in the Taisho years romantic love stories and tales of valiant samurai filled the pages while in the militaristic thirties heroic and patriotic figures, past and present, were featured.

Noma's magazines did not contain serious literature because his readership was in search of entertaining stories. The newspapers also featured popular novels presented in daily strips. Some were lengthy features. *The Mountain Pass of the Great Bodhisattva*, the story of a blind nihilistic swordsman whose karma was to wander about fighting for good over evil, was twice as long as Tolstoy's *War and Peace*. Yoshikawa Eiji (1892–1962) had only elementary education but he became the most widely read popular writer of the mid-twentieth century. He wrote of the exploits of heroic swordsmen like Miyamoto Musashi, the John Wayne of the samurai world, as well as historical tales such as the history of the Taira clan. Yoshiya Nobuko (1896–1973), a precursor to Danielle Steel, wrote prodigious numbers of romantic stories for women.

Serious writers usually did not find outlets in popular journals but most found a large readership. In 1910 a group of aspiring upper-class young men formed a literary circle, the White Birch School. The purpose of life, one of its members, said was to be in harmony with the "will of mankind." There is a commonality between the individual's spirit and the spirit of mankind. The artist has "a heart that dances with nature and mankind." This led some writers to turn inward to their private lives and produce what came to be known as the "I" novel. The object of the "I" novel was to enable the heart of the writer and the heart of the reader to embrace each other.[12]

Among the writers of this circle was Arishima Takeo (1878–1923) who had studied in America at Haverford and Harvard. He was influenced by Christian humanism and socialism but, as someone who was not a member of the working class, he believed he was not qualified to meddle in the lives of the proletariat. His humanism, however, led him to give his thousand acre farm in Hokkaido to tenants on the land. His sense of social impotence led him to fall into nihilistic despair. He concluded that there are three stages to human life – habitual, intellectual, and instinctive. True freedom is to be found in the instinctive phase. Seeking ultimate meaning of life in love he committed suicide along with a female reporter. The heroine of his masterpiece *A Certain Woman* "is totally unlike any previous heroine of modern Japanese fiction – strong-willed, decisive in her actions though capricious, full of intense vitality."[13] Arishima was a strong believer in women's liberation. He believed that women should not be content with merely achieving the right to participate in contemporary cultural life, for by accepting the existing cultural state would mean capitulating to men's taste. They must create feminine geniuses from among themselves.[14]

Another group of writers, who were influenced by Natsume Sōseki, started a literary journal called *Shin Shichō* (New Current of Thought). The most brilliant member of this circle was Akutagawa Ryūnosuke (1892–1927) whose work has been regarded as the embodiment of "pure intellect and refinement." He had a pessimistic view of life but he satirized human frailties in a humorous vein. He believed that unexpected events always prevented people from achieving happiness. This is seen in his *The Hell Screen* (*Jigokumon*) in which an artist is commissioned by his lord to depict on a screen a scene in hell. In order to be able to paint the scene realistically he had the lord arrange to have a woman burned in a carriage. When he arrived to paint the scene he found that the woman chained to the burning carriage was his own daughter. He painted the scene and killed himself. Akutagawa became increasingly pessimistic, was drawn toward death, and finally killed himself. The words he left to his children were: "Do not forget that life is a battle that leads to death. If you are defeated in this battle of life commit suicide like your father."[15] His *Rashōmon*, a medieval story dealing with four differing subjective accounts given about rape and violent death, was turned into an internationally renowned movie by the director Kurosawa Akira.

Another prominent writer of this school was Tanizaki Jun'ichirō (1886–1965) whose writing career extended to the post-1945 years. Like his fellow writers he was opposed to naturalism and concentrated on evoking mood and atmosphere rather than spelling things out in concrete detail. His advice to aspiring writers was: "Do not try to be too clear, leave some gaps in the meaning ... we consider it good form to keep a thin sheet of paper between the fact and object, and the words that give expression to it." "In the mansion called literature I would have the eaves deep and the walls dark. I would push back into the shadows the things that come forward too clearly."[16] Tanizaki worshipped feminine beauty and regarded men as nothing more than manure to nurture it. He was influenced by Western writers but he was also imbued in traditional culture. In his *Some Prefer*

Nettles he dealt with the conflict between the attractions of Western and traditional ways and culture.

The other writer whose work gained renown in the West and eventually won him the Nobel Prize for literature in 1968 was Kawabata Yasunari (1899–1972). The lyrical quality of his writing style is compared to haiku masters by E. G. Seidensticker who translated many of his works. "Haiku seeks to convey a sudden awareness of beauty by mating of opposite or incongruous terms. Thus the classical haiku characteristically fuses motion and stillness. Similarly Kawabata relies very heavily on a mingling of the senses."[17] In his acceptance speech of the Nobel Prize Kawabata spoke of Japanese culture and its oneness with nature. Speaking of a thirteenth-century priest's poem he observed: "Seeing the moon he becomes the moon, the moon seen by him becomes him. He sinks into nature, becomes one with nature."[18] Tanizaki and Kawabata continued their literary work during the Shōwa (1926–1989) years.

A number of woman writers also emerged in the 1920s and 1930s. Among them was Uno Chiyo (1907–1996). She did not concern herself with social issues, as did some women writers of the prewar years, but created novels based on distinctive personalities she encountered. A literary critic said of Uno, "disregarding conventions and time and place, [she] invented a kind of novelistic fantasy world in which the words themselves seem to live by their own strength."[19] Another renowned woman writer was Enchi Fumiko (1905–1986) who reached her most productive period in the postwar years. In one of her major works Enchi depicted the life of Meiji women who suffered with nobility and resourcefulness the oppression of the paternalistic family system. In her old age the heroine "suddenly saw the futility of that somehow artificial life on which she had lavished so much energy and wisdom."[20]

During the Taishō years when socialists and communists were actively fighting for the working class, a number of writers of proletarian literature emerged. *Tsuchi* (Earth) written by Naga-tsuka Takashi (1879–1915) before the Taisho years, in 1910, depicts the hard life of the peasantry. In 1921 a literary journal devoted to proletarian literature, *Tane Maku Hito* (Sowers of Seeds) was published but it did not flourish as a literary magazine or a vehicle to advance working-class interests. One prominent proletarian writer was Kobayashi Takiji, noted earlier. Among women writers who embraced Marxism was Miyamoto Yuriko (1899–1951). She joined the Communist Party in 1931 and married a communist party leader. She was imprisoned in the late 1930s but was released due to poor health. Her first novel, *Nobuko*, a semi-autobiographical account of her life in America, was published in the mid-1920s. But most of her important works were published in the postwar years.

The popularity of leading writers led publishers to bring out multi-volume collections of literary works. In 1926 a thirty-six volume collection of literature appeared. Six hundred thousand people made pre-publication pledges. In 1927 a publisher began publishing pocketbook editions of literary works.

It was not just literary writers who were beginning to produce serious intellectual works. Following the early Meiji thinkers' interest in English and French liberalism, German idealism became the primary philosophy pursued by scholars in the academic circle. The most prominent of this school of thought was Nishida Kitarō (1870–1945). He was influenced by Hegelian and Neo-Kantian philosophy but he was also a student of Zen Buddhism. He set out to formulate a philosophy that included religious elements as well as rational science. In his *Study of Good* he sought to define reality in terms of "pure" or "direct" experience, a point before subject and object are separated. In a subsequent work he posits this as "the place of nothingness" where subject and object exist and consciousness itself is established. Here "the form of the formless is seen and the sound of the soundless is heard."[21]

After being exposed to Western science in the Meiji period an increasing number of scholars took up scientific studies, and Japanese scientists began making significant discoveries. Among the first to do so was Kitazato Shibasaburō (1852–1931) who discovered the bacillus of bubonic plague in 1894. He also isolated the bacilli of dysentery and tetanus, and prepared an antitoxin for diphtheria. Noguchi Hideyo (1876–1928), a bacteriologist, discovered the cause and treatment of syphilis and yellow fever. Others made significant contributions in atomic studies, seismology, and pharmacology.

SOCIO-ECONOMIC DEVELOPMENTS

The second stage of modern economic growth as posited by Rosovsky and Ohkawa extends from 1906 to 1952. They divide this stage into two phases, 1906 to 1930, and 1930 to 1952. In the first phase the modern, industrial-commercial sector increased rapidly because of arms production during the Russo-Japanese War and access to new markets with the acquisition of colonies. In 1925–29 manufacturing production increased three-fold from 1910 to 1914. The traditional, agrarian sector did not grow as rapidly and increased only by two to three percent annually.

The modern sector saw significant increase in the production of textiles, metals and machinery, chemicals, ceramics, electricity and gas. The number of factories equipped with power machinery increased over five-fold between 1909 and 1929. The number of factory workers increased from one million to nearly 2.4 million in 1929. In addition there were millions of workers in small workshops. But the percentage of workers in the primary industries of agriculture, fishing, and mining remained high. In 1880 it was eighty-one percent. It continued to decline but in 1930 it was still 51.1%.

The standard of living did not improve significantly. Wages and working conditions remained poor, especially in the textile plants where the workers were predominantly young girls and women. Efforts to organize unions to improve the plight of the workers, as discussed above, met with resistance by big-business leaders and the government. Urban dwellers enjoyed some improvement in standards of living but modern facilities, like electricity, were slow in reaching the villages. The gap between urban and rural communities continued to increase from the early Meiji years. In 1874 Fukuzawa Yukichi complained that the government "take the fruits of rural labor to make flowers for Tokyo. Steel bridges glisten in the capital ... but in the country wooden bridges are so rotten that one cannot cross them."[22] To the impoverished villagers the urban dwellers appeared to be living a life of luxury. At the end of the century the daily wage of an average tenant farmer came to about 15 sen (0.15 yen) a day. The average daily wage for a male weaver was 30 sen; for a female weaver, 19 sen and an urban day-laborer, 33 sen. A government survey taken of the mid 1920s indicated that farm family income was seventy percent that of white-collar workers and ninety-five percent of urban laborers. Because the urban laborers had to purchase all their food while farm families could consume their own produce, the urban worker was no better off than the farm workers. For the villagers the quality of food consumed did not improve much from the Tokugawa years. Rice, cereal, vegetables, and fish comprised the bulk of the diet. The daily caloric consumption rose from about 2,100 in the 1870s to about 2,300 in the Taishō era. Health care and sanitation facilities showed no significant improvements. In the 1920s the infant mortality rate was well over a hundred for every thousand live births, compared to four in 1996. The death rate in 1920 was twenty-five persons out of a thousand compared to eight in 1993. Life expectancy in 1921–25 dropped somewhat to 42.06 years compared to 43.97 years in 1899–1903 and 44.25 years in 1909–1913. In contrast by 1997 it was over eighty. The major cause of the high death rate was frequent outbreaks of epidemics. For example in 1886 108,400 persons died of a cholera epidemic. A variety of epidemics continued to plague the populace into the Taishō years.

In general the living conditions of the working class, rural and urban, did not improve significantly. Who then was benefiting from the three-fold economic expansion in the first phase of the second period of modern economic growth? The peasant and urban working families constituted eighty-four percent of Japanese families in 1930 but they received only fifty percent of the country's household income. At the top, about twenty-four thousand families (0.0019 percent of the nation's households) had incomes exceeding 10,000 yen or ten percent of the national family income. At the very top, nineteen households had family incomes of over 1 million yen. At the bottom, 2.232 million families had incomes of 200 yen or less per annum.

Concentration of wealth at the top by a few families meant industrial and commercial control of the economy by a handful of corporate giants who constituted the *zaibatsu*, the financial-industrial conglomerates. There were a dozen or so in this category of business giants but at the top there were four: Mitsui, Mitsubishi, Sumitomo, and Yasuda. Unlike corporate complexes in the West these gigantic trusts were family-owned conglomerates.

Their business activities extended across several areas. The largest of these houses, Mitsui, was involved in commerce, banking, mining, lumbering, textiles, shipping, sugar, metals, machinery, and many other business enterprises. The Mitsubishi conglomerate by the 1940s controlled twenty-five percent of the nation's shipping and shipbuilding, fifteen percent of coal and metals, sixteen percent of bank loans, fifty percent of flour milling, fifty-nine percent of sheet glass, thirty-five percent of sugar and fifteen percent of cotton textiles. None had monopolistic control in one area but the handful of the zaibatsu clique had a grip virtually on the nation's entire economic life.

These business conglomerates had close ties to the government and political leaders. Mitsui and Mitsubishi were patrons and moneybags for the two major prewar parties, the *Seiyūkai* and the *Minseitō*. From the outset of the Meiji era when the big business houses were rising there was a direct, personal link between the big four houses and government leaders. Government leaders did nothing to curb the monopolistic thrust of the *zaibatsu*. In fact they were integral to the goal of building "a rich nation and a powerful military." And military and political expansion abroad went hand and hand with *zaibatsu* control of markets and resources.

The agricultural sector also saw a concentration of wealth by a few wealthy landowners. The end of the feudal landholding system in the Meiji era did not mean an end to the concentration of landholding in the hands of the big landowners. In 1935 3,415 landowners controlled 4.7% of the cultivated land while 4,765,000 farm families with smallholdings held only fifty-six percent. Tenant farming had continued to increase since early Meiji and in 1910 forty-five percent of the cultivated land was tilled by tenant farmers. Thirty-nine percent of the tillers owned no land at all.

SEVEN

The Road to War

The two years of the Tanaka government (1927–29) can be seen as the end of the era of nascent democracy and the onset of the road to militarism and war. In the Taishō years there were brief reigns by liberally inclined party leaders but Tanaka began moving vigorously against harborers of "dangerous thought:" communists and communist sympathizers. In external affairs aggressive moves in China began with the confrontation with the emerging Nationalist forces of Chiang Kai-shek. As the Nationalist troops approached Tsinan in Shandung Peninsula in May 1928 Tanaka sent troops to block the Chinese forces. The campaign resulted in thousands of Chinese residents being killed and injured.

As the Nationalist forces moved further north the Japanese leaders began to become concerned about Manchuria which had become a Japanese sphere of influence after the Russo-Japanese War. In the summer of 1927 Tanaka held a conference with officials of the army and foreign office to formulate a China policy. The interventionists who held Manchuria to be Japan's "lifeline" were temporarily restrained. The Manchurian warlord, Zhang Zuolin had cooperated with the Japanese Kwangtung Army in Manchuria. In June 1928 when the Nationalist forces were approaching Manchuria Zhang Zuolin, whose forces were in control in Beijing, decided to pull back to Manchuria in June 1928. On the way back to Manchuria he was assassinated by the Kwangtung Army officers who blew up the train on which he was traveling. Their object was to remove Zhang and extend Japanese control over all of Manchuria. Tanaka did not approve their plan to move beyond the legally sanctioned zone. Zhang was succeeded by his son Zhang Xue-liang who pledged his allegiance to Chiang Kai-shek. This led the Kwangtung Army officers to begin plotting to bring all of Manchuria under Japanese control.

Tanaka was compeled to resign his post when he prevaricated to the Emperor about those responsible for Zhang's death. Thus in July 1929 Hamaguchi Yūkō (1870–1931) the president of the other major party, *Minseitō*, became Prime Minister. The immediate task that confronted Hamaguchi was the economic crisis that followed the bank crisis of early 1927. Many middle- and small-sized banks went out of business and the concentration of financial control by the bigger banks was accelerated. The same happened in the manufacturing sector with smaller firms going out of business and the bigger firms extended their monopolistic control. Tanaka's response to the economic crisis was to stimulate the economy by increasing military spending and intensifying the exploitation of the colonies. But these measures did not solve the nation's economic problems, and soon the Great Depression that shook the world affected Japan adversely also because its exports declined drastically. Exports of silk to the United States dropped sharply as well as exports of cotton textile goods and other items to China and other Asian countries. Japanese exports dropped fifty percent between 1929 and 1931.

The resulting social difficulties that beset the working class and the peasantry contributed to the rising criticism of the establishment and the political parties that were affiliated to big business interests. The government had cracked down on left-wing movements whose voice was somewhat muted but now the attack on the establishment came from the right-wing militarists. Thus the party governments that succeeded Tanaka were confronted with the growing discontent and hostility of the right-wing and militarists.

Prime Minister Hamaguchi sought to deal with the economic crisis by economic retrenchment but to no avail. While the government was confronted with the economic crisis it was also beset by right-wing opponents of its foreign policy of international cooperation that had been pursued since the Washington Conference of 1921. The person identified with this policy of international cooperation was Shidehara Kijuro (1872–1951) who served as foreign minister in a number of cabinets in the 1920s. Tanaka had continued this policy and signed the Kellogg-Briand Pact of 1928. The policy of naval arms limitation adopted at the Washington Conference was continued and, in early 1930, the powers concerned met in London to negotiate reductions in other warships in addition to the Washington agreement on battleships. The negotiations resulted in Japan agreeing to a 10:10:6 ratio (U.S.:Britain:Japan) in heavy cruisers and a 10:10:7 ratio in destroyers. In submarines Japan gained parity with the United States.

The naval leaders opposed this agreement demanding a 10:10:7 ratio of cruisers and destroyers. The opposition *Seiyūkai* played politics and attacked the Hamaguchi government for signing the London agreement. They contended that the government had violated the principle of the independence of the supreme command. The government did not have the right to override the naval general staff on matters of national defense. These party leaders were providing the rationale for the militarists to challenge the civilian governments in the 1930s. The naval leaders who had supported the London agreement were marked for assassination in the 1930s. Among them were admirals Okada Keisuke and Suzuki Kantarō. The immediate victim was Prime Minister Hamaguchi who was shot and seriously injured in late 1930. He resigned his post and died soon after. Shidehara served as acting Prime Minister prior to Hamaguchi's death but was constantly attacked as a traitor for upholding the London agreement.

After Hamaguchi's resignation Wakatsuki Reijirō (1866–1949), who had served as Prime Minister in 1926–7, assumed the premiership in April 1931. But he was beset by right-wing activists who plotted assassinations. In September he was confronted with the outbreak of the Manchurian Incident staged by the Japanese Kwangtung officers. Faced with these difficulties and party dissension he was forced to resign. He was succeeded by the head of the *Seiyūkai*, Inukai Tsuyoshi (1855–1932), who had fought for party government since the outset of his political career but acted demagogically, attacking the Hamaguchi government for signing the London agreement. He too found himself being harassed and harangued by right-wing ultra-nationalists, and targeted for assassination. Thus Japan entered a decade in which domestic political developments and foreign affairs came to be governed by right-wing, militarist, ultra-nationalist elements. Some label this movement fascist though it was not quite like the European version in its ideological or organizational paradigms.

EMERGENCE OF RADICAL NATIONALIST ACTIVISTS

In the 1930s what came to be emphasized was the sanctity of the Emperor system originating with the Sun Goddess, the inviolability of the national polity, the uniqueness and superiority of the Japanese race and its history, and the mission to bring the eight-corners of the world under one roof.

This mode of thinking can be traced back to the thought of the Tokugawa scholars of National Learning though they were not chauvinistic or "fascistic" like the 1930s ultra-nationalists. The notion that Manchuria was important for Japanese interests persisted from the time of the Russo-Japanese war. Among civilian groups that favored Japanese expansion into Manchuria and Mongolia was the Amur River Society which was founded in 1901. After the Russo-Japanese War Tōyama Mitsuru (1855–1944) became the leader of the Amur River Society and emerged as the guru of right-wing nationalists pushing to advance Japanese boundaries to the Amur River. As the economic crisis beset the nation at the end of the 1920s the nationalists and militarists began advocating incursions on the continent more vehemently. The officers of the Kwangtung Army in Manchuria began to adopt a hardline as the possibility that Chiang Kai-shek would unify under the new Chinese government became apparent.

Domestic difficulties bred "fascistic" elements which began to take an anti-liberal stance against the government. Among such right-wing ideologues was Kita Ikki (1884–1937) who started out as a socialist but came to stress the importance of the Emperor system. He believed it was necessary to overthrow the government controlled by the privileged clique and the *zaibatsu*, and restructure the entire political system. Only by doing so would there be a union of the Emperor and the people. What he favored was national socialism with nationalization of the major enterprises and limitation of private landownership. Initially he was in sympathy with China as a victim of Western imperialism. But as Sino-Japanese relations became strained as a result of Japanese militancy against China he focused his attention on internal reconstruction. His ideas were embraced by some of the radical young army officers who staged the kind of coup d'état that Kita advocated. He was convicted for being in league with the military officers who carried out the February 26 (1936) Incident (discussed below pp. 148–9) and was executed.

Another radical nationalist was Inoue Nisshō (1886–1967) who organized extreme nationalist societies, including the Blood Brotherhood League whose object was to assassinate thirteen prominent leaders. An agrarian extremist group also emerged as the depression intensified the poverty and hardship experienced by the peasantry. Among the leaders of this group was Gondō Seikyō (1868–1938) who advocated a policy of agrarian autonomy and agriculture-based economy. He contended that in the late nineteenth century the oligarchy, consisting of the bureaucracy, the *zaibatsu*, and the military, gained control of the society, and a small group of powerful capitalists grasped all the resources of the land. Another radical activist was Ōkawa Shūmei (1886–1957) who founded many right-wing societies and was involved in numerous assassination plots of the 1930s. He was charged as a Class-A war criminal in 1945 but was not convicted because of his mental state. The *Kokuhonsha*, organized by Hiranuma, emphasized the uniqueness of the Japanese national polity, and its membership included top political, business, and military leaders.

In the late twenties and thirties young military officers organized political circles. Military opposition to the political leadership of the 1920s was triggered, in part, by their objection to the disarmament policies pursued by the Taishō and early Shōwa government leaders. Some young military officers, many of whom came from rural communities, were angry at the government for doing little to help the impoverished peasantry while the politicians and the rich were wallowing in luxury. One of the army officers involved in the assassination of Prime Minister Inukai in 1932 stated at his trial: "In utter disregard of the poverty-stricken farmers, the enormously rich *zaibatsu* pursue their private profit. Meanwhile the young children of the impoverished farmers of the northeastern provinces attend school without breakfast, and their families subsist on rotten potatoes."[1] There was a convergence of the right-wing civilians and the military activists.

Officers concerned about the apparent decline in the military's influence in politics since the demise of the old leadership with Yamagata's death in 1922 began to form circles to advance their objectives. They were critical of the party government leaders and the capitalists' indifference to the plight of the impoverished masses. They concluded that radical political reforms were necessary. One of these groups, the *Issekikai* (One Evening Society) was formed in 1929 by middle-level officers, many of whom, like Tōjō Hideki, emerged as national leaders in the 1930s. Another organization of military officers, the Cherry Blossom Society (*Sakurakai*) was organized in 1930. Its objective was the overthrow of the existing government and the establishment of a military regime. In its statement of purpose it condemned the disarmament policy being pursued and accused the political leaders of corruption. They asserted that the political leaders "have forgotten basic principles ... neglect the spiritual values that are essential for the ascendancy of the Yamato people ... The torrent of political corruption has reached its crest ... Now, the poisonous sword of the thoroughly degenerate party politicians is being pointed at the military. This was clearly demonstrated in the controversy over the London treaties ... It is obvious that the party politicians' sword, which was used against the navy, will soon be used to reduce the size of the army ... Hence, we must ... arouse ourselves and wash out the bowels of the completely decadent politicians."[2] The "spiritual values" that these officers exalted were linked to a mystical concept about the superiority of the Japanese national character, the uniqueness of the national polity and the sanctity of the Emperor system, the source of all values.

This mode of thinking was shared by the civilian ultra-nationalists. The military elements emphasized expansion into the Asian continent more than some civilian radicals but they shared the anti-democratic beliefs and favored the establishment of a totalitarian government. Their nationalistic mode of thinking inclined increasingly toward anti-Western nations, Western culture, individualistic life-style, and Western-style capitalist interests that dominated the Japanese economy. They favored the traditional, agrarian values and family centered way of life. In a way the conflict between the ultra-nationalists and the more liberal, Western-oriented sectors was a conflict between rural and urban Japan, the old versus the new, Japanism versus Westernism. In the ultra-nationalists' mind they represented traditional values and the essence of Japan centered on the Emperor while their opponents represented the decadent ways afflicted by selfish Western values.

With the rising emphasis on Japanism the mode of thinking categorized as "dangerous thought" was not restricted to communism but came to include liberalism, and intellectuals, especially scholars who adhered to liberal concepts. Scholars became targets of attack, and were dismissed from university positions. Japanism entailed sanctification and glorification of the Emperor system. Toward the end of the Meiji era a constitutional scholar at the University of Tokyo, Minobe Tatsukichi (1873–1948), had posited the so-called Organ Theory regarding the Emperor. He held the Emperor to be an organ of the state. He was not above the state nor was he the state itself. Initially Minobe's theory was not regarded as being controversial but in the ultra-nationalist era of the 1930s it was singled out for attack by nationalist thinkers and politicians, and he was charged with "lese majesty" in 1935. His theory was condemned, his books were banned, and he was compelled to resign from the University of Tokyo. A fanatical nationalist attempted to murder him but did not succeed. This incident symbolizes the "fascistic" mindset of the thirties. The attack on Minobe and the Organ Theory, condemned as defiling the national polity, in effect meant the end of freedom of thought and expression. Under pressure from the ultra-nationalists the Ministry of Education issued the Fundamentals of Our National Polity in 1937 asserting that the Emperor was a descendant of the Sun Goddess, and he was the fountainhead of life and morality of the people. It emphasized the virtues of loyalty, patriotism, filial piety, harmony, the martial spirit, and *bushidō*. It condemned Western individualism as the root cause of all undesirable movement such as democracy, socialism, and communism.

ASSASSINATION PLOTS

Driven by a sense of righteousness many right-wing nationalists believed that getting rid of leaders who represented inimical ways and obstructed their objectives was perfectly justified as a defense of true values and act of patriotism. A series of assassination plots were hatched by the circle of civilian and military radicals. In March 1931 a group of conspirators planned a coup against the government and placed General Ugaki Kazushige (1868–1956) in power but the plot failed when Ugaki refused to cooperate. They then plotted, in October, to assassinate Prime Minister Wakatsuki and place General Araki Sadao (1877–1966) in power. Araki was highly regarded by the radicals because he was an anti-foreign advocate of Japanism and the Imperial Way (Kōdō). Araki who was at the time inspector-general of military education stifled the effort of the plotters. In neither case were the conspirators punished.

The next conspiracy was initiated by the Blood Brotherhood League, which had a list of thirteen leaders as targets of assassination. In early 1932 they assassinated the minister of finance, and the director of the Mitsui conglomerate. Inoue Nisshō was sentenced to fifteen years in prison for his links to the conspirators but the League's members continued with their plan. Their next move was in conjunction with malcontent naval officers. Inukai Tsuyoshi, who was then Prime Minister, became the prime target. The plotters of his assassination were right-wing radicals desiring domestic "reforms" and militants favoring an imperialistic foreign policy. In September 1931 the Kwangtung Army officers contrived to stage the so-called Manchurian Incident, and launched Japan on an aggressive policy on the continent and eventually a major war. The Manchurian war had broken out during Wakatsuki's premiership. Inukai, as the leader of the opposition *Seiyūkai* party, criticized the "weak-kneed" policy of international cooperation being pursued by foreign minister Shidehara. When he became Prime Minister, however, he too sought to restrict the Kwangtung Army's actions in Manchuria. Upset at Inukai's position the radical army and navy officers joined hands with radical agrarian critics of the ruling establishment of big business, bureaucrats, and politicians. They decided to assassinate top officials and attack key facilities and institutions. They only managed to assassinate Inukai on May 15, 1932. Inukai's assassination was a turning point in Japan's move toward militaristic extremism. It brought about the end to party government and brought a heavy infusion of right-wing military influence into domestic and foreign policy-making.

RIGHT-WING EXTREMISM IN DOMESTIC AND EXTERNAL AFFAIRS

A more militant stance toward China had been initiated by the Tanaka government but it was the Manchurian Incident that led Japan into the Second World War. Manchuria was held to be essential for Japan's national security, and this idea prevailed among the radical nationalists from the time of the Russo-Japanese War.

The Kwangtung Army officers and other army officers were determined to prevent Manchuria from being unified under the new Nationalist government. The Manchurian warlord Zhang Xue-liang, son of Zhang Zuo-lin, was moving toward cooperation with the Nationalist Government. So the top Kwangtung Army officers, Ishiwara Kanji (1886–1949) and Itagaki Seishirō (1885–1948) decided to overthrow Zhang Xue-liang and bring Manchuria under Japanese rule. Some army leaders in Tokyo also concurred with the Kwangtung officers' plan.

As the first step of their campaign the Kwangtung officers blew up a section of the South Manchurian Railroad in Mukden and blamed it on Chinese troops. They then moved Kwantung Army troops into areas beyond the confines of the South Manchurian Railway. When Prime Minister Wakatsuki followed Foreign Minister Shidehara's advice to limit military action the Army General Staff contended that the government did not have the authority to intervene in this matter. It was in the realm of the independence of the supreme command, and the staff of the field armies had the right to make military decisions which they deemed necessary. The Chinese government was not in a position to take military action against the Japanese forces because it was in a state of virtual civil war with the communists. So it appealed to the League of Nations to stop Japanese aggression. After some procrastination the Council of the League passed a resolution calling on Japan to withdraw its troops. The pro-war sentiment in Japan was fired up and Shidehara's efforts to negotiate a settlement found no support. He, therefore, abandoned his efforts and Wakatsuki resigned and was replaced by Inukai whose party had been vociferously criticizing Shidehara.

When Inukai became Prime Minister he too concluded that it was necessary to restrain the army. He hoped to persuade the Kwangtung Army to withdraw to the zone of the South Manchurian Railroad and to start negotiations with the Chinese government. Before he could realize his hopes, the Kwangtung Army advanced further, capturing the key cities of Jinzhou and Harbin, and moved north into Amur Province. In January 1932 Chinese anger at Japanese action in Manchuria resulted in a clash between Japanese forces stationed in the international concession zone in Shanghai and Chinese troops. The Japanese then bombed a densely populated section of Shanghai from the air. This outrageous action aroused world opinion against the Japanese and hardened Chinese determination to fight back. Inukai, following his war minister Araki's advice, dispatched two army divisions into Shanghai. The Japanese forces drove the Chinese forces out of Shanghai and an armistice was concluded in early May. The Shanghai incident aroused jingoistic sentiments in Japan, and Inukai found it impossible to pursue a policy of negotiated settlement. With public opinion on its side the Kwangtung Army officers proceeded to found a puppet state of Manchukuo in August 1932, and placed the former Qing Emperor Puyi on the throne.

The Japanese ignored the initial appeal by the League to cease military action in Manchuria. The League, therefore, dispatched a commission headed by Lord Lytton to examine the situation. The United States, not being a member of the League, on its own initiative issued the so-called doctrine of non-recognition of actions that violated the rights of other nations. The Lytton Commission reported that the Japanese military action was not legitimate and the state of Manchukuo was not founded on a genuine independence movement. It called for the establishment of an autonomous regime under Chinese sovereignty, and the withdrawal of Chinese and Japanese troops. It also recognized Japanese rights and interests in Manchuria. The Japanese found the report unacceptable and when the League adopted the report the Japanese delegation walked out, and the Japanese government withdrew from the League in March 1933.

The Japanese government at this time was headed by Admiral Saitō Makoto (1858–1936), the successor to Inukai. With Inukai's assassination party government ended. Saitō was chosen as Prime Minister by Saionji, now the key adviser to the Emperor. Saitō as a moderate was seen to be acceptable to all factions. He was to be the first Prime Minister to head a "united national government." He was not a strong leader and succumbed to the army's insistence that Japan withdraw from the League, and he allowed the Kwangtung Army to continue to advance into Inner Mongolia and south of the Great Wall. War Minister, General Araki, restrained the Kwangtung forces from moving further into China and, in May 1933, a settlement was effected with the signing of the Tanggu Truce. Jehol Province was incorporated into Manchuria, the Kwangtung Army gained control of the Shanhaiguan Pass on the border of China and Manchuria, and a demilitarized zone was established north of Beijing.

Right-wing nationalists became critical of Saitō's moderate posture, and he was compelled to resign in mid-1934. Saionji conferred with a circle of advisers and selected another admiral, Okada Keisuke (1868–1852) to succeed Saitō. The Okada government in the face of increasing nationalist agitation succumbed to right-wing pressure. It acceded to the demands of the naval expansionists and abrogated the Washington and London naval agreements in 1935. It was during the Okada regime that the attack on Minobe surfaced.

During this period there were two contending factions in the army. The leading proponents of ultra-nationalism in the army were generals Araki Sadao and Mazaki Jinzaburō (1876–1956). They believed in the supremacy of the Japanese soldiers who were imbued with "spiritual power," the Yamato spirit. The military officers who favored violent action to overturn the existing order looked upon them as their leaders. Araki and Mazaki were exponents of the Imperial Way (*Kōdōha*) and critics of Minobe's Organ Theory. Other generals did not favor isolated acts of violence to achieve political ends. Their object was military preparedness by modernizing the army with tanks and airplanes rather than relying on the spiritual force of the soldier. Future wars would require total mobilization of the nation's resources. This would entail comprehensive planning under the controlled, disciplined leadership of army central command. The officers who shared this line of thought came to be known as members of the Control Faction (Tōsei-ha). Among the leaders of this group were Nagata Tetsuzan (1884–1935), and future Prime Minister Tōjō Hideki (1884–1948). The two factions were not formally organized groups but consisted primarily of officers who shared similar views and objectives, one stressing pragmatic military preparedness under disciplined leadership the other violence.

The controversy among the two factions surfaced in mid-1935 when General Hayashi Senjurō (1876–1943), War Minister in the Okada cabinet removed General Mazaki from his post as Inspector General of Military Education, one of the top three army positions (together with the war minister and army general chief of staff). Mazaki had been appointed to that post by General Araki when he was War Minister. Mazaki's followers were outraged at his dismissal and regarded it as a plot by Hayashi and Nagata, chief of military affairs, to weaken the Kōdō-ha. They blamed Nagata in particular. Their bitterness toward him had been festering because in late 1934 he had removed Araki's followers from the army's top positions when a conspiracy by Kōdō-ha officers to assassinate leading statesmen and establish a military government was uncovered. As a result a Kōdō-ha officer decided to assassinate Nagata. He walked into Nagata's office and cut him down with his sword.

The Kōdō-ha officers decided the time was propitious to remove top political leaders. Nagata's assassin was played up by the Kōdō-ha as a patriot. The condemnation of Minobe's Organ Theory and the move to exalt the national polity were moving the public in favor of the "imperial way." Kōdō-ha officers, including those who had been dismissed by Nagata earlier, decided to put their plan into action. They had the implicit support of Mazaki and other generals, and received financial support from right-wing businessmen and politicians. The First Division, to which many of the conspirators were attached, was scheduled to be sent to Manchuria. So they decided to stage a coup before the Division was sent off. They struck on the morning of February 26, 1926.

They ordered the troops of the First Division to occupy key government buildings, and led groups of men to assassinate a number of senior statesmen and government officials. The targeted victims included Prime Minister Okada, former Prime Minister Saitō, Minister of Finance Takahashi Korekiyo (1854–1936), General Watanabe Jōtarō (1874–1936) who had replaced Mazaki as Inspector General of Military Education, Grand Chamberlain Suzuki Kantarō (1867–1948), and former Lord Keeper of the Privy Seal Makino Nobuaki (1861–1949). Genrō Saionji was also on the original list but was dropped when some officers wanted his name removed. Three officials on the list Saitō, Takahashi, and Watanabe were killed. The assassins also believed they had executed Okada but they had assassinated his brother-in-law by mistake, thinking he was Okada. Suzuki was inflicted with several bullet wounds but he survived and later served as Prime Minister at the end of the Second World War. Makino successfully eluded the assassins.

The assassins issued a manifesto condemning government leaders, politicians and some military leaders for undermining the national polity and creating a national crisis. They called on the Minister of War, Kawashima Yoshiyuki (1878–1945), to take charge and to implement the Shōwa Restoration. The generals were divided on how to cope with the situation. Kawashima was indecisive, Araki and Mazaki were opposed to the proposal to quash the rebels. In fact Mazaki wanted Kawashima to persuade the Emperor to accede to the rebels' demands. The officers of the general staff, led by Ishiwara Kanji, one of the plotters of the Manchurian Incident, called for the suppression of the rebels. The person who was most responsible for crushing the rebels was the Emperor. He was adamant against compromising with the rebels and condemned them for killing his close advisers. Martial law was proclaimed and troops were called in from outlying districts. Confronted with strong opposition the rebels decided to surrender. Two rebel officers committed suicide. The rebel leaders were tried in a closed trial and nineteen were condemned to death and executed. Kita did not play a part in the rebellion but he was held responsible for having influenced the rebels, and was tried by a military court and executed. Mazaki, whose ties were much closer than Kita's, was absolved.

After the coup attempt the army leaders purged generals and officers who were linked to the *Kōdō-ha*. Generals Araki and Mazaki were placed on the inactive list. To prevent those placed on the inactive list from serving as war minister, military regulations were revised to make only generals and admirals on the active list eligible for the cabinet. This same regulation had been introduced by Yamagata in 1900 but in 1913 it was revised and inactive generals and admirals became eligible to serve as war or naval ministers.

The officers who took charge of the military after the attempted coup were not simply *Tōsei-ha* officers opposed to the *Kōdō-ha* but were officers who were opposed to zealous, ideologically driven acts of violence. Leadership in the army was taken over by a group of officers who believed in disciplined centralized order. They were not opposed to the army intervening in the political realm. But political action was to be effected through the established order. In fact the army's place in the political order was enhanced by the February 26 activists because it tended to make the political leaders wary of opposing the military openly and vigorously. Thus the army's influence over the government was manifested immediately. The army leaders now had a veto power over any cabinet because they now had control over the appointment of the war minister. By not naming a war minister they could prevent the cabinet from being formed. So they could stymie a Prime Minister designate from forming his cabinet if they disapproved of him or his choice of cabinet members.

The army exercised this power immediately after the coup attempt when Hirota Kōki (1878–1948) was chosen by the Emperor to form the cabinet to succeed the assassinated Saitō. General Terauchi Hisaichi (1879–1946), the army's choice for war minister, prevented Hirota from appointing any liberal cabinet members of whom he disapproved. Among those rejected was Yoshida Shigeru (1878–1967) who was to become a prominent political leader in the postwar years. He was not acceptable not only because he was Makino's son-in-law but he had been critical of the military's action in Manchuria.

Upon assuming office the Hirota government proclaimed its policy objectives in "The Fundamental Principles of National Policy." It held its objectives to be first, the consolidation of the

Japanese empire's position in East Asia and second, the advancement into the region of the South Sea. It posited a moderate stance toward China but a stronger defense stand toward Soviet Russia. The policy regarding the South Sea was advocated by the navy in order to gain access to the oil deposits in South East Asia. The objectives were to be pursued by peaceful means, but ensuing developments eventually contributed to the invasion of China and the outbreak of the Pacific War. Hence the postwar International Military Tribunal held that Hirota had contributed to the ensuing conflicts, and tried and executed him as a Class A war criminal.

That the real wielder of power now was the army was indicated by its ability to approve or disapprove subsequent cabinets. Hirota was forced to resign when he refused the war minister's demand that he dissolve the Diet to get rid of a political party member who criticized the army. When Saionji selected General Ugaki to succeed Hirota as a means to keep the army in line, the hardliners in the army, led by Ishiwara Kanji stymied Ugaki by refusing to name a war minister. Saionji then turned to another general, Hayashi Senjurō (1876–1943), who had served as war minister in the Saitō and Okada cabinets. His government lasted only four months because in the Diet election the opposition political parties won a majority. Faced by a hostile Diet Hayashi resigned.

Saionji then persuaded Prince Konoe Fumimaro (1891–1945) to assume the premiership. Thus in June 1937 he became the head of the government. Konoe was a descendant of the five regency families of the Heian court, and was held in high regard by all sectors of the society. The political parties, the military, and business interests all approved of his selection. Saionji had hopes that Konoe would eventually succeed him as the chief adviser to the Emperor. He was seen as a moderate capable of bringing the contending groups together and providing political stability. But he had been expressing hardline views in foreign affairs and distancing himself from the policy of international cooperation. Japan had to adopt an autonomous foreign policy, he asserted. "All the nations have formed blocs. Japan too must organize a bloc to compete with them." The "have nations" must recognize the demands of the "have-not nations," he contended. He believed that the Emperor was too liberal and too rigid in his stance toward the army.[3] His thinking was in tune with the *Kōdō-ha* and he appointed Araki as Minister of Education. His hardline on international relations contributed to the outbreak of the China War that started a month after he assumed office.

The move toward military aggression in China had, of course, been set in motion by the Manchurian Incident. This directed the Japanese economy toward greater emphasis on production of war goods. Some of the advocates for expansion on the continent stressed the need for an outlet for the growing population. The solution to the economic distress caused by the Great Depression was also seen in military expansion. By the outbreak of the China War in 1937 the industrial-financial conglomerates, the *zaibatsu*, were ready to cooperate with the militarists to partake of the fruits of imperialism. As noted earlier, the army radicals were hostile to big capitalistic conglomerates because of the gross inequality in the country. Some peasants in hardhit communities were on the verge of starvation. The wages of the factory workers declined in the first half of the 1930s. Real wages dropped from index 100 in 1931 to 87.8 in 1933 and 75.7 in 1937. Despite this situation a Japanese businessman operating a textile factory in China held that the capitalists in Japan were not dealing with trouble-making workers harshly enough. In Shanghai, he claimed, trouble-making workers were apprehended and shot. One Mitsui executive complained that Japanese workers were overpaid. In Manchuria workers survived on ten sen a day while Japanese workers were being paid fifty sen a day, They should cut their food costs by eating only rice and tofu, he contended.

The business tycoons did not need to trim their lifestyle for they benefited from the expanding defense production. The Kwangtung leaders initially sought to keep big business companies out but in order to develop the Manchurian economy, infusion of Japanese capital was necessary. So Japanese business interests came to hold 84.1% of the capital investments in Manchuria by 1940. The economic buildup in Manchuria was accompanied by a ruthless exploitation of Chinese laborers who were paid one-third the wages of Japanese workers.

At home the big conglomerates, Mitsui and Mitsubishi, cooperated with the military interests and built up the defense industries. This resulted in the expansion of heavy industries linked to strategic war industries. The *zaibatsu* firms, as usual, gained dominance in the field. In shipbuilding Mitsubishi came to produce thirty percent of the tonnage. It also engaged in aircraft production and began to produce the Zero fighter plane that played an important part in the Pacific War. While the big companies prospered small and middle-sized enterprises, engaged in the production of non-essential goods, suffered because they were unable to obtain the necessary raw materials, capital, and workers. At the same time the export market was shrinking because the Depression caused many nations to raise tariffs. This practice was employed in Asian and African markets controlled by the Western nations. For this reason the militarists would call for the establishment of Japan's own imperial market or Konoe's "autonomous bloc." Economic expansion in the second half of the second stage of modern economic growth, the period from 1931 to 1952, depended largely on military expansion.

ON THE PATH TO THE PACIFIC WAR

The course that led to the China War (called China Incident by Japan) had commenced in the early 1930s with incursion into Manchuria. To establish the autonomous bloc the Japanese government proclaimed the "Asiatic Monroe Doctrine." The Chinese government, of course, refused to recognize Manchukuo as an independent state. The Japanese government continued to call for friendly relations among China, Japan, and Manchukuo – under the leadership of Japan. In 1935 the Chinese government established diplomatic relations with Japan. But the Kwangtung Army and the Japanese garrison in Tianjin (stationed there since the Boxer incident) set out to try to bring North China under Japanese control. In mid-1935 protesting the outburst of anti-Japanese demonstrations the Japanese government compelled the Chinese government to accede to its demand that Nationalist troops be withdrawn from two provinces north of Beijing, Hebei and Chahar. The Japanese army leaders then endeavored to tighten their control over that region by insisting on the establishment of an autonomous zone. The Nationalist government did create the Hebei-Chahar Political Council but it was not an autonomous political unit. It remained an administrative unit of the Nationalist government.

When Hirota became Prime Minister he formulated the Fundamental Policy which entailed a stronger defensive posture toward Soviet Russia. In accordance with this policy Hirota concluded an Anti-Comintern Pact with Germany in 1936. It was designed to combat subversive activities by the Communist International and was not a military pact. However, in case one of the parties got involved in a conflict with the Soviet Union the second party was not to aid the Soviet Union. Italy also joined the pact. Thus to anti-fascist nations, it appeared that Japan was aligning itself with the fascist powers.

A month after Konoe assumed the premiership the war with China broke out. It was triggered by what appeared to be a minor clash between Japanese and Chinese troops at Marco Polo Bridge outside Beijing on the night of 7 July 1937. Initially the Konoe government regarded it as an incident to be settled locally. But there were hardliners in the army who wanted to use this incident to establish a North China state under Japanese control. War Minister Sugiyama Hajime (1880–1945) proposed sending additional divisions to China. Those like Ishiwara who was more concerned about the Soviet Union opposed the idea of getting involved in a major conflict in China which could evolve into a long war of attrition. Some foreign ministry officials sought to persuade Foreign Minister Hirota to oppose dispatching additional troops to China but Hirota did not oppose the army's hardliners. Konoe also went along with the army hawks. He called a press conference and blamed the Chinese for the troubles in North China and announced a mobilization plan.

Japan's move naturally aroused Chinese public opinion and the Nationalist government set out to strengthen its position in North China. Further incidents and skirmishes aggravated the situation. An incident in Shanghai led the navy, which initially had favored a policy of moderation, to insist on dispatching troops. The army, more concerned about North China than the Shanghai area that the navy considered to be its own sphere of interest, reluctantly agreed to send additional forces there. By mid-August Japanese and Chinese forces began exchanging fire in Shanghai. The Chinese government initiated a policy of general mobilization and the Japanese government abandoned its policy of localizing the conflict and began preparing for a general war. Thus the Marco

Polo Bridge incident quickly led to a major conflict. Public opinion in both countries was marked by great patriotic fervor. The Japanese press lauded the army's hardline and called for the "castigation of China."[4] The Japanese forces were better prepared for the conflict. There had been a strong military force since the Meiji period. The Chinese government, on the other hand, had just managed to establish a national government in 1927. From then on it had been confronted with regional warlords as well as the Communist forces. It had lost Manchuria to the Japanese and was forced to make concessions in North China. Consequently it was not able to turn back the Japanese forces and, by the end of 1937, the Japanese controlled North China.

On the Shanghai front the Chinese forces put up a stiff resistance but by November Japanese forces drove the Chinese defenders out. Then the Konoe government gave the army permission to attack the Chinese capital, Nanjing. The Japanese forces captured Nanjing by mid-December and committed one of the most horrendous atrocities of the war. The troops roamed through the streets, killing men, women, and children indiscriminately. They rounded up males of military age and shot them, raped women, and killed Chinese soldiers who had surrendered. Estimates of the number of victims vary but the Tokyo War Crimes trial concluded that over two hundred thousand civilians and prisoners-of-war were killed in Nanjing and the surrounding area, many by brutal means. The citation of the number of victims does not provide us with the sense of the heinous suffering the victims endured. One woman, Xia Shu-chi who was seven at that time recounted her experience to a Japanese scholar fifty years later in 1987. She recalled that twenty to thirty Japanese soldiers broke into her family house, shot and killed her father, then chased her mother who was running away with her small baby. She was caught, raped, and shot. The baby was thrown on the ground and died. She and her grandparents and two sisters fled to the back room but they were caught. The grandparents were shot to death, and her two older sisters were raped and then shot. Ms. Xia was hiding in the bed but she was stabbed three times with a bayonet. Of the nine members of her family seven were killed. She kept repeating, "Why did they have to kill them?"[5] The commanding general Matsui Iwane (1878–1948) and other officers did nothing to restrain the troops. Matsui was executed as a war criminal after the war.

To explain why the Japanese troops behaved in such a brutal manner would require a detailed analysis of traditional Japanese mores. The inculcation of the samurai spirit in which brutal behavior was idealized was an integral part of military training. Absolute submission to authority and harsh treatment of those lower in rank governed military life. The tight discipline enforced in the military keeps the soldier in line but what happens when the bonds of discipline are loosened? In society in general respect for the strong, and contempt for the weak prevailed. The persistence of insular parochialism which characterized Japanese society may have been a factor. People identified themselves narrowly with members of their own circle and village. Thus concern and compassion toward others were not likely to be fostered. A sense of individuality and individual responsibility were not values stressed. Thus when mob violence breaks out people may become part of the mob.

When the government indoctrinated the school children with nationalistic sentiments it instilled in them a sense of pride and superiority in being a Japanese. No effort was made to foster a common sense of humanity with other people. Ignoring the enormous cultural debt that Japan owed China there was a tendency to hold modern China in low regard ever since Japan's victory in the Sino-Japanese War of 1894–95. Wars induce brutal activities. Soldiers, regardless of nationality, may commit vicious actions indiscriminately. Other atrocities were committed by Japanese forces during the campaign in China but the Nanjing atrocities were among the most horrendous and appalling. The army authorities did little to prevent or restrain atrocities that occurred on other fronts. Only on rare occasions did the commanding generals restrain their forces. Among them was General Hata Shunroku (1879–1962) who led the forces against Hanguo on central Yangzi River. He issued strict orders to the troops not to commit atrocities.[6]

The Nanjing atrocities strengthened the Chinese will to resist the Japanese aggressors. The Nationalist government appealed to the League of Nations for assistance but the League issued only a lukewarm condemnation of Japanese aggression. The signatories of the Nine Power Treaty met but accomplished nothing. The only nation to give some assistance was the Soviet Union but it was not in a position to provide massive aid. In October 1937 President

Roosevelt proclaimed the need to quarantine aggression but took no action. In November some Japanese army officers, hoping to start a conflict with Britain and America, attacked American and British gunboats but the Japanese government quickly apologized and paid reparations.

Germany, more concerned about getting Japan to serve as a check against the Soviet Union rather than getting bogged down in China, offered to mediate to end the conflict but the Japanese terms were too stringent. When the Chinese government did not immediately accept the terms the Japanese government terminated the negotiations. Konoe issued a statement saying that the Japanese government would have no further dealings with the Nationalist government and the campaign to subdue the Chinese government continued. The Japanese controlled the coastal region from north to south and expanded inland to Hangou where the Chinese government had moved the capital after the fall of Nanjing. It then moved further inland to Chongquing. There the Chinese government continued its resistance and the Japanese were unable to push further into the mountainous region so the conflict settled in to a long drawn-out war of attrition with both sides paying a heavy price with the lives of men on the front. On both sides the soldiers conscripted to do the fighting were young peasant men and boys. The Japanese soldiers were indoctrinated since elementary school to give their lives to the Emperor. Like all political leaders who remain safely at home while they sent young men, mostly from poor families, to die, the Emperor and Konoe were ensconced safely in Tokyo.

In July 1938, while Japan was ensnared in an interminable quagmire in China, some army officers who were concerned about Soviet power in East Asia engaged the Soviet forces in a border dispute at Changkufen where Siberia, Manchuria, and Korea converge. Contrary to their expectation of dealing a crushing blow to the Russians the Japanese suffered a decisive defeat. They had to withdraw and accept a negotiated settlement. Still not convinced of the superiority of the Russian forces, in the following May the Kwangtung Army leaders engaged in a border clash with the Russians in Nomonhan on the border of Manchuria and Outer Mongolia. This developed into a major conflict. When the Japanese forces launched a large-scale attack against the Soviet forces, the latter launched a major counter-offensive utilizing mechanized forces supported by air power. Having suffered a decisive defeat the Kwangtung Army asked for reinforcements but in September Hitler invaded Poland, so after the defeat neither the Japanese government nor the Soviet Union, concerned over Europe, wanted to get involved in a major war in the Far East. A cease-fire was arranged. At Nomonhan Japan had committed fifty-six thousand troops and suffered losses of 8,400 dead and 8,766 wounded while the Soviet and Mongolian forces suffered nine thousand dead and wounded. The Japanese assumption that the Soviet forces had been weakened by Stalin's purge of the army leaders proved to be illusory. Strained relations between the two countries existed until they concluded a neutrality pact in April 1941. They did so because Japan's relationship with Britain and America was worsening while Soviet Russia's strained relations with Germany were becoming acute, and neither wanted the other nation to be aligned with its potential adversary.

INCREASING TENSIONS: DOMESTIC AND EXTERNAL

As the conflict with China dragged on and relations with other powers became increasingly strained the Japanese government began to adopt stringent measures to tighten its control over internal affairs to ensure public support of its military actions. In February 1938 the Konoe government enacted a National Mobilization Act to marshal resources and manpower for national defense. All workers were called on to dedicate themselves to the national effort. The labor unions, regarded as instruments to serve the interests of the workers not the nation, were compelled to dissolve. The government intensified its censorship activities and set out to curb all harborers of dangerous thoughts, including liberal-minded scholars. The news media were tightly controlled and unfavorable news about the military campaign in China was suppressed. Books that were deemed pacifistic, anti-military, or negative about the National Polity, the imperial court or the sacrosanct national history were banned. Textbooks were revised to instill in the children nationalistic, militaristic sentiments.

With the intensifying war-like mindset a cheerless, grim, stern atmosphere began to pervade Japanese society. The "frivolous"

Western-style activities of the "*mo-bo* and *mo-ga*" era virtually disappeared. Romantic love songs were replaced by patriotic war-songs. All things Western came to be rejected. Baseball, which had become a favorite national pastime, was condemned, and Babe Ruth who was the idol of baseball lovers came to be booed. Women were discouraged from getting permanent waves (some patriotic women went about snipping off hairs of women who had permanent waves) or wearing stylish Western clothes. Soon all men came to wear khaki-colored "people's uniform" and women stepped into pantaloons.

The political situation worsened as the conflict in China remained unresolved and international frictions intensified. In the hope of undermining the Chinese Nationalist government in early 1940 the Japanese established a puppet government under Wang Jingwei who was persuaded to defect from the Nationalist government. However this had no effect on Chinese resistance. During the same period a movement to form an alliance with Germany and Italy was being pushed by the hardline nationalists. But just before Hitler invaded Poland he concluded a non-aggression pact with the Soviet Union. This stunned the advocates of the Axis alliance because the purpose of the alliance was to curb the Soviet Union. However, Hitler's military successes in Europe revived the move to conclude an alliance with the Axis powers. An alliance, the expansionists contended, would enable Japan to move into South East Asia and gain control of the European colonies there. In September 1940 the Japanese government, under Konoe's leadership, concluded the Axis Alliance with Germany and Italy.

Konoe had resumed the premiership in July 1940 after an interlude of a year and a half. He had the support of the militarists and ultra-nationalists, and the policies that he pursued led Japan directly to the Pacific War. His cabinet included General Tōjō Hideki as War Minister, and American-educated Matsuoka Yōsuke (1880–1946), who had led the Japanese delegation out of the League of Nations in 1933, as Foreign Minister. Konoe and his ministers formulated "The Main Principles of Basic National Policy." It called for the establishment of a new order in Greater East Asia based on the alleged nation's founding principle of "eight corners of the world under one roof." Matsuoka explained that this means the establishment of the "Greater East Asia co-prosperity sphere." To prepare for this the officials asserted that there must be a military build-up, settlement of the China conflict, administrative reforms, economic planning, and educational measures to reinforce the principles of national polity and eliminate "selfish thoughts."

A conference of the cabinet and the supreme command in late July adopted the statement. The members also agreed on moving south towards South East Asia by recourse to arms if necessary. They anticipated encountering British Military opposition to this move, but they agreed that they must also be prepared for a possible conflict with the United States. Hence military preparedness had to be accelerated. This decision to move south by force set the stage for the Pacific War.

The navy was more adamant about the move south than the army because of its interest in gaining access to the oil supplies in South East Asia. The navy's desire to gain access to the resources in the south was motivated, in part, by the United States' abrogation of the commercial treaty in the preceding January. The army was more concerned about the Soviet Union to the north.

In the realm of political restructuring, Konoe initiated the plan to form a single, unitary political party in place of the existing parties. The hardline army leaders favored the formation of a Nazi-type party that would underpin the establishment of a "national defense state," namely a military state. Many "reformists" favored the establishment of a mass party to build a new social order. The existing parties voluntarily dissolved themselves and joined the movement. In October 1940 the Imperial Rule Assistance Association was formed, with Konoe at its head, but because of divergent interests and elements involved, the organization failed to function as an effective political party and it became merely a vehicle to guide the people to invigorate the "Yamato spirit."

The move to the south had commenced even before the Konoe government adopted the "Main Principles." In order to block the entry of supplies to China through French controlled Indochina (Vietnam) the Japanese government under Admiral Yonai requested the French governor-general to allow Japanese military observers in Hanoi to end all shipment of war materials to China.

France, having been defeated by Germany, was in no position to resist the Japanese and agreed to the request in June 1940. When the Konoe government emerged with its decision to move south it demanded that the French allow Japan to dispatch troops into Indochina. The French were unable to resist and Japanese troops occupied northern Indochina by late September 1940. The United States and Britain felt compelled to adopt retaliatory measures against Japan. The former placed an embargo on shipment of iron and steel scrap to Japan, and Britain decided to reopen the Burma Road, a supply route into China, which it had agreed to close earlier.

Japan was most interested in gaining access to the Dutch East Indies (Indonesia) for its petroleum. Negotiations with the Dutch authorities in Batavia continued from September 1940 to June 1941 but the Dutch, aligned with Britain, did not accede to Japanese demands. This reinforced the Japanese militarists' argument that force must be resorted to to break through the so-called A.B.C.D. (America, British, China, Dutch) encirclement. As the possibility of confrontation with Britain and America became more acute Foreign Minister Matsuoka decided to ensure that stable relations would prevail with the Soviet Union. Since the Soviet Union and Germany had concluded a neutrality pact in August 1939 Matsuoka hoped to link the Soviet Union to the Axis Alliance. Therefore in March 1941 he traveled to Germany only to find that German-Soviet relations had deteriorated. Instead of effecting a rapprochement with Russia the Germans sought to persuade Japan to enter the war against Britain by attacking Singapore. Matsuoka abandoned the plan for a quadruple military alliance and, on his way back to Japan, concluded a neutrality pact with Russia on April 13. Stalin told him, "Now Japan can move south."

Two months later Germany launched a war against Russia. After having concluded the pact with Soviet Russia Matsuoka proposed to the liaison conference of the cabinet and the supreme command that Japan should abandon its plan to move south and should join Germany in the war against Russia. The conference rejected Matsuoka's proposal and proceeded with the plan to move south.

Nomura Kichisaburō, who was foreign minister when the United States declared its decision to abrogate the commercial treaty in January 1940, had planned to negotiate a new commercial treaty but the cabinet fell and he was unable to proceed with his plan to improve U.S.-Japanese relations. In early 1941 he was appointed by Konoe to serve as ambassador to the United States. He set out to improve relations between the two nations and began discussions with the U.S. Secretary of State Cordell Hull. The latter posited four basic principles: respect for territorial integrity, non-interference in the internal affairs of other countries, equality of opportunity, and non-disturbance of the *status quo* in the Pacific. Specific issues to be resolved were the renewal of the commercial treaty, Japanese occupation of China, Japan's South East Asian policy, and its alliance with Germany and Italy. The discussions continued from March through November. The China question proved to be the most difficult issue to resolve. The United States insisted that Japan must withdraw from China. Japan maintained that complete withdrawal was not feasible.

While the negotiators were talking the Japanese government decided to proceed with the plan to occupy the southern section of Indochina, although Nomura warned that such a move would be regarded as a preliminary act in the plan to invade Singapore and the Dutch East Indies. At the end of July the Japanese government compelled the French Vichy government to acquiesce to the Japanese occupation of southern Indochina. The United States government responded by freezing the Japanese assets in America and imposed a total embargo on exports to Japan except for cotton and food. Britain and the Dutch East Indies followed suit. This in effect meant a total economic blockade by the countries that Japan was heavily dependent upon for imports. In 1939 66.4% of Japan's imports came from regions under Anglo-American economic control. Japan was heavily dependent on the United States for oil, a commodity crucial for the navy. In 1939 eighty-five percent and in 1940 eighty percent of Japan's oil came from the United States. Without access to the major source of oil the Japanese navy's oil reserves were expected to last two years, and a year and a half if Japan were to engage in a full-scale war. This turned the navy leaders, who had been opposed to the idea of a military conflict with Britain and America, into advocates of military action to gain access to the oil fields of the Dutch East

Indies. They realized this meant war with the United States and Britain but if the blockade continued the navy would be immobilized. Japan would be like "a fish in a pond from which the water was gradually being drained away."[7]

The situation was approaching a critical stage in which war between Anglo-American nations and Japan seemed inevitable. Konoe decided to seek a conference with President Roosevelt to negotiate an agreement. The army leaders refused to agree to any settlement unless the United States discontinued aiding China, accepted the Tripartite Pact, and resumed trade with Japan. But Konoe decided to confer with Roosevelt. Before such a meeting could be held Secretary Hull insisted that Japan must withdraw from the Axis Pact and also agree to pull out all its troops from China. President Roosevelt agreed with Hull so the summit conference did not materialize. He, Hull, and others agreed that China could not be abandoned, and Japan had to sever its ties with Germany which was at war with Britain and Russia. The Japanese, the militarists in particular, were determined not to withdraw from China after the heavy losses in what they had persuaded the people was a "righteous war." Tōjō contended that Japan could not agree to withdraw from all of China "after having sacrificed so many precious lives on the continent."[8] The failure of Nomura and the negotiators to make any progress led the military leaders to begin preparing for war with the United States and Britain. The army and navy staff officers decided that if the negotiations were not successful by early October the decision to go to war should be made. They presented their proposal to the liaison conference between the cabinet and the supreme command. The conference members agreed with the proposal and submitted it on September 6 to the imperial conference which was presided over by the Emperor.

At the conference the Emperor expressed his preference for diplomatic negotiations rather than war. The conference agreed on the continuance of negotiations but voiced a determination not to be deterred by the possibility of war if Japan's demands were not accepted by the United States. Japan's demands included non-interference in the settlement of the China Incident by the United States and Britain; that they were not to provide aid to the Chinese government; and not to establish military bases in Thailand, the

Dutch East Indies or China; and that they had to resume trade with Japan. If these demands were met Japan would promise not to use French Indochina as a base of operations against any neighboring country; would guarantee neutrality of the Philippines; not automatically invoke the Tripartite Pact should the United States enter the European war; and abide by the neutrality pact with the Soviet Union. If by early October negotiations proved fruitless war preparations were to be started.

Konoe continued his effort to have a meeting with President Roosevelt. The United States ambassador to Japan urged the U.S. government to agree to such a meeting; otherwise the Konoe government would fall and a military dictatorship would be established. But Secretary of State Hull insisted that a Konoe-Roosevelt meeting could not be arranged unless the four principles he submitted earlier were agreed upon, and he sent a note to this effect to Japanese authorities on October 2. Thereupon the army leaders insisted that Konoe make the decision to go to war. The navy leaders procrastinated saying the decision was up to the Prime Minister. Unable to get the army to agree to make some concessions Konoe resigned his post. The court adviser Kido Kōichi (1889–1977) advised the Emperor to appoint General Tōjō as Prime Minister because he believed that only Tōjō could keep the chauvinistic army officers under control. On October 18 Tōjō became Prime Minister.

Tōjō convened the liaison conference toward the end of October. The army general staff officers contended that the decision to go to war must be made and they must be prepared to commence fighting by early December. However, they were persuaded by the foreign minister, Tōgō Shigenori (1882–1950), to continue negotiations. If the negotiations failed to make any progress they wanted them terminated by November 13 but agreed to extend the deadline to December 1. The liaison conference agreed on submitting proposals that were favorable to Japan and required the United States to accept Japanese occupation of certain areas of China such as North China and Inner Mongolia. If these proposals were rejected a *modus vivendi* was to be presented which in essence involved the *status quo* in South East Asia and the South Pacific so far as military deployments went. In return commercial relations between United States and Japan were to be restored, and the U.S. was not to intervene in a Chinese–Japanese settlement of the conflict. The imperial conference decided to go to war in early December if these proposals did not produce positive results. As the hardliners expected the United States rejected the proposals.

Secretary Hull proposed that the United States submit a *modus vivendi* of its own to delay a breakdown in the negotiations for at least three months. The proposal, as envisioned by President Roosevelt, entailed renewal of some trade between the two countries; Japan was to refrain from dispatching additional troops to Indochina, to the Manchurian border, or any place south; Japan was not to invoke the Tripartite Pact should the United States get involved in the European War; the U.S. would foster Chinese and Japanese discussions. However, Britain and China objected to this plan so it was dropped.

Secretary Hull's desire to delay the possible collapse of the negotiations for several months was based on the lead time needed by the United States to prepare for possible military confrontation. This contrasts with the position of the Japanese militarists who were convinced that delay would only weaken Japan's position because of the oil embargo.

With the abandonment of the planned *modus vivendi* the U.S. authorities decided to reiterate the original U.S. position. On November 26 Secretary Hull handed the Japanese envoys a note restating his four basic principles, and withdrawal of all Japanese troops from China and Indochina, and recognition of the Nationalist government as the only legitimate government of all China, including Manchuria. Thus the negotiations returned to ground zero. Secretary Hull realized that this meant war was likely. He told Secretary of War Stimson, "I have washed my hands of it, and it is now in the hands of you and Knox, the Army and Navy."[9]

The Hull note played into the hands of the hawkish Japanese military leaders who were set to go to war when negotiations failed. The members of the liaison conference agreed with Tōjō that the Hull note was an ultimatum and agreed to go to war. The imperial conference met on December 1 and ratified the decision for war and set December 8 (7th, U.S. date) as the date to attack Pearl Harbor. The Japanese fleet under the command of Admiral

Yamamoto Isoroku (1884–1943) left the base in the Kurlies on November 26, the day the Hull note was sent, and headed for Hawaii to stage an attack on December 8th. Yamamoto believed that the Japanese navy could be successful in a short war but not in a prolonged war. Thus, a quick victory over the U.S. navy by a surprise attack on Pearl Harbor underpinned his strategy.

The decision was made to deliver the declaration of war as close as possible to the commencement of the attack but due to the delay in deciphering the message by the Japanese embassy in Washington, the message was delivered to the Secretary of State an hour after the bombs began falling at Pearl Harbor. Thus the great Pacific War commenced.

THE PACIFIC WAR AND DEFEAT

The surprise attack on the U.S. fleet at Pearl Harbor, from the Japanese standpoint was successful. The air attacks had sunk or heavily damaged eighteen American naval vessels, and close to 350 planes were destroyed or damaged. The aircraft carriers escaped because they were at sea. The American casualties numbered 2,403 dead and 1,178 wounded. The Japanese losses were minor: twenty-nine planes and about a hundred casualties. Japanese authorities hailed this as a great victory. But naval historian Samuel Eliot Morison concluded: "The surprise attack on Pearl Harbor ... was a strategic imbecility ... On the tactical level, the Pearl Harbor attack was wrongly concentrated on ships rather than permanent installations and oil tanks. On the strategic level it was idiotic. On the high political level it was disastrous."[10] For one thing it shook American opinion out of its isolationist mind-set and the country moved to a full-scale war-footing immediately.

Simultaneously with the attack on Pearl Harbor, Japanese attacks were launched against Guam, Wake Island, the Philippines, Hong Kong, and Malaya. In the Philippine campaign Japanese planes destroyed the U.S. planes sitting on Clark Field in Manila and launched campaigns in Luzon and Mindanao. General MacArthur was compelled to declare Manila an open city and withdraw to Bataan Peninsula, thus setting the stage for the infamous Bataan death march when the Japanese captured the U.S. forces. The death toll of that march came to twenty-three hundred

American and twenty-nine thousand Filippino troops. General MacArthur withdrew to Australia, leaving the forces at Corregidor under the command of General Wainwright who was compelled to surrender in May 1942. The Philippine campaign was over but guerrilla warfare was continued by the Filippinos.

Guam, Wake Island, and Hong Kong fell to the Japanese by late December 1941. Japan concluded an alliance with Thailand and launched a campaign down the Malay Peninsula against Singapore and captured the city on February 15, 1942. Earlier the battleship *Prince of Wales* and the cruiser *Repulse* guarding the city had been destroyed by the Japanese. After the fall of Singapore the Japanese forces invaded Burma and brought it under control by mid-May.

The coveted target of the entire campaign was the Dutch East Indies and its oil deposits. The Dutch were unable to resist the Japanese forces and surrendered by early March 1942. The battle for the Dutch East Indies involved naval control of the seas in the region. The Japanese fleet won a series of encounters on the Java Sea against the allied naval forces of America, Britain, and the Netherlands, and gained control of the seas of the southwest Pacific by April.

Having established control of South East Asia and the southwest Pacific more quickly than they had anticipated the liaison conference proposed the establishment of a defense perimeter in anticipation of the American counter-offensive. A portent of things to come was demonstrated by Colonel James H. Doolittle's air raid on Tokyo by a squadron of B-25s, launched from an aircraft carrier on April 18, 1942. The damage was slight but it signified that Japanese air and land were not invulnerable.

After the initial successes the Japanese marked off a defensive perimeter in the Pacific extending from the Aleutian Islands in the north through the mid-Pacific along the Midway Atoll to the Solomon Islands and New Guinea to the south. The first sea battle in defense of the perimeter took place on May 8, 1942 in the Battle of the Coral Sea. This was the first naval battle in history in which combat was undertaken mainly by carrier-based planes. Both sides claimed victory but Japan failed to achieve its objective of capturing Port Moresby in New Guinea.

The next major sea battle, and the battle that in effect turned the tide against the Japanese in the Pacific War, was the Battle of

Midway, which took place in June 1942. The Japanese fleet led by Admiral Yamamoto was set to launch a surprise attack on the American naval base on Midway Island. But the Americans had broken the Japanese code and were prepared for the Japanese attack. In the battle on June 4 the American carriers, including the *Yorktown* that the Japanese believed had been sunk in the Coral Sea battle, launched dive bombers. The American forces succeeded in sinking four Japanese carriers, half a dozen naval vessels, and destroyed 332 planes. In contrast the American losses came to one carrier, a destroyer, and 147 planes. Human lives lost came to 3,500 Japanese and 307 Americans. Among the Japanese losses were one hundred skilled navy pilots which reduced the number of able pilots who were in short supply compared to American forces. Suffering a major defeat Yamamoto turned back. News of this disaster was kept from the Japanese public.

After the Battle of Midway Japan was forced on the defensive. The United States, which was concentrating on the European war and was devoting its military resources primarily to that front, was able nevertheless to begin breaking through the Japanese defense perimeter. The campaign was conducted primarily by the navy which began regaining the islands occupied by the Japanese forces. In the naval battles off the Solomon Islands in August 1942 both sides lost a considerable number of combat ships but the United States was able to gain naval and air supremacy in this region. At the same time a grisly land battle on Guadalcanal was taking place. After a six-month campaign the Japanese were forced to withdraw from the island in February 1943. Japan lost 893 planes and 2,362 airmen in the half-year battle of the Solomon Islands. In the following year Japan lost 6,203 planes and 4,824 aviators, resources it could ill-afford to lose. Lacking the productive capacity of the United States, Japan found it increasingly difficult to replace its losses. The U.S. while fighting a two-front war was able to build up its naval and air power substantially. By the end of the war it had 40,893 first-line planes and sixty aircraft carriers.

The campaign to dislodge the Japanese forces from the Solomon Islands continued with the United States continuing to inflict heavy losses on Japanese naval and supply ships. One Japanese victim of U.S. air power was Admiral Yamamoto while on a flight to the Solomon Islands. By the end of 1943 the U.S. was able to prevent the Japanese from sending supplies and reinforcements to their holdings in the Solomon Islands.

In May 1943 the United States devised a three-pronged offensive strategy. The first phase, the campaign to regain the Aleutian islands of Kiska and Attu, was quickly accomplished. The second phase involved an offensive through New Guinea, the Celebes, and the Sulu to Hong Kong. General MacArthur was in charge of this campaign. The Allied forces gained control of the Japanese-held bases in New Guinea, isolating the Japanese forces. Their isolation continued to the end of the war. Of the 140,000 troops sent to New Guinea only thirteen thousand survived to the end of the war. General MacArthur continued his campaign to return to the Philippines which had fallen to the Japanese.

The third phase, a naval campaign through the Central Pacific islands was led by Admiral Chester Nimitz. This was to inflict the heaviest damage on Japanese forces and Japan itself. In the first campaign in November 1943 the U.S. forces captured Makin and Tarawa in the Gilbert Islands. The amphibious battle for Tarawa was one of the bloodiest struggle of the war. American casualties numbered a thousand dead and over two thousand wounded. All the Japanese marines, 4,800 men, died in this battle. Then Admiral Nimitz launched a campaign in the Marshall Islands, capturing Kwajalein and Eniwetok in early February 1944.

While the battle on the Pacific front was taking place fighting resumed in Burma as the Japanese sought to cut off the British and American supply route to China by attacking Imphal in Assam in the spring of 1944. Beset by an early monsoon and with their supply lines cut, the Japanese withdrew, suffering heavy losses at the hands of advancing British-Indian forces. During this period General Joseph Stilwell and the Chinese forces launched an offensive in northern Burma gaining firm control of the supply line to China. The Allied forces continued the offensive and in May 1945 recaptured Rangoon. In the Burma campaign from the Fall of 1944 to May 1945 the Japanese dead, resulting from combat, epidemic diseases, and starvation, came to two hundred thousand men. Fighting on mainland China was limited during the Pacific War though Japan had to station one million troops there. They engaged in occasional encounters with Nationalist forces, and the Chinese Communist guerrillas harassed Japanese troops occupying the northern villages.

In June 1944 an enormous U.S. naval task force, consisting of 535 vessels, proceeded to the Mariana Islands to attack the Japanese held islands of Guam, Tinian, and Saipan. After saturation bombing by air and naval forces the United States marines landed on Saipan and secured a beachhead. The Japanese fleet led by Admiral Ozawa Jisaburō launched major air attacks on the U.S. but the Japanese planes were intercepted and shot down. American submarines sank the Japanese flagship and a carrier. Ozawa decided to withdraw to the north but the U.S. task force inflicted blows on his carriers and planes. He fled to Okinawa with only thirty-five carrier planes left.

Over three weeks of ferocious fighting took place on Saipan. The Japanese forces resisted to the bitter end conducting *banzai* (suicidal) charges. When the U.S. forces claimed victory on July 9, 1944 only one thousand of the thirty-two thousand Japanese troops survived. Ten thousand civilians also perished as the troops encouraged them to commit suicide rather than surrender just as the soldiers had been indoctrinated never to surrender or become prisoners of war.[11] "Men, women and children cut each others' throats, deliberately drowned themselves ... Parents dashed babies' brains out on the cliffs and then jumped over themselves; children tossed hand grenades to each other."[12] American casualties were also high: 3,426 dead and 13,099 wounded.

The United States forces captured Tinian, using napalm bombs for the first time. Guam was also taken by 10 August 1944 after a three-week combat. For Japan the loss of the Mariana Islands did not simply mean heavy losses in troops but Tokyo became vulnerable. The U.S. had bases in Saipan and Tinian from whence it could attack Tokyo by air. Guam became an important naval base for the Pacific fleet. The first flight to conduct air raids on Tokyo took place on November 24, 1944, and from Tinian the fateful flights over Hiroshima and Nagasaki took off in August 1945.

The unfavorable tide of war began to undermine Tōjō's standing at home. At the outset of the war when Japan could celebrate victory after victory the public was euphoric and Tōjō's control of the political domain was firm. But he did not have complete control over war planning; the army general staff insisted on the "independence of the supreme command." Petty rivalry between the army and navy continued and they refused to coordinate the war efforts. Hoping to coordinate matters Tōjō assumed the post of chief of the army general staff in February 1944 but the unfavorable turn of the war led some senior statesmen to seek Tōjō's removal from office. The defeat at Saipan and opposition from senior statesmen and his own cabinet members caused Tōjō to resign on July 18, 1944.

General Koiso Kuniaki (1880–1950) succeeded Tōjō but the course of the war continued to worsen. Koiso was concerned about the possibility of the Soviet Union joining the war against Japan and he sought to get Soviet reassurance on the neutrality pact but was unsuccessful. In November 1994 Stalin denounced Japan as an aggressor and, at Yalta in February 1945, he agreed to enter the war against Japan after Germany's defeat. In April 1945 the Soviet government announced that it would not renew the neutrality pact. Koiso also sought to initiate negotiations with the Chinese Nationalist government to settle the war but this effort failed. Immediately after U.S. troops landed in Okinawa in April 1945 Koiso resigned. He was succeeded by the retired admiral Suzuki Kantarō, who had been attacked by the February 26 (1936) army rebels.

The fall of Saipan was not the only portent of unfavorable things to come for the Japanese forces. On the southwestern Pacific front General MacArthur continued his march to return to the Philippines to live up to his earlier vow: "I shall return." Together with the naval fleet, under the command of Admiral William F. Halsey, the General was able to sever Japanese links to the East Indies by making air and submarine attacks on Japanese vessels and bases. Then in mid-October 1944 a massive force was marshalled to land Allied troops on Leyte in the Philippines. A decisive, four-day naval battle ensued at Leyte Gulf and Surigao Straits, and the heavy losses of naval ships of all categories rendered the Japanese navy an ineffective force. In January 1945 U.S. forces landed in Luzon and captured Manila in early March. The resistance of about 170,000 Japanese troops under General Yamashita's command continued. Some troops fled into the mountains and, scrounging for food, some even turned to cannibalism. By the end of June the Japanese had lost over 250,000 men through battle, starvation, and disease. United States losses numbered 8,140 killed and 29,557 wounded.

Meanwhile the battle for the key islands on the approach to Japan continued. The most renowned of these was the battle for Iwo Jima which lies midway between Saipan and the Japanese islands. After sustained bombing U.S. marines landed on the island on February 19, 1945, and bitter fighting took place for a month. When the U.S. conquered the eight-square mile island it had lost 6,821 lives with nineteen thousand wounded. Virtually the entire Japanese garrison, 22,500 men died in battle. The base was immediately used by U.S. fighter planes to escort B-29 bombers to Japan.

After conquering Saipan B-29 bombers were sent over Tokyo to raid major factories. Then the targets shifted from factories to civilians in the major cities to compel the Japanese government to surrender. From March 1945 densely populated areas became targets of fire-bombing. On March 9, 334 bombers destroyed a quarter of Tokyo, leaving 83,793 dead and 40,918 injured and a million homeless. Similar fire-bombings were launched against other major cities, and continued until the end of the war. By the end of the war sixty-six cities had been attacked from the air and sea. Although the U.S. air force targeted civilian residential sections in all the air raids, the seat of power and the primary locus of responsibility for the war, the imperial palace, remained untouched.

The final land battle of the war took place in Okinawa. On April 1, 1945 U.S. marines landed and confronted some one hundred thousand troops entrenched in the rugged interior. The vicious battle raged into June with the Japanese forces determined to fight to the end. In the battle 110,000 Japanese soldiers and Okinawa militiamen (conscripted by the Japanese authorities) died. Also one hundred thousand Okinawa civilians perished during the battle as U.S. troops set out to wipe out all "hostile" elements, little realizing that Okinawans were victims of Japanese colonialism too. In fact eight hundred Okinawans were executed by the Japanese military as pro-American.[13]

During the Okinawan campaign air and naval encounters took place off Kyushu and on the Inland Sea. The Japanese launched "kamikaze" attacks by suicide planes against U.S. naval vessels and destroyed and damaged a number of warships. But the U.S. was able to down a large number of the Kamikaze planes. The U.S. navy also sank the super battleship *Yamato* and most of the destroyers escorting it, thus decimating the last of the Japanese navy.

The protracted war not only virtually eliminated the Japanese navy and hundreds of thousands of land troops but the U.S. navy and air force had crippled the Japanese economy which depended on South East Asian resources. Compared to the United States Japanese economic resources were miniscule; it was one seventy-eighth that of the United States. It was estimated in 1941 that three million metric tons of non-military shipping would be necessary to maintain adequate war production. But because of the U.S. success in sinking Japanese vessels and cutting off the sea lanes by the end of the war it was down to 1.56 million metric tons. The U.S. submarines were especially effective in crippling the Japanese merchant fleet. This meant serious shortage of essential raw materials. The supply of scrap iron and steel dropped from 4.468 million metric tons to 0.449 million metric tons. More critically the supply of crude and refined oil dropped from 48.89 million metric tons in 1941 to 4.946 million metric tons in the first half of 1945. This in essence demobilized the Japanese navy. Similar shortages developed with other mineral resources.

From the outset U.S. productive capacity was far greater than Japan's. In aircraft production during 1941–44 Japan produced a total of 58,822 aircraft while Germany produced 92,656, Britain 96,400 and the United States 261,826. The conscription of workers into the military resulted in shortages of skilled workers and a decline in per capita productivity. As a result of the shortage of raw materials there was a general drop in the production of war goods as well as consumer goods. So even before the massive air attacks Japan's economy was in dire straits.

With the U.S. military in Okinawa and the possibility of U.S. invasion of Japan proper, some Japanese leaders began to contemplate ways of ending the war. With Germany's surrender on May 7, 1945 the situation became even more ominous. The Suzuki government sought to get the Soviet Union to mediate between Japan and the Allied powers to end the war short of unconditional surrender. But the Soviet Union had agreed to enter the war against Japan at Yalta and the agreement was firmed up at the Potsdam meeting in July. On July 26 the United States, Great Britain and China issued the Potsdam Declaration calling on Japan to end the war on the basis of unconditional surrender. The terms called for elimination from authority those responsible for the war; occupation of Japan; limitation of Japanese sovereignty to the Japanese islands; complete disarmament; punishment of war criminals; political reform, and restriction on Japanese industries.

The cabinet members discussed the Declaration but for public consumption Suzuki declared that the government would ignore the Declaration. This was taken by the United States as an outright rejection and President Truman decided to employ the atomic bomb. On the morning of August 6 the bomber Enola Gay flew over Hiroshima and dropped an atomic bomb with a force of twenty thousand tons of TNT on the center of the city. A huge mushroom cloud spread overhead while the city was turned into a living inferno. One eyewitness recollected: "It was a horrible sight. Hundreds of injured people who were trying to escape to the hills passed our house ... Their faces and hands were burnt and swollen; and great sheets of skin had peeled away from their tissues to hang down like rags on a scarecrow." The victims, those who died instantly and those who died of radiation soon after, numbered about 140,000. Tens of thousands of others suffered injury and radiation sickness. One doctor observed: "Many people who appeared to be healthy ... were beginning to die with symptoms of vaginal bleeding, nose bleeds, bloody sputum, bloody vomitus, and hemorrhage beneath the skin and in the tissues."[14]

Even this horrific devastation failed to persuade the militarists to end the war. They insisted that "one hundred million" must sacrifice themselves. But before the impact of this new bomb could be fully assessed, the Soviet Union, as promised, joined the war against Japan on August 8, and advanced rapidly into Manchuria. This caused the Supreme Council to consider ending the war by accepting the terms laid down by the Potsdam Declaration but the militarists insisted on having the terms modified so that the implementation of the terms would be left to Japan. Before the issue could be resolved a second atomic bomb was dropped on Nagasaki on August 9. The Peace Memorial Park in Nagasaki lists the number of victims as dead 73,884, injured 74,909, sufferers 120,820. A medical doctor in Nagasaki who eventually died of the effects of radiation noted the terrible effects of the bomb. "Five hundred meters from the explosion lay a mother with her stomach split open while her future baby attached by the umbilical cord dangled between her legs. There were corpses with the belly gaping and the entrails exposed. Seven hundred meters away were heads that had been torn from the trunks of bodies. There were broken skulls with blood dripping from the ears." Some of those exposed to atomic radiation died of hemorrhage in about a week but some with less exposure did not die right away. They experienced diarrhoea for a while but after a few weeks they became fatigued, suffered from high fever, the skin turned white, ulcers prevented them from eating or drinking, purplish red spots began to appear on the skin which grew in size, the white blood cells diminished and they died in about nine days.[15]

Even after becoming aware of the terrifying effects of the atomic bombs the militarists refused to budge from their position of fighting until the hundred million Japanese were all vanquished. As a result Prime Minister Suzuki asked the Emperor to make the decision. The Emperor agreed with the advocates of peace and advised that the Allied terms be accepted. The Japanese government communicated its acceptance of the Potsdam terms with the proviso that the Emperor's prerogatives as a sovereign ruler should not be compromised. The Allies responded that the imperial institution would be allowed to remain but it was to be subject to the authority of the supreme command. The military leaders opposed having the Emperor being made "subject to" the authority of the supreme command. Suzuki again asked the Emperor to make the final decision. The Emperor recommended compliance with the Allied terms. The military leaders accepted his decision but some fanatical middle-grade officers attempted a coup d'etat to remove the Emperor's "evil advisers." The plot failed because the military leaders did not support it. Instead the top army leaders committed hara-kiri. A total of about five hundred army and naval officers committed suicide.

On August 15 the Emperor went on the air announcing his decision to terminate the war. On September 2 the Japanese signed the terms of surrender on board the battleship *Missouri*. Thus the war that cost the people of Asia and Japan horrendous suffering and enormous loss of life ended. Japanese aggression in China and in other Asian countries led to millions of deaths and injuries. The United Nations' estimate was that nine million Chinese were killed in the war with Japan between 1937 and 1945. Loss of life due to Japanese military actions, including those killed by Japanese troops, death resulting from forced labor, starvation, and disease in South East Asia was estimated to number millions. It is thought that three million people lost their lives in Java alone. The brutal treatment of prisoners (POW) of war and forced laborers compelled to work on the bridge over the River Kwai is well known. That project was part of the railroad construction between Thailand and Burma. Fourteen thousand POWs and over thirty-three thousand forced laborers perished in the project.[16] Korea which had been colonized by Japan since 1910, paid a heavy price in the Japanese military campaign. Koreans were drafted into the army and used as forced laborers. Over two hundred thousand of the Koreans compelled to serve in Japanese campaigns died. Among the victims were thousands of "comfort women" who were conscripted to serve the Japanese troops.

The Japanese army casualties from the beginning to the end of the Pacific War came to 1.14 million dead (two hundred thousand of whom died in *banzai* suicide attacks), and the naval dead came to 415,000. Japanese civilian deaths in the Pacific War zone may have been as high as 650,000. The victims of air raids over Japan numbered 393,000 dead and 310,000 injured. A large percentage of the physical structures in the cities subjected to air raids was destroyed. For example Tokyo lost fifty-seven percent of its dwellings. The destruction of the industrial plants reduced Japan's industrial production to ten percent of the prewar level.

The high-level perpetrators of war thought nothing of sacrificing the lives of the Japanese people as well as the targets of Japanese aggression for some high-flown notion of bringing the "eight corners of the earth" under imperial rule.

EIGHT

Postwar Reform and Reconstruction

The acceptance of the Potsdam Declaration meant acquiescence to military occupation by the Allied powers, mainly by U.S. forces. The first contingent of the troops arrived on August 28 1945 and two days later the Supreme Commander of the Allied Powers (S.C.A.P.) General MacArthur arrived. In theory the occupation was under the Far Eastern Commission consisting of eleven Allied powers but the U.S. government held the ultimate authority. S.C.A.P. was to be the supreme political authority in Japan during the occupation period (which lasted until April 28, 1952). The Emperor and the Japanese government were to be subordinate to S.C.A.P. The reform measures to be implemented were to be carried out by the Japanese government. The basic policies were decided upon by the Washington policy makers. The basic objectives were to demilitarize and democratize Japan. General MacArthur explained in his memoirs his policy objectives. "First destroy the military power. Punish war criminals. Build the structure of representative government. Modernize the constitution. Hold free elections. Enfranchise the women. Release political prisoners. Liberate the farmers. Establish a free and responsible press. Liberalize education. Decentralize the political power. Separate Church from State."[1] This was a tall order but he and his staff set about implementing these policies.

The country that General MacArthur arrived to govern was in a state of chaos with large sections of major cities devastated. There were acute shortages of food and necessary goods but the people were surprisingly placid and cooperative toward the occupation forces. The fear of fanatical Japanese resisting with suicide attacks was unwarranted. The people, accustomed to obedience to higher authority, submitted to the new ruling authority. Undoubtedly the friendly attitude of the American troops also contributed to the relatively harmonious relationship that characterized the occupation era. And S.C.A.P. aided the populace by importing food to avert mass starvation.

S.C.A.P. immediately set about implementing the policies listed above. Demilitarization proceeded with the demobilization of the 3.7 million troops in Japan, and repatriation of the 3.3 million troops from abroad. Japanese military installations and equipment were destroyed. The task of punishing top political leaders for war crimes was carried out by the International Military Tribunal for the Far East created by the Allied powers.

The trial of the top leaders by the Military Tribunal entailed trying twenty-eight Class A criminals for "crimes against peace." They were seen as a "criminal, militaristic clique" that had dominated the Japanese political world from 1928 to 1945. The trial, presided over by eleven justices from the Allied powers commenced on May 3, 1945 and continued until April 1948. In November 1948 seven leaders, including General Tōjō, were sentenced to death by hanging. The only civilian leader hanged was Hirota Koki, Prime Minister from 1936–37. Prince Konoe avoided being tried by committing suicide when he was about to be arrested. Sixteen of the Class A suspects were sentenced to life imprisonment but their sentences were commuted in 1957. Three justices dissented from the tribunal's decision, two on specific aspects while Justice Radhabinod Pal of India held that the accused were innocent of all counts because aggressive war was not a crime under international law. Two generals held responsible for atrocities committed in the Philippines were executed by a military court established by General MacArthur in the Philippines.

About twenty high-ranking military officers who were charged with command responsibility for the troops' atrocities were classified as Class B criminals. They were all acquitted. Lower-ranking officers and soldiers accused of committing atrocities were classified as Class C criminals. They were tried by Allied military authorities where the crimes were committed. Of the 5,702 persons who were classified as Class B and Class C war criminals

920 were executed and a large number of the others were sent to prison. Among the executed were 150 Koreans and 170 Taiwanese who had been conscripted by the Japanese.[2]

The question of trying the Emperor as a war criminal was raised but it was rejected by American officials because this would make the task of the occupation forces impossible. General MacArthur asserted that if this took place it would require one million men to impose military rule in Japan.

In addition to trying war criminals S.C.A.P. instituted a policy of purging all those who had been in positions of responsibility or were exponents of militarism and aggression. Thus all army and navy officers as well as high government officials, and leaders of business and industry were removed from key positions. At the same time S.C.A.P. got the Japanese government to release all political prisoners, including Communist party leaders like Tokuda Kyuichi.

To implement political reforms and foster democracy, the Ministry of Home Affairs that had authority over the nation's police force and operated the political police was abolished, and jurisdiction over the police was turned over to local authorities. The tight control central government had over local and prefectural governments was loosened. Formerly prefectural governors were appointed by the central government but now they were to be elected by the prefectural voters.

To protect the civil rights of the people S.C.A.P. introduced the Bill of Rights in the constitution (see p. 182) and in 1948 it introduced the concept of *habeas corpus*, an act which General MacArthur considered to be among the most significant of the reforms introduced. Another important reform was the enhancement of women's rights. In 1946 women were granted the right to vote, and the voting age was lowered from twenty-five to twenty. The Civil Code provided for equal rights of women and men. To foster freedom, freedom of the press and speech was introduced. This policy enabled the Japanese press to criticize S.C.A.P. policies. This placed General MacArthur in the awkward position of having to curb "irresponsible" statements in the press, and insist on a "free and responsible press." S.C.A.P. censorship came to include any publication that showed America in an unfavorable light. This included books such as Erskine Caldwell's *Tobacco Road*.

Major reforms were introduced in the economic domain. The issue of reparations to be paid to countries victimized by Japanese aggressors was resolved by S.C.A.P. without compelling Japan to pay huge indemnities. The major object was to institute democracy and freedom in the economic sector. This meant breaking up the huge business conglomerates, the *zaibatsu*. Among the top conglomerates were Mitsui, Mitsubishi, Sumitomo and Yasuda. These had huge holding companies with a total of 761 subsidiaries. Eventually eighty-three holding companies were dissolved. The Mitsui and Mitsubishi conglomerates were dissolved into 240 separate firms. After S.C.A.P. pulled out of Japan in 1952 the old *zaibatsu* firms began to reunite, albeit in a looser form. The other step taken to prevent excessive concentration of economic power was the passage of the anti-monopoly law. The law, however, was full of loopholes and was not effective in curbing the emergence of monopolistic enterprises.

The other major economic reform introduced by S.C.A.P. was the land reform program. By the end of the Second World War seventy percent of the farmers were tenants or partial tenants. Forty-six percent of the cultivated land was under tenancy. But there were no huge landowners. Only about two thousand landowners owned as much as one hundred acres. Most landowners owned no more than ten acres. In October 1946 the Farm Land Reform Law was passed. Absentee landlordism was prohibited. The land that could be owned by a landlord living in the community was limited to 2.5 acres. An active farmer could own a maximum of 7.5 acres for his own cultivation and an additional 2.5 acres that he did not cultivate. The government purchased land from the landowners and sold it to the former tenants. By August 1950 4.75 million acres of rice and upland farms had been acquired from 2.34 million landowners and sold to 4.75 million tenant and small farmers. As a result only twelve percent of the arable land remained under tenancy and the number of full tenants dropped to about five percent. The land reforms were the most successful of the S.C.A.P. reforms ending the historical condition of tenant farmers who had barely managed to feed their families.

Labor reforms were also designed to democratize the economy and society. In December 1945 a trade union law was enacted granting all workers in the private and public sectors the right to organize, engage in collective bargaining, and strike. In 1946, however, a law was enacted denying public-safety and administrative employees the right to strike. In 1947 the Labor Standards Laws regulating working conditions and ensuring worker benefits was passed. The law exceeded the U.S. Fair Labor Standard Act in coverage. As a result of these reforms the number of unions and union members burgeoned. By 1949 there were 6.5 million industrial workers in thirty-five thousand unions.

EDUCATIONAL REFORMS

In education liberalization entailed removing militaristic and ultranationalistic elements that characterized the curriculum, and introducing democratic values. The practice of reciting the Imperial Rescript on Education in schools was ended, textbooks were revised, and moral education was removed from the curriculum. Compulsory education was extended from six to nine years, and centralized control of education was replaced by control by local boards. The Ministry of Education's power to issue public school textbooks was terminated and approval of textbooks was left to the prefectural boards. The Ministry of Education, however, continued to certify textbooks. In a move to foster higher education a number of new colleges and universities were established in 1949.

Teachers acquired the right to organize unions and a national union, the Japan Teachers' Union, a militant activist organization emerged. At the college level the National Student Federation was organized in 1948, and it became an activist organization fighting for political causes.

THE NEW CONSTITUTION

The most significant political reform initiated by S.C.A.P. was the formulation of a new constitution. The object was to remove the sovereignty lodged in the Emperor under the Meiji Constitution, and vest it in the hands of the people. The Japanese officials worked on constitutional revision but the constitution was ultimately drafted by officials of S.C.A.P. on the basis of U.S. government directives. The new constitution that was approved by the Diet in August 1946 retained the Emperor simply as "the symbol of the state." Sovereignty was vested in the people. The members of the two-house Diet were now all elected by the people, and the cabinet was responsible to the Diet, not the Emperor as it was under the Meiji Constitution. The new constitution has extensive provisions for the rights of the people. In addition to the rights provided for citizens in the American constitution, the Japanese constitution provides for social welfare and equality between husband and wife. It also has a "no-war" clause. Article 9 states, "The Japanese people forever renounce war as a sovereign right of the nation ... land, sea, and air forces, as well as other war potential, will never be maintained." This clause later placed the U.S. in an awkward position as the tensions of the Cold War inclined the U.S. to favor some degree of Japanese rearmament. So it was contended that the "no war clause" did not preclude the maintenance of "self-defense forces."

In line with the liberalization of the society, the family system formerly under the tight control of the family head was relaxed. Primogeniture was ended and daughters gained equal rights with sons to inherit the family property. As noted above, the constitution provided equality of husband and wife. A male at age eighteen and a female at age sixteen could marry without parental consent. Public brothels which had remained a fixture in Japanese society for ages were banned with the anti-prostitution law of 1956. Abortion was legalized in 1949 ending the tendency to have large families.

POLITICAL DEVELOPMENTS DURING S.C.A.P. RULE

During the Occupation Years (1945–1952) the Japanese government enacted the reforms initiated by S.C.A.P. The first government to undertake the reforms was headed by Shidehara (the proponent of international cooperation in the 1920s). Confronted with opposition to some reforms, such as the adoption of a new constitution, Shidehara dissolved the Diet. With the advent of the new democratic era a whole slew of political parties emerged. In the April 1946 election Shidehara's Progressive Party failed to gain a majority and Shidehara resigned. Hatoyama Ichirō (1883–1959), the head of the Liberal Party with the largest number of seats in the Diet, was purged by S.C.A.P. because of his prewar political activities. Yoshida Shigeru was then chosen to head the government.

Yoshida continued implementing the S.C.A.P.-initiated reforms. With the new constitution scheduled to take effect in May 1947 S.C.A.P. ordered that a new election be held. In that election the Socialist Party won the largest number of seats so the head of the Socialist Party in a coalition with the new Democratic Party formed a Socialist government. But factional disputes led to its fall. The head of the Democratic Party formed another coalition government but he too was forced to resign, as a result of charges of graft and bribery, in October 1948. Yoshida then became Prime Minister again as head of the newly coalesced Democratic-Liberal Party. Yoshida was destined to remain in office until 1954, paving the way for the dominance of the political scene by the conservative party until 1994.

Yoshida dissolved the Diet upon taking office and, in the following election his party won 264 of the 466 seats gaining an absolute majority. Many of the members of his party who won Diet seats were former bureaucrats. This election is seen as marking the emergence of the triangular power bloc consisting of conservative party members, bureaucrats, and big business interests which dominated the Japanese scene into the 1990s.

Yoshida concentrated on maintaining political stability and working for the nation's economic recovery. Some of the measures he favored were seen as a move to "reverse" the course of postwar reforms, and the left-wing groups, led by the Communist leaders, challenged his policies. In mid-1950 he began to purge communists from government positions, and with the outbreak of the Korean War in June 1950 S.C.A.P. got Yoshida to purge Communist party leaders who were compelled to go underground. The Korean War caused the United States to shift its initial policy of guarding against the revival of militarism to making Japan an important component of the anti-Communist bloc. This move coincided with the U.S. decision to conclude a peace treaty with Japan and end the occupation.

General MacArthur favored an early end to the occupation because he believed a prolonged occupation would have an adverse effect. Preparations for the peace treaty started in early 1950 by John Foster Dulles were complete by September 1951 and the powers concerned convened in San Francisco to sign the treaty. The Soviet Union refused to participate in the conference. China was not a participant because the United States and Great Britain disagreed about which government to invite, Taiwan or Communist China. Forty-eight nations signed the treaty. On the same day a security pact was signed by the U.S. and Japan. This pact provided for the continued stationing of U.S. troops in Japan to protect it from external aggression. The treaty was ratified by the Japanese Diet in October 1951 despite opposition from the left-wing parties. It went into effect in April 1952 thus ending the era of S.C.A.P. occupation which had resulted in revolutionary changes in Japan such as demilitarization, democratization, extension of freedom, a new constitution, and bill of rights.

POST-OCCUPATION POLITICAL DEVELOPMENTS

From the time of Yoshida's premiership the conservative parties virtually dominated the political world for nearly a half a century. The Cold War contributed to the ascendancy of the conservatives because of their anti-communist posture. Left-wing opposition to conservative policies was seen as partisanship in favor of the Communist powers, and the "reverse course" policies pursued by the conservatives were viewed as a move to counter this. Among the measures advanced by Yoshida in pursuing the "reverse course" were those to curb the influence of communism in the public school system, the enactment of a subversive activities law, centralization of police authority, and the establishment of the National Police Reserve as a security force which was soon transformed into ground, maritime, and air self-defense forces.

Confronted with opposition from fellow conservatives Yoshida resigned in late 1954. In 1955 the two major conservative parties joined to form the Liberal Democratic Party. This party dominated the political scene from this point to 1993, and is referred to as the "1955 system."

Following two cabinets after Yoshida, Kishi Nobusuke (1896–1987) assumed the premiership in 1957. Kishi had been indicted as a Class A war criminal for his prewar political activities and was imprisoned for three years. After he was released and "de-purged" he resumed his political life. He followed Yoshida's conservative political line in domestic affairs, and in foreign affairs he favored maintaining close ties with the United States. The most controversial issue that confronted him was the revision of the

Mutual Security Pact to place Japan on a more equal footing with the United States. The revision he concluded provided for continued use of Japanese bases by the United States. In return the U.S. agreed to confer with Japan before dispatching American troops based in Japan for military operations abroad. This agreement met with fierce opposition from liberal and left-wing groups who contended that it drew Japan into a military alliance against the Communist nations. In late 1959 massive demonstrations were staged against the treaty by students, intellectuals, left-wing political parties, and labor unions. The demonstrations continued into mid-1960 and took an increasingly anti-American tone, and the projected visit by President Eisenhower had to be cancelled.

Kishi rammed the treaty revision through the Diet but he was compelled to resign the premiership in July 1960. He was succeeded by Ikeda Hayato (1899–1965) who had risen through the bureaucracy. Ikeda's major accomplishment was the accelera- tion of Japan's economic recovery. Japan's economic growth from the 1960s strengthened support for the conservative party and weakened the left-wing parties. In 1964 Ikeda resigned when he became ill with throat cancer. He was succeeded by Satō Eisuke (1901–1975), Kishi's brother, who had also risen as a bureaucrat. He remained in office for nearly eight years, the longest tenure of any Prime Minister. He followed Ikeda's policy of fostering economic growth, and also played a more active role in foreign affairs. He visited the United States and negotiated the return of Okinawa and the Bonin Islands to Japan. He followed the anti- Chinese Communist line in accordance with what he believed was United States policy but he lost face when the U.S. without any advance notice to Japan changed its policy and President Nixon visited China to establish friendlier relations with Beijing.

Satō was succeeded in 1972 by another highly ambitious political leader, Tanaka Kakuei (1918–1993). He had only an elementary school education but had made a fortune in the construction business, and climbed the political ladder as an expert political manipulator relying on "money politics," patronage, and "pork barrel" allocations. The gravest problem he faced while in office was the oil crisis of 1973. Japan imported 99.7% of its oil, and the difficulties caused by the crisis resulted in inflation and threatened the economic growth that had been in motion since the

1960s. Satō's downfall came about, however, because of the shady financial and political deals in which he was involved. His major accomplishment while in office was the introduction of free medical care for the elderly, so 1973 is regarded as "year one" of the welfare system.

Even after his resignation Tanaka remained the true wielder of power, a "shadow shōgun," despite his involvement in the Lockhead bribery scandal of 1976. It was revealed that high government officials, including Tanaka, had taken bribes to facilitate the sale of Lockhead's Tristar passenger planes to a Japanese airline.

After Tanaka's resignation a series of Prime Ministers from the L.D.P. followed, most of whom served only two years or so. The L.D.P.'s monopoly of government leadership ended when it failed to gain a majority in the 1993 Lower House election. Hosokawa Morihiro, grandson of Prince Konoe, formed a coalition of minor parties and became Prime Minister. A series of coalition governments followed until 1996 when Hashimoto Ryūtarō, head of the L.D.P. formed a government with the support of minor parties.

The predominance of the L.D.P. after 1955 was partly the result of the expanding economy, the support of big business interests, and ties with the bureaucrats, and the farming communities whose interests were catered for by price supports on rice and stringent import restrictions on farm products. The frequent shifts in party leadership resulted from factional divisions based on personal and regional ties. The success of the faction leaders depended on the money that they could dispense to their followers to enable them to win elections. So "money politics" was important.

The opposition parties like the Socialist and Communist parties failed to gain much public support, partly because of the economic expansion from the 1960s onward. The split between the left and right wings of the Socialists did not help them in their struggle against the L.D.P. The socialist party, the Social Democratic Party, held 144 seats in the lower house in 1963 and remained in the lower hundreds during the 1970s and 1980s, then dropped to seventy seats in 1993, and in 1996 it won only fifteen seats. During the immediate postwar years of economic hardship and during the height of the Cold War the Communist Party was able to rally the unions, students, and intellectuals to its cause by staging demonstrations and strikes. As the demonstration challenged

S.C.A.P. a Red Purge was instituted in May 1950 and the party leaders were driven underground until 1955 when the "purge" was lifted. They continued to raise their voice against American imperialism and Japanese monopoly capitalism but their vociferous actions failed to win support from the general public. They had gained thirty-six seats in the Diet in 1949 but in the 1952 election they failed to gain a single seat. In subsequent elections they usually managed to win several seats and they reached a high of thirty-eight seats in 1972 and subsequently held seats numbering between twenty and thirty. The collapse of the Soviet Union in 1989 weakened the Communist Party's place in the Japanese political scene further and by 1993 its lower house seats were down to thirteen. The economic recession of the 1990s, however, resulted in the party gaining more public support. In the 1996 lower house election it won twenty-six of the five hundred seats, and after the 1998 upper house election the party came to hold twenty-three of the 252 seats. Although the Communist Party was unable to do well in national elections they were more successful in local elections in major cities. In 1998 the party held over four thousand seats in city councils nationally, compared to the 3,600 held by the L.D.P.

The bureaucrats play an important political role, and not simply because of their ties to the L.D.P. They have been an important source of power since the Meiji years. In the thinking of the masses, government officials are the reincarnation of the feudal ruling samurai, the actual wielders of power. Political leaders come and go but bureaucrats remain entrenched in key positions with lifetime tenure. Lodged in the various ministries bureaucrats exercise regulatory authority over all facets of life, including the minutest matter. Hosokawa Morihiro, who was Prime Minister during 1993–94, complained that when he was a prefectural governor he had to get permission from the Transportation Ministry to move a bus stop by ten meters (10.94 yards). The most powerful bureaucrats are in the Ministry of International Trade and Industry, and the Finance Ministry. Together they regulate the course of the nation's economy. M.I.T.I. exercises tight control over foreign trade. The Finance Ministry regulates the securities industry. The collapse of the bubble economy in the mid-1990s resulted in the exposure of illegal financial dealings between ministry bureaucrats and securities firms. The seemingly incorruptible bureaucrats were exposed as having taken bribes and a number of them committed suicide.

ECONOMIC DEVELOPMENT

The most serious problem facing Japan at the end of the war was the economic crisis with acute shortages, inflation, and unemployment. In 1946 industrial production was 30.7% of the 1934–36 level. S.C.A.P. sought to implement measures to revive the economy and the United States government injected more than $2 billion into the Japanese economy by 1951. But what triggered the economic recovery was the outbreak of the Korean War which resulted in huge U.S. procurements of war materials. Industrial production began to increase. Taking 1949 as index 100 by 1954 it had risen to index 240.

Following the departure of S.C.A.P. the Japanese government began to relax the anti-monopoly measures and the former conglomerates of the *zaibatsu* circle began to reemerge in the form known as *keiretsu*, cartel-like enterprise groups. There are horizontal and vertical *keiretsu*. Many of the old *zaibatsu* conglomerates constitute the horizontal *keiretsu*. At the core are large banks or trading companies with major industrial firms affiliated with them. Thus Mitsui and Mitsubishi conglomerates re-emerged. Horizontal *keiretsu* consist of postwar industrial giants like Toyota, Honda, Sony and Matsushita with a complex of satellite firms that supply them with necessary parts. For example, in the mid-1980s seventy percent of Nissan Motors' production costs were absorbed by subcontractors. During a recession the major companies reduce payments to subcontracting firms. Hence the bankruptcy rate of small companies increases while the firms at the top of the *keiretsu* survive.

At the same time the laissez-faire policy introduced by S.C.A.P. was gradually replaced by the old system of managed economy with M.I.T.I. and the Finance Ministry determining economic policies. The stimulus by the Korean War, growth in foreign trade, higher farm productivity, lower unemployment rates, and increasing consumer spending triggered what is referred to as the period of high-speed economic growth which began about 1955. In the second half of the 1950s the economy grew at 9.3% per year but in the 1960s it began to grow at a phenomenal pace under the leadership of Prime Minister Ikeda who pursued an income-doubling plan. Capital investments were made in public works, including the construction of the bullet train railway between Tokyo and Osaka. In 1964, the last year of Ikeda's regime, G.N.P. grew by 13.9%. Ikeda's policies were continued by his successors and the economy continued to expand. The growth was particularly spectacular from 1965 to 1974 when industrial production more than doubled. Then it was stalled briefly by the oil shortage of 1974–75.

Throughout the 1960s the G.N.P. growth averaged eleven percent per year compared to four percent growth rate in the U.S. In 1970 Japan's G.N.P. was the second-highest among the capitalist nations. Growth was especially significant in heavy industries as well as in the field of high technology. The oil crisis of 1974 led to a shift away from oil consuming industries to high tech production such as electronic products. Recovery from the oil crisis resulted in continued economic growth. The automobile industry, in particular, benefited from the oil crisis because smaller, fuel-efficient Japanese cars found a tremendous growth in the U.S. market as they came to replace the high consumption American cars. In 1950 Japan manufactured only 1,593 passenger cars but in 1990 it produced 9,948 million. In 1990 twenty-five percent of Japanese cars, including those manufactured in the United States, were sold in the U.S. market. Japanese high tech products like cameras, TV's, radios, V.C.R.'s, quartz watches, computers and computer chips, semiconductors, precision machinery, and so on, also constituted important export items. Japan's share of the international market, which was less than four percent in 1960 rose to about eight percent during the 1980s. The United States remained the biggest trading partner. In 1991 29.1% of Japanese exports went to the U.S. By 1995 this had dropped slightly to 27.3%. In 1995 22.4% of its imports were from the U.S. The balance of trade steadily increased in Japan's favor. In 1993 it reached $59.3 billion. By 1995 it decreased somewhat to $45.5 billion. With economic expansion overseas investments increased, including investments in the United States. Heavy investment was made in Asia. In the mid-1990s it was estimated that forty to sixty percent of the funds for Asian projects came from Japan.

The sustained economic growth since the 1960s resulted in Japan achieving the world's highest per capita Gross National Product by 1991 at $26,920 compared to $22,560 for the United States. But by 1992 the Japanese economy entered a state of recession. Gross National Product that had increased at an annual rate of over ten percent during the period of high-speed growth dropped to 0.4% in 1994 and fell even further during the following years,[3] hitting a low of minus 1.9% in 1998. Automobile production began to decline from the 1990 high and by 1995 it dropped to below seven million. Banks which had over-extended bad loans began to face difficulties by 1997. They had invested heavily in hyperinflated property which by 1998 had tumbled as much ninety percent in value. Prime properties in Tokyo fell to ten percent of their peak value. The government which traditionally buttressed banks in trouble shifted its policy during the late-1990s bank crisis and allowed some banks to go under. The stock market which had hit a high of 39,000 yen in the Nikkei average in 1989 dropped to 15,000 yen and lower by mid-1998. One of the major securities firms, Yamaichi Securities, went bankrupt in the Fall of 1997.

The economic slowdown resulted in an increase in unemployment. It was 2.1% in 1990 but it reached 4.3% by June 1998. The recession compelled many firms to reduce their staff which, viewed from Western business perspectives are overstaffed, such as banks where "row upon row of workers with seemingly little to do can be spotted behind the tellers."[4] The tradition of life-time employment began to erode somewhat.[5]

Agriculture

With rapid growth in the industrial sector in the postwar years fewer people worked in agricultural production.

In 1950 48.3% of the workforce was in agriculture but by 1994 it had dropped to 5.2%. Young people tended to leave farm work for urban jobs. Hence those aged sixty-five or older constituted 38.8% of the farm workers. In 1960 agriculture accounted for nine percent of the G.D.P. but by 1994 it was down to 1.6%. The government, considering the interests of rural districts, which tended to support its conservative policies, was inclined to institute measures to support farmers, such as purchase of surplus rice. It also set strict import restrictions on farm products that competed with Japanese products, especially rice, so keeping food prices high. But international pressure led to the relaxation of restrictions on imports of some farm products, and by 1995 apples from Washington state began to enter Japan. Restrictions on rice imports remained but the equivalent of four percent of the rice harvest could be imported with the quota to rise to eight percent in year 2000. On non-competitive products, however, imports have remained high. With the importation of corn, soybean, beef, and pork Japan became the largest importer of American farm products.

Reasons for economic growth

Numerous explanations are offered for Japan's postwar economic expansion. The economy had been growing since the early Meiji years. For example, between the First and Second World Wars Japanese manufacturing output grew by six hundred percent. None the less, the Japanese economy was seen to be weak compared with other industrial nations, and Japanese products were not in the high tech industries. Textile products were the chief items of export, and Japanese goods were regarded as low cost items sold in five-and-dime stores. All this has changed since the 1960s.

One of the chief reasons for Japan's rapid economic recovery and growth was the U.S. policy of helping Japan rebuild its economy. The most important factor was the U.S. policy of opening its market to Japanese products, and encouraging other noncommunist nations to follow suit. Some credit the managerial class for the success by focusing on modern technology, to increase productivity, and quality control (following the advice of W. Edwards Deming). Investments in research and development were important in big corporations. Japanese propensity toward saving plus the abandonment of militarism, made capital available for investment. Management is also willing to accept low levels of short-term profits and company officials are not subject to constant pressure by stockholders for immediate, high level profits and dividends. They can, therefore, engage in long-term planning.

Government agencies like the Ministry of International Trade and Industry regulate economic activities stringently to foster growth. In particular they impose strict regulations to control imports that compete with domestic producers. The general policy of assisting business interests is related to the close personal ties that exist between the government officials in M.I.T.I. and the Finance Ministry, and big business executives. The leaders of the big conglomerates and these ministries constitute a kinship-like circle. The leaders usually come from similar backgrounds and educational environment. Most are graduates of elite universities. Top bureaucrats are often provided with personal favors which in America would be considered bribes. After retirement they are given "cushy" positions by conglomerate firms.

Management and labor relations are less acrimonious than in the United States. In the immediate postwar years the labor unions, whose activities were curtailed in the 1930s, revived. Led by Communist party leaders, they linked labor demands with political objectives and staged numerous strikes. With the rapid economic growth, however, the militancy that characterized labor unions subsided, and labor adhered to a policy of cooperation with business and industrial firms to advance Japan's economic expansion. Among the workers the tradition of a sense of loyalty and commonality with the interests of the employers reemerged. The practice of life-time employment, which remained common (especially prevalent in the managerial and office staff) until the mid-1990s, underpinned this sense of identity and loyalty. The unions are also enterprise or company-based so the workers identify more with the company than with workers in other companies. Hence, days lost in labor dispute are miniscule. The traditional work ethic remains strong. An American observer notes, "the single most important ingredient in Japan's success is the Japanese attitude toward work."[6] The benefits of job security, higher wages and bonuses, and various paternalistic benefits that accrue in mainstream companies sustain a sense of loyalty among the workers.

Unlike the major conglomerates at the top tier there is a lower tier of small companies and family-type businesses. The major companies reduce production costs by subcontracting work to smaller satellite companies. The same benefits do not prevail among workers in these companies. The pay is lower, hours are longer, and working conditions are poorer. Still, in the small workplace, a tighter sense of personal attachment to the employer and enterprise prevails and the workers are likely to remain loyal.

The practice of life-time employment which provides the employees with a sense of security tends to enable "deadwoods" to survive but in periods of expansion and prosperity the negative elements remain obscure. In the recession of the early 1990s, however, the system began to erode somewhat with more companies beginning to eliminate some positions and foster early retirement or transfer workers to lesser posts. Some companies even began to close some plants.

The recession of the 1990s weakened the image of rational business management that boosted the Japanese economy. Some of the less than savory business practices came to the surface. For example links between the *yakuza* gangsters and business leaders were exposed. Among the practices resorted to have been payoffs, and undercover loans to the *yakuza*. Notable in this field was the world's largest securities firm, Nomura Securities, which made payoffs and manipulated stock prices on behalf of *yakuza* clients. Also Dai Ichi Kangyō Bank extended illicit loans to *yakuza* groups. Nomura Securities had a list of special clients including politicians and bureaucrats who were given special benefits. It arranged for political leaders to collect funds through stock manipulations. Among other scandals that came to light in 1998 were bribes involving Finance Ministry officials and major bank officials. This led to some officials committing suicide. All of these developments revealed the shadowy alliances that prevail among politicians, bureaucrats, and business executives to advance their special interests.

FOREIGN RELATIONS AND TRADE

The United States

Since the end of the war and the Occupation era Japan has remained closely aligned with the United States. In the 1950s opponents of the Mutual Security Pact staged demonstrations charging the government with affiliating with the U.S. in the Cold War. However, the economic growth resulting from close ties with the U.S. cooled much of the anti-American fervor. As Cold War tensions eased the ideological confrontation subsided and the issues that concerned the U.S. and Japan came to focus on the burgeoning imbalance of trade in favor of the latter.

In order to help assist Japan's recovery the United States had opened its market to Japan. As Japan's economy grew rapidly in the 1960s the imbalance in trade between the two countries grew enormously. In 1960 the balance was still in favor of the United States but by 1970 the balance began to shift in Japan's favor. In 1998 in dollar terms Japanese exports to the U.S. came to 30.5% and imports amounted to 23.9% of her total trade. The imbalance came to $51.5 billion, a drop from the high of $59.3 billion in 1993. Japanese cars and electronic products flooded the U.S. market. Japanese cars found a ready market after the oil crisis of 1973. In 1983 close to 2.4 million passenger vehicles were exported to the U.S. To curb the rising imports of Japanese cars the Japanese government established voluntary quotas in 1986. Then the Japanese auto manufacturers began establishing automobile factories in the U.S. in order to circumvent import restrictions. By 1993 Japanese auto manufacturers held about thirty percent of the U.S. car market.

Because Japanese exports exceeded its imports in its trade with other nations international pressure led Japan to float the yen on international exchange. So the yen dropped from 360 yen to a dollar to eventually 100 and lower by 1995 but it still did not result in reducing the imbalance of trade with the U.S. and other countries. Neither did the slight relaxation in import restrictions. Failure of U.S. manufacturers to make much headway in the Japanese market was not due simply to the stringent regulations imposed by the Japanese government. The U.S. manufacturers were unwilling to make adjustments to Japanese needs. For example, Japanese drive on the left side of the road and favor right-hand drive. United State's manufacturers failed to make the necessary change until the 1990s.

Japan's relations with the Soviet Union remained somewhat strained initially because Japanese foreign policy during the Occupation era was essentially determined by the United States. The Soviet Union refused to sign the peace treaty, and the question of ownership of the four southern Kurile islands continued to remain unresolved. At Yalta the U.S. had agreed to turn over the Kuriles, held by the Japanese, to the Soviet Union. The Japanese government has held that the four southern islands were not part of the Kuriles but are part of Japan's Northern Territories.

Subsequent discussions by the two governments failed to resolve the island issue and a formal peace treaty has not been concluded but diplomatic relations have resumed since the mid-1950s, and the Soviet Union consented to Japan entering the United Nations.

Relations with China remained a delicate matter because after the victory of the Communists, the Nationalist government fled to Taiwan and claimed to be the legitimate government of China. Japan followed the U.S. policy of recognizing the Taiwan government as the Chinese government. Thus it supported the U.S. policy of opposing the admittance of the People's Republic into the United Nations. But trade relations with the People's Republic resumed in the 1960s. The sudden reversal of U.S. policy toward China with President Nixon's visit to China in 1971 resulted in Prime Minister Tanaka's visit to Beijing in 1972 and the signing of an agreement to normalize relations. A peace treaty was not concluded until 1978 but trade between the two countries continued to grow, and Japanese investments in China steadily increased. With the establishment of formal relations with the People's Republic, diplomatic relations with Taiwan were severed in 1972 but an agreement to sustain economic and cultural relations through non-governmental organizations was concluded.

The other sensitive area of foreign relations was Korea which had been colonized by Japan in the prewar years. Essentially Japanese relations with Korea were determined by U.S. policy toward North and South Korea during the Occupation years. The outbreak of the Korean War turned Japan into a U.S. base and Japan benefited from U.S. procurements. Issues that hindered the establishment of formal diplomatic relations with South Korea could not be resolved until 1965 but once diplomatic ties were established economic relations between the two countries steadily strengthened. Efforts to establish formal relations with North Korea have not been successful to date.

Japanese activities during the war years, such as the exploitation of forced laborers, have caused bitter memories among the South East Asian countries but Japan has worked on building economic ties to these countries, and has managed to increase trade, and make significant investments. Japanese businessmen have been accused of displaying a lack of sensitivity and respect for the people of South East Asia, and showing little regard for their well being. A German Catholic priest observed the Japanese "do not seem to show much responsibility for other people, unless it will bring them profit."[7] When the Vietnamese boatpeople were fleeing the Communists the Japanese virtually locked out the refugees unlike America and other countries. The Japanese leaders have been responding to these criticisms by increasing Japan's contribution to international economic aid programs and a number of political leaders have traveled to South East Asian countries and expressed contrition for past actions.

Middle East and Europe

Japan has steadily increased its commercial ties with Australia as well as Middle Eastern countries. It is heavily dependent on oil from the Middle East so it seeks to maintain amicable relations with nations of this region. For example it sought to avoid involvement as far as possible in the American actions in the Persian Gulf War of 1990.

Relations with European countries have seen their ups and downs, again because of the imbalance of trade. The Japanese have long admired French culture so they were disheartened when the former Prime Minister, Edith Cresson, remarked in 1991: "Japanese are short yellow people who stay up all night thinking of ways to screw the Americans and the Europeans."[8] France has kept tight restrictions on Japanese imports but commercial relations with Germany have been extensive and political relations have been amicable. Japanese economic links to the United Kingdom have also been important with Japan making substantial investments in Britain. The Japanese imperial court sought to play up its affinity with British royalty, and Emperor Hirohito visited England in 1971, and Emperor Akihito in 1998. Financial ties with Netherlands and Switzerland have also been extensive.

SOCIAL CONDITIONS

The reforms introduced by S.C.A.P. and the economic growth since the 1960s resulted in the resolution of many prewar social difficulties and a higher standard of living. For example the per capita national income which was about $500 in 1955 rose to

$29,244 by 1994, compared to $20,382 in the United States and $13,366 in the United Kingdom. In 1935 life expectancy for men was 46.92 and for women 49.63. In 1997 the figures were 77 and 83.6 respectively. This has resulted in an increase in the percentage of people over the age of sixty-five and the younger generation's percentage steadily declined as the birth rate declined. In 1997 those over the age of sixty-five outnumbered children under fifteen. The birth rate per thousand population in 1920 was 36.2. In 1997 it was 9.5. The average number of children per woman of child-bearing age in 1947 was 4.54. In 1997 it was 1.39, less than the 2.1 needed to sustain the current level of population. But with a low infant mortality rate of four per one thousand live births in 1996, longer life expectancy, and better health care the population continued to rise in the postwar years. In 1950 the population was 83.586 million and in 1998 126.4 million. Immigration laws are still restrictive, so the increase in population did not result from extensive immigration.

The general state of affluence resulted in a higher standard of living with families having modern facilities for home, business, and recreational purposes. The number of people traveling abroad increased annually. It rose from less than half a million in 1969 to about 16.8 million in 1997.

Despite the rise in living standards problems of overcrowding, housing shortages, poorer sanitation facilities compared to other industrial nations, and pollution continue to plague the populace. Housing shortage has resulted in exorbitant prices for real estate in the major cities, especially the Tokyo metropolitan area, where close to thirty million people, 23.7% of the nation's population, converge. In 1996 7.8 million people lived in the Tokyo city limits constituting a population density of 32,850 per square mile. (In New York it was 23,705.) The cost of family-size apartments in Tokyo in 1990 was over $516,000, and residential land prices in Tokyo were estimated to be eighty-nine times higher than in New York. Before the overpriced real estate market tumbled in the 1990s one square meter of commercial space in Tokyo cost $251,000 (1990 figure). The high cost of goods placed many items beyond the reach of the lower classes. A top grade cut of beef cost $100 a pound or more, a perfect musk melon $150 in 1996. Compared to the U.S., gasoline prices remained high at well over $4 a gallon.

Conspicuous consumption was engaged in by those who became wealthy with expenditure such as $104,000 for a BMW car and $22,900 for a Swiss Corum wristwatch. Some collectors of art boosted the price of art to unheard of levels. At a 1990 auction Vincent van Gogh's *Portrait of Doctor Gachet* starting at $25 million was raised to $82.5 by a Japanese collector. When the bubble burst the family sold a Renoir purchased at $78.1 million for $50 million. But even with the recession of the mid-1990s, sale of luxury items did not decline. While such sales declined in other parts of Asia they continued to rise in Japan. In mid-1998 Tiffany & Company's sales increased by thirty percent over the same period the previous year while it dropped by ten percent in the rest of Asia. The Gucci Group opened a number of new stores in Japan in 1998 expecting ever-increasing sales in the midst of the economic decline as some people remained willing to pay several thousand dollars for handbags.[9] In the early stages of economic expansion serious problems of pollution, especially chemical pollution occurred. The most infamous case was the mercury pollution of the waters of Minamata Bay in northwestern Kyushu by a chemical plant in 1953. People consuming fish from the bay area suffered serious physical illness such as paralysis and loss of vision. Other instances of chemical pollution compelled the government to pass strict anti-pollution laws in 1970. Also strict auto-emission standards were established. The highly polluted air of cities like Tokyo became safe to inhale.

Other measures to ensure the health and welfare of the people in line with constitutional provision were introduced. Social security provisions, welfare benefits for the elderly and needy, public health and medical care programs have been established. For those over the age of seventy national health insurance covers entire medical costs, even when surgery, such as open-heart surgery, costs over $30,000. The tradition of the family caring for the elderly and needy members persists though the percentage of such practice is declining somewhat. In 1996 fifty-five percent of those older than sixty-five lived with their children, a decline from eighty percent in 1970. But it is more favorable than less than twenty percent in other industrialized countries such as the United States.

SOCIAL PROBLEMS

Because of pressures of work, overcrowding, and general social pressures the suicide rate increased in the years of economic growth. The rate was especially high among older men. For men over sixty-five the rate of suicide in 1998 was 53.3 per 100,000 persons in the age group whereas for males between the ages of fifteen to nineteen it was 10.6. Some ascribe the high rate of suicide among older men to the lack of meaningful life after retirement. The elderly are seemingly not honored as in the past in the fast paced high tech age and this may be a contributory factor.

The image of a socially harmonious Japan has been shattered from time to time as violent protest movements erupted in the 1950s and 1960s. Reports of juvenile crimes and violence in the schools occur occasionally, even student assaults on teachers. But overall student behavior at school conforms to the ideal of obedience, propriety, and conformity. Crimes committed on the streets is miniscule compared to other highly industrialized societies. People can walk safely late at night without fear of being molested. Firearms are controlled strictly so murders by guns are rare. In 1991 firearms were used in only seventy-four murders and twenty-two robberies. In 1994 the rate for gun deaths was 0.05 per 100,000 persons compared to 14.24 in the United States. Drug use has also remained low. In 1991 there were only 397 arrests for use of narcotics.

The wholesome image of morally upright Japanese is sullied by the presence of a group of gangster-type organizations, the *yakuza*, involved in activities such as gambling, drugs, prostitution, extortion, racketeering, and petty crimes. They also engage in acts of violence. In 1992 *yakuza* members attacked and slashed the film-maker Itami Jūzō for depicting them unfavorably in his film. The bigger *yakuza* syndicates are tied in with business ventures like construction. As noted above, a large percentage of major firms have paid money or extended loans to the *yakuza* to avoid trouble with them.[10] Many political leaders also have ties to the *yakuza*. In 1963 former premier Kishi put up bail money for a *yakuza* boss convicted of murder. Another former Prime Minister got the aid of the *yakuza* to quash public protests against him. One writer reports: "*Yakuza* have deep roots in virtually very nook and corner of Japanese society. Yet, politicians, bureaucrats and business leaders continue to maintain a 'don't see, don't say and a don't hear' attitude."[11]

Another social blight that has continued to beset Japanese society is the persistence of discrimination against minority groups like the *burakumin*, Ainu, and resident Koreans. The discrimination against the *burakumin* can be traced to the pre-modern era but despite paying lip-service to the idea of non-discrimination, social and economic discrimination against them continues. In the postwar reforms the practice of identifying *burakumin* as "new commoners" in the family registers was ended but the practice of ascertaining whether or not a job applicant or a marriage candidate is a *burakumin* continues with some private agencies specializing in this task. Thus job discrimination results in *burakumin* families having lower incomes than the national average, and the Buraku Liberation League continues to receive reports of discrimination. In October 1991 a high school girl committed suicide because her plan to marry her fiance, a *burakumin*, was opposed by those around her.[12] A *burakumin* educator visiting the United States in 1991 explained: "We face discrimination at work, in school and in marriage ... We are ten times more likely to be on welfare than the general population ... As a people we have been vilified, shunned and segregated."[13] In 1997 there were about two to three million *burakumin*.

The other minority group who have suffered discrimination from the Tokugawa era to the present are the Ainu, the indigenous residents of Hokkaido. Currently there are about fifty thousand Ainu people. During the Tokugawa years a northern feudal lord extended his authority over Hokkaido and deprived the Ainu of their economic rights and reduced them to semi-slavery. The Meiji government brought Hokkaido under its direct administration and deprived the Ainu of their land, and fishing and hunting rights. To Japanize the Ainu the Meiji government in 1899 enacted the Hokkaido Former Aborigine Protection Law. The law remained in effect until the 1990s. Under this law the government banned traditional Ainu practices and compelled Ainu children to forsake their native language and learn Japanese. In the postwar era Ainu leaders have endeavored to preserve Ainu culture, language, and way of life.

Another group of people who continue to experience discrimination are the Koreans, many of whom are residents of several generations. After being colonized many Koreans were made to serve as forced laborers in the mines, and on construction projects including military projects overseas during the Pacific War. During the war about a million Koreans were brought to Japan to work as virtual slave laborers. Many worked on military bases and as many as one hundred thousand Korean women were forced to serve the Japanese troops as "comfort women." At the end of the war many returned to Korea but in the mid-1990s there were about seven hundred thousand Koreans in Japan. They are denied Japanese citizenship though born in Japan. Until 1992 they were fingerprinted as alien residents. Recently citizenship was made open to Koreans if they can meet complex regulations. Job discrimination and bias against inter-marriage with Japanese continues. About twenty thousand Koreans died in the Hiroshima a-bomb attack but permission to build a memorial for the Korean victims in the Hiroshima Peace Park was denied. Also two thousand of the Nagasaki A-bomb dead were Korean. The 137,000 or so Chinese experience similar discrimination.

Regarding the Japanese bias against Koreans a longtime American resident of Japan observed, "No minority in the world (no minority that I know anything about) is treated more badly by a majority than the Koreans and Chinese by the Japanese ... it is so pervasive and so insidious and it's an absolute blanket condemnation."[14]

During the period of booming economy and growing labor shortage immigration restrictions were relaxed somewhat and people from South East Asia and South Asia were allowed in to engage in unskilled work. The number of illegal immigrants also began to increase. Thousands of young women were persuaded by *yakuza* gangs to come to Japan with the promise of attractive jobs and then were compelled to work as prostitutes. Many were held in virtual captivity.

Surprisingly a slight shift in prejudice toward foreigners began to occur in the rural, farming communities where provincial bias tends to be strong. Young women flock to the cities, and prefer to marry urban workers, "somebody in a suit," rather than a farmer. Hence a shortage of wives for the young farmers who remain in the countryside developed. As a result marriage brokers began to bring in women from South East Asia and South Asia to marry, sometimes against their will, young farmers in remote villages.

If racial bias weakens in the rural areas perhaps the cosmopolitan areas will become more open too.

The urban poor

Despite the economic growth and general rise in the standard of living there have been pockets of poverty and loci of homeless people. Homeless people sleep in cardboard cocoons in rail and subway stations and in the streets, or in flophouses (cheap inns for transients). The authorities are determined to sweep them off the streets and periodically destroy their cardboard nests. Sections where the homeless and poor settle can be found in major cities like Tokyo and Osaka. In San'ya in Tokyo *yakuza* gangs go to hire day laborers for construction work. Hundreds line up every morning hoping to get hired. Many are aged and sick. The government agencies extend little help to the needy if they are under sixty-five and healthy. The needy are reluctant to apply for welfare aid because it is considered shameful. The consensus is that the family rather than the government should take care of the aged, sick and needy. Hence in 1994 less than one percent of the population was on welfare compared to five percent in the United States.[15]

THE STATUS OF WOMEN

The new constitution mandates gender equality but in the social and economic realm women continue to be at a disadvantage. In occupational positions women tend to hold lower level, low paying jobs. Many tend to be part-time or temporary employees. Many women employed by business firms were classified as "office ladies" whose primary function was to serve tea and perform secretarial tasks for the male bosses. Even though women's rights is pursued by some women, higher level positions for women remain scarce. As soon as a woman married she was expected to leave her post and perform her function at home as a dutiful wife. As the economy continued to expand and the need for educated, highly trained workers increased more opportunities for women began to open up in the 1980s. But in 1981 forty-five percent of companies surveyed said they did not promote women to supervisory positions. In 1985 the Diet passed the Equal Employment

Opportunity Law but it did not provide for penalties against companies that did not comply with the law. But, together with the economic boom, it is credited with opening up more opportunities for women. In 1986 2.6% of middle management positions were held by women. By 1993 the figure had risen to 3.6%. In 1991 in administrative and managerial positions it was 8.2%. In contrast 41.7% of such positions were held by women in the United States. Salaries for full-time women employees averaged 60.2% of men's in 1995, up from 56.1% in 1985. In the U.S. women's wages were seventy-five percent of men's.

Since the Meiji era a large number of women have been employed in textile mills but in the postwar years the textile industry declined and jobs in automobile plants, mechanical industries and high tech plants accounted for most of the factory jobs. In 1998 39.6% of the workers in major industries were women. Few women are employed in automobile factories but many are employed in the electronics industry. The economic slowdown in the early 1990s resulted in a decline in the number of women being hired, especially in management-track positions. In 1992 Mitsubishi hired 213 men and only four women, and women began to be laid off before men.

Women in the political arena have not made significant advances since they gained suffrage in 1946. In 1946 women won thirty-nine seats in the lower house of the Diet but the number dropped in subsequent elections, hovering around ten. In the 1996 election for the Lower House women gained twenty-three of the five hundred seats. A woman was not appointed to a cabinet post until 1989. In 1989 Doi Takako became the first woman to head a political party, the Social Democratic Party.

The academic world has also been an exclusive domain of male professors and the doors have been inching open very slowly. In 1980 there was only one female professor at the University of Tokyo. As discussed earlier, education for women was not given equal emphasis as that for men. In the postwar years more women began going to college but their enrollment tended to be primarily in junior colleges. Thus fewer women are in professional fields though the number has been increasing. For example in 1979 there were fourteen thousand women engineers. In 1990 there were sixty-two thousand.

The conventional view that women's place is in the home persists, but the younger generation is becoming more independent minded. The idea of sacrificing oneself for the good of husband and family is weakening. This is seen in the growing divorce rate in which one in three to four marriages ends in divorce. In 1997 222,635 marriages ended in divorce, compared to 95,937 in 1970. The rate was 1.78 per 1,000 people, an increase over 1.66 of the previous year. The divorces were not just among newly weds. Sixteen percent of the divorces in 1996 were couples married for over twenty years. The majority of the divorces were initiated by the wives, indicating their rejection of the traditional endurance of the husband's infidelity as well as the growing sense of individualism. Also unlike the prewar years when, by law, the children remained with the husband's family now the wife has gained the right of child custody. While the number of divorces have been increasing the number of marriages have begun to decrease. Women are marrying later with the average marrying age approaching twenty-seven. They are having fewer children. Abortion was legalized in 1949 and in the 1980s one abortion for every three births was performed. Although arranged marriages are still common the plight of the young wife has become less stressful because the nuclear family has become more prevalent and she no longer has to cater to members of the extended family.

INTELLECTUAL AND CULTURAL DEVELOPMENTS

The prewar Japanese *weltanchauung* was shattered by defeat in the Second World War. Hearing the Emperor on August 15, 1945 announce Japan's surrender the writer Ōe Kenzaburō writes: "The adults sat around their radios and cried. The children gathered outside in the dusty road and whispered their bewilderment. We were most surprised and disappointed by the fact that the Emperor had spoken in a human voice ... How could we believe that an august presence of such awful power had become an ordinary human voice?"[16] The sense of uniqueness and superiority, the value system, the mode of life, the natural order of things had all been desolated. The whole moral and psychological edifice had turned into an empty shell. The only object of life was physical survival, finding enough to eat and shelter. People still embraced haunting images of lost family members. Then the cultural and moral vacuum was filled by the Occupation authorities with their ways and values. Liberalism, democracy, freedom, equality became the watchwords. Thus a new age of "enlightenment and civilization" dawned.

Itami Jūzō, a movie director recalled: "We were told that the whole nation would fight to death. But within one month of the end of the war, it was suddenly 'Banzai democracy! Banzai MacArthur!' The U.S. forces were treated as if they were liberators. Praise was directed toward all things American."[17] The young in particular embraced American culture. Murakami Haruki, a contemporary writer recalled that in the 1960s, "American culture was so vibrant back then, and I was very influenced by its music, television shows, cars, clothes, everything."[18]

It was not just in the world of pop culture but serious scholars were now able to pursue learning without fear of censure. The departure from the traditional intellectual and cultural framework struck some critics as being a form of anarchism. One scholar returning to Japan after years in America observed: "The most significant change in the past few years has been the emergence of a kind of social and psychological anarchy ... Before Second World War my generation had the Emperor, but today there is nobody for young Japanese to look up to. There is a lack of spiritual force ... an absence of purpose and meaning."[19] The traditional sense of hierarchy manifested in the mode of speech and behavior appear to be adhered to less conscientiously among the young. Some believe that the family system is "disintegrating ... more rapidly in the cities, more slowly in rural areas."[20] Postwar legal changes contributed to weakening the traditional extended and stem families with fewer young couples living with their parents. This also contributed to the weakening of traditional attitudes and values.

The seeming decline of traditional mores has led some to emphasize the need to return to Japanism and stress the uniqueness of Japanese culture and national character. But traditional values and mores have not vanished completely. The prewar generation retain them, and the young pursuers of pop culture do not reject them completely. A survey conducted in the late 1980s indicated that filial piety and the concept of *on* (social and moral obligation) were still valued by the vast majority. A book calling for the rejection of consumerism and return to the simplicity of old Japan became a best seller in 1993. But consumerism continued to flourish even in face of the impending recession. Unlike the old authoritarian era diversity of choice remains a reality.

This diversity is prevalent in the popular cultural and intellectual arena with a plethora of newspapers, weekly and monthly magazines, fiction and non-fiction books, movies, T.V. and radio programs, and comic books. The daily circulation of newspapers numbered 53.67 million in 1998; 65,513 books and 3,271 monthly magazines were published.[21] Popular and serious Western works are quickly translated and published.

Writers continued to have a wide readership. Prewar writers, like Tanizaki and Kawabata, gained greater readership in the postwar years than before. Their novels were translated into English and they gained international renown. Ibuse Masuji was not well-known abroad until his *Black Rain*, in which he depicts the horrors of the effects of the Hiroshima atomic bomb, was translated into English.

A generation of new writers emerged in the postwar years. The most prominent among these was Mishima Yukio (1925–70) whose many works were translated into English. In the opinion of Donald Keene, an authority on Japanese literature, Mishima is "the most gifted and achieved the most of all the writers who appeared after the war."[22] Mishima delved into the manners and mores of the postwar generation, their sense of emptiness and despair. In *The Temple of the Golden Pavilion* a physically handicapped acolyte burns down the Golden Pavilion, an embodiment of perfect beauty, because it stands there to remind him of his imperfection. "If beauty really did exist there, it meant that my own existence was a thing estranged from beauty."[23] Mishima, although familiar with Western civilization, believed in traditional values and institutions, including the Emperor whom he saw as "the symbolic moral source of loyalty and culture."[24] Influenced by Wang Yang-ming's teaching he believed that a person should act on his convictions. Thus in November 1970 after he failed to rouse the members of the Self-Defense Force he committed hara-kiri in classical samurai fashion.

A number wrote novels based on their wartime experiences. Noma Hiroshi fought in the Philippines but was detained in army prison barracks because of his communist leanings. In his major work, *Zone of Emptiness*, he depicts the brutalities of army life.

Later he turned from Marxism to Buddhism, in particular to Shinran's teaching regarding universal salvation, including great sinners. Buddhism, Noma believed, is embedded in the Japanese body. Another writer who depicted the horrors of war is Ōoka Shōhei. He was a soldier in the Philippines and was captured by the Americans. After the war he wrote of the plight of the soldiers in Leyte in his *Fires on the Plain*. The soldiers in flight wander in the jungles foraging for food and end up killing their fellow soldiers and eating their flesh.

In the postwar years when traditional moorings had been decimated many writers dealt with the problem of alienation and the search for meaning in life. The most prominent of these is Ōe Kenzaburō.

His characters seek meaning in "sex and violence and political fanaticism." In his *Personal Matter* the protagonist contemplates killing his infant son born with serious brain damage. He changes his mind, however, and strives for his son's well-being. The story is based in part on his own experience. His son was born with severe brain damage, and evidently Ōe identified with his son's pain. "Whatever pain his son was feeling communicated to him through their clasped hands and never failed to produce in his own body a tremor of pain in unison."[25] In 1994 Ōe was awarded the Nobel Prize. The Swedish Academy noted that Ōe, "creates an imagined world where life and myth condense to form a disconcerting picture of the human predicament today."[26]

A writer who is firmly grounded in his faith is Endō Shūsaku (1923–96), a Catholic whose renowned work *Silence* deals with the Christians persecuted during the early seventeenth century. A Jesuit is told that the torturous persecution of the Japanese converts, bound and hanged upside down in a pit, will not cease unless he steps on the image of Christ. He does so after he hears Christ tell him to. A Western critic writes that Endō, "remains firmly Catholic in spite of guilt and doubt, and for all his divided feelings about East and West, he remains firmly and mysteriously Japanese."[27]

Women writers also remained active in the literary world. Prewar writers like Uno Chiyo (1897–1996) and Enchi Fumiko (1905–1986) continued their writing career. Uno defied the social conventions of prewar Japan, having a series of love affairs. In 1927 she cut her hair in a short bob, a radical move that caused neighborhood children to run away shrieking. In her acclaimed prewar novel Uno wrote a semi-autobiographical story of thwarted love, *Confessions of Love*. Her prominent postwar novel of 1957 *Ohan* (translated as *The Old Woman, the Archer and the Wife*) is based partly on the life of a shopkeeper, and his wife and lover. Uno said the three were the models: the impetuous geisha, the patient wife, and the husband who can't resist temptation. Donald Keene says Ohan, "is enjoyable because it gives off the kind of flavor one gets from a reading of Chikamatsu."[28]

Enchi Fumiko's major work, *Onnazaka* (translated as *The Waiting Years*) written in 1957, depicts the life of a Meiji woman who endures the oppression of the paternalistic family system with nobility and resourcefulness. The heroine lives the life of a docile, selfless wife, tolerating her husband's mistress in the household and his affair with the daughter-in-law. But in her old age she concludes that her life serving a self-centered profligate husband for the sake of the family had been meaningless. "She had suddenly seen the futility of that somehow artificial life on which she had lavished so much energy and wisdom."[29] Hayashi Fumiko (1903–51) was also a popular prewar novelist. She grew up in poverty with her itinerant peddler parents. During the war years she travelled to the war zones to support the war effort. Among her postwar novels is *Bangiku* (*Late Chrysanthemum*) about a geisha and her former lover. Donald Keene concludes: "Of the innumerable stories about geishas ... none rings truer than 'Late Chrysanthemum.'"[30]

A number of woman writers embraced Marxism. Among these was Miyamoto Yuriko (1899–1951). In 1918 she accompanied her father to New York. She wrote a novel, *Nobuko*, about her experience in New York, marriage, return to Japan, and divorce. The novel is essentially about personal liberation in a society that expected women to suppress their individuality. Miyamoto traveled to Russia, joined the Communist Party in 1931, married Miyamoto Kenji (postwar Communist Party chief) and was sent to prison in the late 1930s. Her major postwar work, *Banshū Heiya* (*Banshū Plains*), depicts the suffering inflicted on the people by the Japanese military.

The younger women writers do not deal with the plight of women under traditional imperatives but focus on women in the new age who can chart their own course of life. Women must learn to communicate their true feelings one young writer, Tsushima Yuko, contends. Writers before her time wrote of women who did not speak their true feelings or who did not want to be independent. One of her themes deals with the "stifling nature of family and blood relationships."[31]

CINEMA

Film-making had flourished since the 1920s as the public became avid followers of movies both Japanese and American. Romantic tales, sword swinging samurai, and modern military exploits were depicted by Japanese movie-makers. And viewers of Hollywood films filled the movie theaters right up to the outbreak of the Pacific War. Robert Taylor was as popular as Japanese movie star Uehara Ken. In the postwar years Japanese movies began to gain international recognition. The director who is credited with having drawn the West's attention to Japanese movies is Kurosawa Akira (1910–98). He joined the ranks of the world's great directors. The first movie to gain recognition in the West was *Rashomon*, depicting four contradictory accounts of medieval rape and murder. *Seven Samurai,* a tale of seven samurai who defend a small village from bandits, has been called "the finest Japanese film ever made." Kurosawa says: "If I look at the pictures I've made, I think they say, 'Why is it that human beings aren't happy?'" He is regarded as a master at producing scenes of striking pictorial beauty.[32] He continued to produce movies well into the 1980s. Among these was *Ran*, an adaptation of *King Lear,* An American critic says Ran ranks with "the greatest epics of Sergei Eisenstein, D. W. Griffith and Abel Gance ... It's a movie by a man whose art stands outside time and fashion."[33] There are a number of other prominent directors like Mizoguchi Kenji and Ōtsu Yasujirō whose works gained renown in the West

Following the couple of postwar decades, the "golden age" of Japanese filmmaking lost its lustre, undoubtedly because of the competition from television. But a new generation of creative directors continued to produce high quality movies. Among them was Itami Juzo who created satirical films like *Tampopo* depicting a woman who sets out to become Tokyo's best noodle-maker. He sees the Japanese not as stoic, tragic victims of fate but as "comically fallible, heedless guests at an extraordinary party."[34] In 1992 he was knifed by *yakuza* gangsters for making a film that parodied them. In 1997 director Imamura Shōhei won the grand prize for his film *Unagi* (*Eel*) at the Cannes film festival. This was his second prize. He had won the prize in 1983 for his *Narayama-bushi-kō* (*Ballad of Narayama*) dealing with the legend that in feudal years in some regions old people were abandoned in the mountains to die. He also created *Karayuki-san* (*Those Sent Abroad*) dealing with young girls who were sent to other Asian nations to serve as prostitutes. A young woman director, Kawase Narumi, won the new director prize at Cannes in 1997 for her film depicting rural mountain villagers forced to leave their homes.

ART AND ARCHITECTURE

A number of architects rose to prominence in the postwar years. Among the first to gain international renown was Tange Kenzō who combines the traditional post-and-lintel configuration with the styles of modern Western architects. Isozaki Arata has designed numerous architectural projects in America and Europe, including the Olympic Hall in Barcelona. In 1993 Maki Fumihiko won the Pritzker Architecture Prize, akin to the Nobel Prize, and in 1995 Andō Tadao won the prize. Maki was credited with using "light in a masterful way, making it as tangible a part of every design as walls and roofs."[35] Andō is known for his concrete constructions. In his work he is credited with paying "meticulous attention to form, structure, space and geometry."[36]

Ceramic art has flourished since the Middle Ages. A distinctive style developed as Korean ceramics began to influence the creators of tea cups and bowls for the tea ceremony. The tradition persisted into the postwar era. Among the renowned ceramists was Hamada Shōji (1894–1978). He studied under the English potter Bernard Leach who said of Hamada's work: "His pots articulate like an oak tree, the bones of structure are not concealed, the modulation of forms are intuitive, and all his pots stand firm on their feet."[37]

Woodblock printing also continued to be pursued from the Tokugawa era to the present. Among prominent contemporary artists in this domain was Munakata Shikō (1903–75), a Zen Buddhist. Hence much of his work deals with traditional religious images but he also creates prints akin to modernist expressionism. He endows his prints with strength of design, movement of line, and dramatic tension. Another artist, Saitō Kiyoshi (1907–) with his distinctive style in the portrayal of snowy landscape and Buddhist temples and gardens, gained a popular following.

EDUCATIONAL CHANGES SINCE 1956

The reforms introduced by S.C.A.P. to decentralize the education system were gradually revised to enable the central government to regain some of its former authority in this area. In 1956 elected school boards were replaced by board members appointed by prefectural governors and mayors. The Ministry of Education reasserted its authority over the curriculum and commenced accrediting textbooks for use in the public schools. The Ministry lays down precise guidelines to teachers regarding what and how to teach. In certifying textbooks the Ministry sought to eliminate information or analyses unfavorable to Japan. The denial of certification for a history textbook written by Professor Ienaga Saburō became a *cause celebre*. The Ministry objected to his inclusion of data such as the Nanjing massacre of 1937. It took Ienaga twenty years to have the courts uphold his case.

The traditional importance accorded to education has resulted in a large number of young people going to college. A person's success is seen to be linked to attendance in a prestigious institution so competition to gain admittance to "name" schools results in strenuous preparation to pass entrance examinations at colleges like the University of Tokyo. Cramming and memorization are stressed. Deviation from conventional modes of teaching and learning is not fostered. An American educator notes: "What is absent in far too many Japanese classrooms is the searching and probing for the spark of creativity, innovativeness, and originality."[38]

School life for the students meant not only adhering strictly to the prescribed mode of learning but also enforcement of rigid rules and strict discipline, and recourse to corporal punishment. In recent years, however, junior and senior high school students have tended to reject orderly conduct. From the 1980s violence, bullying and truancy began to increase. In 1996 there were over 10,500 cases of violent incidents in the schools, up thirty-two percent from the previous year. Student activism at the college level had burgeoned in the 1950s and 1960s over political issues such as the Mutal Security Pact. Some students also turned against the feudalistic domain of the university administrators and professors, and engaged in riots and demonstrations. The academic establishment endured, however, and with the advent of the era of high-speed economic growth student political activism abated. Students began to concentrate more on getting ahead in the business world.

END OF THE TWENTIETH CENTURY

In a way the reign of Emperor Hirohito (now referred to as Emperor Shōwa) can be equated to Japan in the twentieth century. He was born in 1901 and died in 1989. In 1921 he became regent to the ailing Emperor Taishō and became Emperor in 1926, and remained on the throne for sixty-two years, the longest reign in Japanese history. His reign saw the rise of democracy in the twenties, militarism in the thirties, the Pacific War in the forties, and the ascendancy of democracy and freedom since the end of the War. The sacrosanct image of the Emperor on a white horse changed to a dowdy-looking symbol of the nation in the postwar years. Soldiers fought and died in his name but he was not held responsible for the war and war crimes, and was not tried by the International Military Tribunal. Although there were critics of the imperial institution there was no move to remove the institution and the public generally accepted its presence as integral part of the nation and its history. His death can be seen in a way as a *de facto* end to the legacy of militarism, imperialism, ultra-nationalism and totalitarianism because he was identified with these principles and practices, and as long as he remained on the throne they lingered on as a reminder of the years when these concepts ruled the Japanese *weltanschauung*. Upon Hirohito's death in 1989 Crown Prince Akihito ascended the throne and the Heisei era began symbolizing closure to the twentieth century, the Hirohito era.

Notes

CHAPTER ONE

1. Wada Atsumu contends hereditary monarchy started with Ingyō (early fifth century) or Yūryaku (mid-fifth century). *Taikei Nihon no Rekishi* (Comprehensive History of Japan) (Tokyo: Shōgakukan, 1992), V. II, p. 163. On Koreans and the ruling classes cf. Watanabe Mitsutoshi, *Tennō-ke no Toraishi* (History of the Arrival of the Imperial Family) (Tokyo: Shin Jimbutsu Oraisha, 1989), and Shiba Ryōtarō *et al.* eds. *Nihon no Chōsen Bunka* (Korean Culture in Japan) (Tokyo: Chuo Koronsha, 1972).
2. Murasaki Shikibu, *The Tale of Genji*, trans. Edward C. Seidensticker (New York: Knopf, 1976), p. 620.
3. W. G. Aston in Joseph Campbell, *The Mask of God: Oriental Mythology* (New York: Viking, 1962), p. 475.
4. *Manyoshu*, trans. by Nippon Gakujutsu Shinkōkai (New York: Columbia University Press, 1965), p. 142.
5. Shikubu, *The Tale of Genji*, p. 581
6. Ivan Morris ed. and trans., *The Pillow Book of Sei Shōnagon*, 2 vols. (New York: Columbia University Press, 1967), vol. I, p. 258.
7. Quoted in Earl Miner, *An Introduction to Japanese Court Poetry* (Stanford, CA: Stanford University Press, 1968), p. 18.
8. Donald Keene, *Anthology of Japanese Literature* (New York: Grove Press, 1955) p. 196.

CHAPTER TWO

1. W. G. Aston, *A History of Japanese Literature* (New York: Appleton, 1899), p. 149.
2. William Barrett, ed., *Zen Buddhism: Selected Writings of D. T. Suzuki* (Garden City, NY: Doubleday, 1956), p. 61.
3. Philip Kapleau, *The Three Pillars of Zen* (New York: Harper & Row, 1966), p. 138.

4. Daisetsu T. Suzuki, *Zen and Japanese Culture* (New York: Pantheon, 1959), p. 78.
5. Donald Keene, ed., *Japanese Literature* (New York: Grove Press, 1955), p. 78.
6. Arthur Waley, *The No Plays of Japan* (London: Allen & Unwin, 1911), p. 21.

CHAPTER THREE

1. Furushima Toshio, *Nihon Hōken Nōgyōshi* (Japanese Feudal Agricultural History) (Tokyo: Shikai Shobo, 1931), p. 83.
2. Ienaga Saburō, *Nihon Dōtokushisō-shi* (History of Japanese Moral Thought) (Tokyo: Iwanami, 1951), p. 120.
3. Howard Hibbett, *The Floating World in Japanese Fiction* (New York: Grove Press, 1960), p. 37.
4. Tsuchikata Tetsu, *Hi-sabetsuburaku no Tatakai* (The Struggle by the Discriminated Hamlets) (Tokyo: Shinsensha, 1973), pp. 11–12.
5. Ibid., p. 14.
6. Michael S. J. Cooper, ed., *They Came to Japan*, (Berkeley, CA: University of California Press, 1965), p. 62.
7. Donald Keene, trans. *The Major Plays of Chikamatsu* (New York: Columbia University Press, 1961), p. 76.
8. Basil H. Chamberlain, *Things Japanese* (London: Routledge & Kegan Paul, 1939), pp. 503–505.
9. Ienaga Saburō, *Nihon Dōtokushisō-shi* pp. 143–147.
10. Kim Yil-men, *Nihon Jyosei Aishi* (Japanese Women: History of Sorrow) (Tokyo: Gendaishi Shuppankai, 1980), pp. 17 ff.
11. Arnold Toynbee, "How to Change the World without War," *Saturday Review*, May 12, 1962, p. 17.
12. Tsunoda, Ryusaku, *et al.* ed., *Sources of Japanese Tradition* (Columbia University Press, 1958), pp. 376–377.
13. Masao Maruyama, *Studies in the Intellectual History of Tokugawa Japan* (Tokyo: University of Tokyo Press, 1974), p. 162.
14. Nippon Gakujutsu Shinkokai, *Manyoshu* (Tokyo: Iwanami, 1940), p. 177.
15. Tsunoda, *Sources of Japanese Tradition*, p. 596.
16. Ibid., p. 571.
17. Uchida Takeshi and Miyamoto Tsuneichi, eds., *Sugae Masumi Zenshū* (Collected Works of Sugae Masumi), 12 vols. (Tokyo: Miraisha, 1971–1978), vol. I, pp. 274–275
18. Maruyama, *Studies in the Intellectual History*, pp. 249–264.
19. Keene, *The Major Plays of Chikamatsu*, p. 332.
20. Mitsui Takafusa, "Some Observations on Merchants," trans., E. S. Crawcour in *Transactions of the Asiatic Society of Japan*, vol. 8, pp. 103, 115.
21. Engelbert Kaempfer, *History of Japan*, 3 vols., trans. J. G. S. Schenchzer (Glasgow: MacLehose, 1906), vol. 3, p. 6.
22. Daisetsu T. Suzuki, *Zen and Japanese Culture* (New York: Pantheon, 1959), pp. 225–227.

23. Donald Keene, *Japanese Literature* (New York: Grove Press, 1955), pp. 39–41.
24. Faubion Bowers, *Japanese Theatre* (New York: Hill & Wang, 1959), p. 177.
25. Lawrence Binyon, *Painting in the Far East* (New York: Dover, 1959), p. 266.
26. Robert T. Paine & Alexander Soper, *The Art and Architecture of Japan* (Baltimore: Penguin, 1955) p. 153.
27. Maruyama, *Studies in the Intellectual History*, p. 124.
28. *The Complete Journal of Townsend Harris* (Rutland, VT: Charles E. Tuttle, 1959) pp. 538–543.
29. Maruyama, *Studies in the Intellectual History*, p. 310.
30. Ibid., p. 360.

CHAPTER FOUR

1. Toyama Shigeki, *Meiji Ishin to Tennō* (Meiji Restoration and the Emperor) (Tokyo: Iwanami, 1991) pp. 91–95.
2. Arnold J. Toynbee, *Civilization on Trial and the World and the West* (New York: Meridian Books, 1958) p. 172.
3. Tsunoda, Ryusaku, *et al.* ed. *Sources of Japanese Tradition* (Columbia University Press, 1958), pp. 376–377.
4. Kazushi Ohkawa and Henry Rosovsky, "A Century of Japanese Economic Growth," in William W. Lockwood, ed., *The State and Economic Enterprise in Japan* (Princeton, NJ: Princeton University Press, 1965), pp. 52–53.
5. Fukuji Sigetaka, *Kindai Nihon Jyoseishi* (History of Modern Japanese Women) (Tokyo: Sekkasha, 1963), pp. 33–34.
6. Inoue Kiyoshi, *Nihon Jyoseishi* (History of Japanese Women) (Tokyo: Sanichi Shobo, 1967), p. 224.
7. Kaigo Tokiomi, ed. *Nihon Kyōkasho Taikei* (Grand Compendium of Japanese Textbooks), 43 vols. (Tokyo: Kodansah, 1961–1967) vol. 2, p. 198.

CHAPTER FIVE

1. Donald Keene, *Dawn to the West* (New York: Henry Holt, 1984), p. 76.
2. Mitsuo Nakamura, *Modern Japanese Fiction, 1868–1926* (Tokyo: Kokusai Bunka Shinkokai, 1968), part 2, p. 19.
3. Tatsuo Arima, *The Failure of Freedom* (Cambridge, MA: Harvard University Press, 1969), p. 79.
4. Takasaka Masaaki, *Meiji Bunkashi* (Meiji Cultural History) (Tokyo: Yoyosha, 1955), vol. 4, p. 436–437.
5. Keene, *Dawn to the West*, p. 180.
6. Toki Yoshimaro, *Meiji Taishō-shi, Geijutsu-hen* (Meiji-Taishō History, The Arts) (Tokyo: Asahi Shimbunsha, 1931), p. 199.
7. Harold G. Henderson, *An Introduction to Haiku* (New York: Doubleday Anchor, 1958), p. 181.

8. Yamamoto Shigemi, *Aa, Nomugi Tōge* (Ah, Nomugi Pass) (Tokyo: Kadokawa, 1977), p. 328.

9. Cited in Mikiso Hane, *Peasants, Rebels and Outcastes* (New York: Pantheon, 1982), pp. 33–34.

10. Ibid, p. 18.

11. Morisaki Kazue, *Makkura* (Pitch Dark) (Tokyo: San'ichi Shobo, 1977), p. 161.

12. Chōsenjin Kyōsei Renkō Shinsō Chōsadan, ed., *Chōsenjin Kyōsei Renkō* (Compulsory Roundup of Koreans) (Tokyo: Gendaishi Shuppankai, 1974), pp. 191–195.

13. Cited in Mikiso Hane, *Reflections on the Way to the Gallows* (Berkeley, CA: University of California Press, 1988), pp. 7–8.

14. Shidzue Ishimoto, *Facing Two Ways. The Story of My Life* (New York: Farrar & Rinehart, 1935), p. 78.

15. Fukao Sumako, *Yosano Akiko* (Tokyo: Jimbutsu Oraisha, 1968), pp. 85–86.

16. See Hane, *Reflections on the Way to the Gallows*, p. 53.

17. Ibid., p. 56, p. 63.

18. Sumiya Mikio, *Dai Nipponteikoku no Shiren* (The Crucible of Imperial Japan) (Tokyo: Chuo Koronsha, 1966), p. 444.

19. Kakuzo Okakura, *The Awakening of Japan* (New York: Japan Society, 1921), pp. 191–192.

20. E. H. Norman, *Japan's Emergence as a Modern State* (New York: Institute of Pacific Relations, 1940), p. 8.

21. Lafcadio Hearn, *Japan, an Attempt at Interpretation* (New York: Macmillan, 1904), p. 420, p. 428.

CHAPTER SIX

1. Bill Hosokawa, *Nisei: The Quiet American* (New York: William Morrow and Co., 1969), p. 86.

2. Masumi Junnosuke, *Nihon Seitōshiron* (Discourse on the History of Japanese Political Parties), 4 vols. (Tokyo: Tokyo Daigaku Shuppankai, 1965–1968), 4, pp. 142–143.

3. Buraku Kaihō Dōmei staff, *Sabetsu no naka of ikite* (Living in the Midst of Discrimination) (Tokyo: Kaiho Shuppansha, 1978), pp. 63–64, p. 278.

4. Cf. Mikiso Hane, *Reflections on the Way to the Gallows* (Berkeley, CA: University of California Press, 1988), p. 29 ff.

5. Ibid., pp. 20–21

6. Ibid., pp. 22–23.

7. Ibid., p. 124.

8. Ibid., pp. 126–127.

9. Ibid., pp. 209–210.

10. Mikiso Hane, *Peasants, Rebels and Outcastes* (New York: Pantheon, 1982), pp. 34–35.

11. Shibuya Teisuke, *Nomin Aishi* (The Sad History of the Peasants) (Tokyo: Keiso Shobo, 1970), p. 264, p. 440.

12. Mitsuo Nakamura, *Modern Japanese Fiction, 1868–1926* (Tokyo: Chuo Koronsha, 1966), Part II, pp. 32–33.
13. Donald Keene, *Dawn to the West* (New York: Henry Holt, 1984), p. 485.
14. Ibid., p. 490.
15. Kadokawa Genyoshi, *et al.* eds., *Nihon Bungaku no Rekishi* (History of Japanese Literature), 12 vols. (Tokyo: Kdokawa Shoten, 1967–1968), vol. II, pp. 199–215.
16. Junichiro Tanizaki, *Some Prefer Nettles*, trans. Edward G. Seidensticker (New York: Knopf, 1955), p. xv and Junichiro Tanizaki, "In Praise of Shadow," in *Perspective of Japan,* an *Atlantic Monthly* supplment (New York: 1954), pp. 48–49.
17. Yasunari Kawabata, *Snow Country*, trans. Edward G. Seidensticker (New York: Knopf, 1956), pp. 6–7.
18. *Japan Report*, New York Consulate General of Japan, January 31, 1969.
19. Keene, *Dawn to the West*. p. 1136.
20. Enchi Fumiko, *Waiting Years*, trans. John Bestor (Tokyo: Kodansha, 1971), p. 190.
21. Cf. Torataro Shimomura, "Nishida Kitaro and Some Aspects of His Philosophical Thought," in Kitaro Nishida, *A Study of Good*, trans. V. H. Viglielmo (Tokyo: Japanese Government Printing Bureau, 1960), p. 191 ff.
22. Kunio Yanagida, ed. *Japanese Culture in the Meiji Era,* vol. iv, trans. Charles S. Terry (Tokyo: Toyo Bunko, 1957), pp. 96–97.

CHAPTER SEVEN

1. Masao Maruyama, *Thought and Behaviour in Modern Japanese Politics* (London: Oxford University Press, 1963), p. 45.
2. Ōuchi Tsutomu, *Fasshizumu e no Michi* (The Road to Fascism) (Tokyo: Chuo Koronsha, 1967), p. 297.
3. Shigeru Honjo; *Emperor Hirohito and his Chief Aide-de-camp: The Honjo Diary*, trans. Mikiso Hane (Tokyo University of Tokyo Press, 1982), pp. 37–38.
4. Ishii Itarō, *Gaikōkan no Isshō, Taichugoku Gaikō no Kaisō* (Life of a Diplomatic Official, Recollections on Foreign Policy Relative to China) (Tokyo:Taiheiyo Shuppansha, 1972), pp. 236 ff.
5. Eguchi Keiichi, *Futatsu no Taisen* (Two Major Wars), vol. 14 of 15 volume series: *Taikei Nihon no Rekishi* (Outline of Japanese History) (Tokyo: Shogakukan, 1993), pp. 307–308.
6. Frank Dorn, *The Sino-Japanese War, 1937–41* (New York: Macmillan, 1974), p. 222.
7. Robert J. C. Butow, *Tojo and the Coming of the War* (Stanford, CA: Stanford University Press, 1961), p. 245.
8. Hayashi Shigeru, *Taiheiyō Sensō* (The Pacific War) (Tokyo: Chuo Koronsha, 1967), pp. 240–241.
9. Herbert Feis, *The Road to Pearl Harbor* (Princeton, NJ: Princeton University Press, 1950), p. 321.

10. Samurel Eliot Morison, *History of the United States Naval Operations in Second World War*, 15 vols. (Boston: Little Brown, 1983), vol. 3, p. 132.
11. Example of the "no surrender" philosophy is Yokoi Shōichi who hid for twenty-seven years in the jungles of Guam after the end of the war. Another officer lived in the Philippine jungles until 1974. *New York Times*, Sept. 26, 1997.
12. Morison, *History of the United States*, vol. 8, p. 338.
13. Eguchi Keiichi, *Futatsu no Taisen*, p. 431.
14. Michihiko Hachiya, *Hiroshima Diary: The Journal of a Japanese Physician* (Chapel Hill, NC: University of North Carolina Press, 1955), pp. 14–15, p. 69.
15. Takashi Nagai, *The Bells of Nagasaki*, trans. William Johnston (Tokyo: Kodansha, 1974), p. 64, pp. 90–91.
16. Eguchi Keiichi, *Futatsu no Taisen*, p. 410.

CHAPTER EIGHT

1. Douglas MacArthur, *Reminiscences* (New York: McGraw Hill, 1964), pp. 282–283.
2. *Japan Times Weekly*, June 22–28, 1998.
3. Japan changed the statistical base from G.N.P. to G.D.P. in 1993 because the former includes overseas investments, which were large. The latter includes only domestic economic activities. Asahi Shimbun, *Japan Almanac*, 1997, p. 73. G.D.P. dropped to minus 0.7% in 1997, lower than minus 0.5% of 1974. *Japan Times Weekly*, June 22–28, 1998.
4. *Far Eastern Economic Review*, April 16, 1998, p. 61.
5. The statistics on the economy are based primarily on data from annual publications of *Nippon: A Chartered Survey of Japan* (Tokyo: Kokuseisha), *Statistical Handbook of Japan* (Statistics Bureau, Prime Minister's Office, Japan), *Japan Almanac* (Asahi Shimbun), *Facts and Figures of Japan* (Foreign Press), and data from the *Far Eastern Economic Review; New York Times; Japan Times Weekly*, and other journals and newspapers.
6. Jared Taylor, *Shadows of the Rising Sun* (New York: Quill, 1983) p. 171.
7. Ronald Bell, *The Japanese Experience* (New York: Weatherhill, 1973), p. 96.
8. *Japan Times Weekly, International Edition*, July 8–14, 1991, p. 1.
9. *New York Times*. Oct. 29, 1998
10. In 1997 the president of Dai-Ichi Kangyō Bank, the world's fourth largest bank was arrested for having extended large loans to the *yakuza*. *Japan Times Weekly*, June 30–July 6, 1997.
11. *Japan Times Weekly*, June 30–July 6, 1997.
12. Buraku Liberation News (Osaka: Buraku Liberation Research Institute), November 1997.
13. *Intersect Japan*, a monthly publication of PHP Institute. May, 1991, pp. 25–26.

14. Donald Richie in Bell, *The Japanese Experience*, p. 60.
15. *New York Times*, Sept. 10, 1996.
16. Oe Kenzaburo, *Teach Us to Outgrow Our Madness*, trans. John Nathan (New York: Grove Press, 1977) pp. xiii–xiv.
17. Quoted in Vincent Canby, "What's So Funny About Japan," *New York Times Magazine*, June 18, 1989, p. 26 ff.
18. *New York Times,* Book Review, September 27, 1992.
19. *Chicago Tribune*, June 16, 1991.
20. Bell, *The Japanese Experience*, p. 142.
21. *Japan Almanac*, 2000, pp. 263–266.
22. Donald Keene, *Dawn to the West* (New York: Henry Holt, 1984), p. 1216.
23. *The Temple of the Golden Pavilion*, trans. Ivan Morris (Rutland, VT: Charles E. Tuttle, 1959), p. 27.
24. *New Yorker*, December 12, 1970, p. 40.
25. Oe Kenzaburo, *Teach Us to Outgrow Our Madness,* p. 186.
26. Yoshiko Yokochi Samuel, *The Life and Works of Oe Kenzaburo* (Ann Arbor MI: University Microfilms International, 1981), p. 10.
27. A. N. Wilson, "Firmly Catholic and Firmly Japanese," *New York Times* Book Review, July 21, 1985, p. 21.
28. Keene, *Dawn to the West*, p. 1136.
29. Enchi Fumiko, *The Waiting Years*, trans. John Bester (Tokyo: Kodansha, 1980), p. 90.
30. Keene, *Dawn to the West*, p. 1144.
31. *This Kind of Woman*, eds. Yukiko Tanaka & Elizabeth Hanson (New York: Perigee Books, 1982), p. 226.
32. Donald Richie, *Japanese Movies* (Tokyo: Japan Travel Bureau, 1961), p. 161.
33. *New York Times*, December 15 & 29, 1985.
34. Vincent Canby, "What's So Funny About Japan," pp. 26ff.
35. *Chicago Tribune*, April 26, 1993.
36. Peter Mcgill, "Boxing Ando," in *Intersect*, November 1993, p. 36.
37. Bernard Leach, *Hamada, Potter* (Tokyo: Kodansha, 1975), p. 125.
38. Benjamin C. Duke, *The Japanese School: Lessons for Industrial America* (New York: Praeger, 1986), p. 200.

Bibliography

PREMODERN JAPAN

Historical and biographical dictionaries and encyclopedias

Bowring, Richard J. and Kornicki, Peter F., eds. *Cambridge Encyclopedia of Japan*. Cambridge: Cambridge University Press, 1993.

Campbell, Alan, Noble, David S., *et al*. eds. *Japan: An Illustrated Encyclopedia*, 2 vols., Tokyo: Kodansha, 1993.

Goedertier, Joseph M. *Dictionary of Japanese History*. New York: Weatherhill, 1968.

Hisamatsu, Senichi. *Biographical Dictionary of Japanese Literature*. Tokyo: Kodansha, 1976.

Huffman, James L., ed. *Modern Japan: An Encyclopedia of History, Culture, and Nationalism*. New York: Garland, 1998.

Hunter, Janet. *Concise Dictionary of Modern Japanese History*. Berkeley, CA: University of California Press, 1984.

Itasaka, Gen, general editor, *Japan Encyclopedia*, 9 vols. Tokyo: Kodansha, 1978.

Iwao, Seiichi. *Biographical Dictionary of Japanese History*. Tokyo: Kodansha, 1978.

O'Neil, P. G. *Japanese Names*. Tokyo: Weatherhill, 1972.

Roberts, Laurance P. A. *Dictionary of Japanese Artists*. Tokyo: Weatherhill, 1976.

Geographical works

Cressey, George B. *Asia's Land and Peoples*. New York: McGraw Hill, 1963.

Dempster, Prue. *Japan Advances: A Geographical Study*. New York: Barnes & Noble, 1968.

Ishida, Ryutaro. *Geography of Japan*. Tokyo: Kokusai Bunka Shinkokai, 1969.

Trewartha, Glenn T. *Japan: A Physical, Cultural and Regional Geography*. Madison, WI: University of Wisconson Press, 1965.

General histories and multi-volume series on Premodern and Modern Japan

Hall, John W., *et al*. ed. *The Cambridge History of Japan*, 6 vols. New York: Cambridge University Press, 1989–1999.

Hall, John W. *Japan: From Prehistory to Modern Times*. New York: Delacorte, 1970.

Hall, John W. and Beardsley, Richard K., eds. *Twelve Doors to Japan*. New York: McGraw Hill, 1965. Twelve studies on diverse aspects of Japanese history.

Hane, Mikiso. *Premodern Japan: A Historical Survey*. Boulder, CO: Westview Press, 1991.

Reischauer, Edwin O. *Japan: The Story of a Nation*. New York: McGraw Hill, 1990.

Sansom, Sir George B. *A History of Japan*, 3 vols. Stanford, CA: Stanford University Press, 1963.

Totman, Conrad. *Japan Before Perry*. Berkeley, CA: University of California Press, 1981.

Transactions of the Asiatic Society of Japan. Tokyo: Asiatic Society of Japan, 1872–1998.

Special aspects of Japanese history and culture

Anseaki, Masaharu. *History of Japanese Religion*. Rutland, VT: Tuttle, 1963.

Benedict, Ruth. *The Chrysanthemum and the Sword: Patterns of Japanese Culture*. Boston, MA: Houghton Mifflin, 1946.

Chamberlain, Basil H. *Things Japanese*. London: Routledge & Kegan Paul, 1939.

Craig, Albert M. and Shively, Donald H. *Personality in Japanese History*. Berkeley, CA: University of California Press, 1971.

Earhart, H. Bryan. *Japanese Religion: Unity and Diversity*. Rutherford, NJ: Farleigh Dickinson University Press, 1974.

Holtom, Daniel C. *The National Faith of Japan: A Study in Modern Shinto*. New York: Dutton, 1938.

Hearn, Lafcadio. *Japan: An Attempt at Interpretation*. New York: Macmillan, 1913.

Kapleau, Philip. *The Three Pillars of Zen*. New York: Harper & Row, 1966.

Keene, Donald, ed. *Anthology of Japanese Literature from the Earliest Era to the Mid-nineteenth Century*. New York: Grove, 1955.

——. *Japanese Literature: An introduction to Western Readers*. New York: Grove, 1955.

——. *Seeds in the Heart: Japanese Literature from the Earliest Times to the Late Sixteenth Century*. New York: Henry Holt, 1993.

Kitagawa, Joseph. M. *Religion in Japanese History*. New York: Columbia University Press, 1966.

Morris, Ivan. *The Nobility of Failure: Tragic Heroes in the History of Japan.* New York: Holt, 1975. A discourse on tragic heroes from a fourth century prince to the twentieth century kamikaze pilots.

Munsterberg, Hugo. *The Arts of Japan: An Illustrated History.* Rutland,VT: Tuttle, 1957.

Nakamura, Hajime. *Ways of Thinking of Eastern People: India, China, Tibet, Japan.* Honolulu: East-West Center Press, 1964.

Nitobe, Inazo. *Bushido, the Soul of Japan.* New York: Putnam, 1905.

Okakura, Kakuzo. *The Book of Tea.* Rutland, VT: Tuttle, 1956.

Paine, Robert T. and Soper, Alexander C. *The Art and Architecture of Japan.* Baltimore, MD: Penguin, 1955.

Sumiya, Mikio and Taira, Koji. *An Outline of Japanese Economic History: 1602–1940.* Tokyo: University of Tokyo Press, 1979.

Sugimoto, Masayoshi and Swain, David L. *Science and Culture in Traditional Japan.* Cambridge, MA: MIT Press, 1978.

Suzuki, Daisetsu T. *An Introduction to Zen Buddhism.* New York: Grove, 1964.

——. *Zen and Japanese Culture.* New York: Pantheon, 1959.

Tsunoda, Ryusaku, *et al.* eds. *Sources of Japanese Tradition.* New York: Columbia University Press, 1958.

Reference works from the early years to the Heian Era

For the *early historical* era see:

Brown, Delmer M., ed. *Ancient Japan*, Cambridge History of Japan, vol. I. New York: Cambridge University Press, 1993.

Kidder, Edward: *Japan Before Buddhism.* New York: Praeger, 1959.

Komatsu, Isao. *The Japanese People: Origins of the People and the Language.* Tokyo: Kokusai Bunka Shinkokai, 1962.

Sansom, Sir George B. *History of Japan to 1334.* Stanford, CA: Stanford University Press, 1958.

Shively, Donald H. and McCullough, William H., eds. *Heian Japan*, Cambridge History of Japan, vol. 2. New York: Cambridge University Press, 1999.

Heian Era

Aston, W. G., trans. *Nihongi* (Chronicles of Japan from the Earliest Time to A.D. 697) New York: Paragon, 1956.

Philippi, Donald L., trans. *Kojiki.* Princeton NJ: Princeton University Press, 1968.

Wheeler, Post, ed. and trans. *The Sacred Scriptures of the Japanese.* New York: Abelard-Schuman, 1952.

On *Heian court life* see:

Morris, Ivan I. *The World of the Shining Prince: Court Life in Ancient Japan.* New York: Knopf, 1964.

For the late *Heian political developments* refer to:

Hurst, Cameron. *Insei: Abdicated Sovereigns in the Politics of Late Heian Japan, 1086–1185*. New York: Columbia University Press, 1976.

For the *social state* of this period see:

Farris, William W. *Population, Disease, and Land in Early Japan, 645–900*. Cambridge, MA: Harvard University Press, 1985.

On the *literary works* of the Heian writers and poets there is the classical:

Murasaki, Shikibu. *The Tale of Genji*. There are two translations:

Waley, Arthur. New York: Random House, 1960, and a more recent translation by Edward G. Seidensticker. New York: Knopf, 1978.

For an analysis of *The Tale of Genji* see:

Field, Norma. *The Splendor of Longing in the Tale of Genji*. Princeton, NJ: Princeton University Press 1987.

OTHER LITERARY WORKS OF THE HEIAN ERA

McCullough, Helen C., trans. *Tales of Ise: Lyrical Episodes from Tenth-Century Japan*. Stanford, CA: Stanford University Press, 1968.

Miner, Earl. *An Introduction to Japanese Court Poetry*. Stanford, CA: Stanford University Press, 1968.

Nippon Gakujutsu Shinkokai, pub. *Manyoshu: One Thousand Court Poems*. New York: Columbia University Press, 1965.

Seidensticker, Edward G., trans. *The Gossamer Years: A Diary by a Noblewoman of Heian Japan*. Rutland, VT: Tuttle, 1964.

Sei Shonagon. *The Pillow Books of Sei Shonagon*, 2 vols. Trans. and ed. by Ivan Morris. New York: Columbia University Press, 1967. This is considered to be one of the two masterpieces of the zuihitsu (flowing brush) genre of poetic essays.

Rise of the military to 1600

On the *rise of the samurai class* and development of "feudalism":

Duus, Peter. *Feudalism in Japan*. New York: Knopf, 1969.

Farris, William Wayne. *Heavenly Warriors: The Evolution of Japan's Military, 500–1300*. Cambridge, MA: Harvard University Press, 1992.

Hall, John W., *et al*. eds. *Japan Before Tokugawa Consolidation and Economic Growth*. Princeton, NJ: Princeton University Press, 1981.

Mass, Jeffrey P. *Warrior Government in Early Medieval Japan*. New Haven, CN: Yale University Press, 1975.

Mass, Jeffrey P. and Hauser, William B., eds. *The Bakufu in Japanese History*. Stanford, CA: Stanford University Press, 1985.

For the *general political and social state of affairs* see:

Elison, George and Smith, Bardwell, eds. *Warlords, Artisans and Commoners: Japan in the Sixteenth Century*, Honolulu: University of Hawaii Press, 1981.

Mass, Jeffrey P. *The Origins of Japan's Medieval World: Courtiers, Clerics, Warriors, and Peasants in the Fourteenth Century*. Stanford, CA: Stanford University Press, 1997.

Yamamuro, Kozo, ed. *Medieval Japan*. vol. 3 of Cambridge History of Japan. New York: Cambridge University Press, 1990.

On the *arrival of the Westerners* in the 16th century see:

Boxer, Charles R. *The Christian Century in Japan, 1549–1650*. Berkeley, CA: University of California Press, 1951.

Cooper, Michael, S. J., ed. *They Came to Japan, An Anthology of European Reports on Japan, 1543–1640*. Berkeley, CA: University of California Press, 1965.

Rodrigues, Joao S. J. *This Island of Japan: Joao Rodrigues' Account of 16th Century Japan*. trans. Michael Cooper. Tokyo: Kodansha, 1973.

On *Japanese-Korean relations* in the Medieval to early Modern years:

Kang, Etsuko Hae-jin. *Diplomacy and Ideology in Japanese-Korean Relations: From the 15th to the 18th Century*. New York: St. Martins, 1997.

For a *biography* of Hideyoshi see:

Berry, Mary Elizabeth. *Hideyoshi*. Cambridge. MA: Harvard University Press, 1982.

For *literary works* of this period:

Keene, Donald, trans. *Essays in Idleness: The Tsurezuregusa* of Kenko, a priest. This is regarded as one of the masterpieces of the zuihitsu (flowing brush) genre.

Kitabatake, Chikafusa. *A Chronicle of Gods and Sovereigns*, trans. H. Paul Varley. New York: Columbia University Press, 1980.

McCullough, Helen C., trans. *The Taiheiki: A Chronicle of Medieval Japan*. New York: Columbia University Press, 1959.

——. trans. *The Tale of the Heike* (a literary account of the Taira clan). Stanford, CA: Stanford University Press, 1988.

For the *Noh plays* that emerged in this period there are:

Keene, Donald, ed. *Twenty Plays of the No Theatre*. New York: Columbia University Press, 1970.

Waley, Arthur. *The No Plays of Japan*. London: Allen & Inwin, 1911.

Tokugawa Era

General histories of this era include:

Hall, John W., ed. *Early Modern Japan*, vol. 4 of the Cambridge History of Japan. New York: Cambridge University Press, 1991.

Sansom, Sir George B. *A History of Japan, 1615–1867*. Stanford, CA: Stanford University Press, 1963.

On the founder of the *Tokugawa reign* see:

Totman, Conrad D. *Tokugawa Ieyasu*. South San Francisco: Heian, 1982.

And a study of an influential *Tokugawa official*:

Ooms, Herman. *Charismatic Bureaucrat: A Political Biography of Matsudaira Sadanobu*. Chicago: University of Chicago Press, 1975.

On *political and institutional studies* see:

Hall, John. W. and Jansen, Marius, eds. *Studies in the Institutional History of Early Modern Japan*. Princeton, NJ: Princeton University Press, 1968.

Totman, Conrad. D. *Politics in the Tokugawa Bakufu, 1600–1843*. Cambridge, MA: Harvard University Press, 1967.

——. *Early Modern Japan*. Berkeley, CA: University of California Press, 1993.

For *social and economic* developments see:

Bix, Herbert. *Peasant Protest in Japan, 1590–1884*. New Haven, CN: Yale University Press, 1986.

Borton, Hugh. "Peasant Uprisings in Japan of the Tokugawa Period," in the *Transactions of the Asiatic Society of Japan*, series 2, vol. 16 (1938).

Hanley, Susan B. *Everyday Things in Premodern Japan: The Hidden Legacy of Material Culture*. Berkeley, CA: University of California Press, 1997.

Jannetta, Ann B. *Epidemics and Mortality in Early Modern Japan*. Princeton, NJ: Princeton University Press, 1987.

Ooms, Herman. *Tokugawa Village Practice: Class, Status, Power, Law*. Berkeley, CA: University of California Press, 1996.

Roberts, John C. *Mitsui Empire: Three Centuries of Japanese Business*. New York: Weatherhill, 1973

Sheldon, C. D. *The Rise of the Merchant Class in Tokugawa Japan*. Locust Valley, NY: Augustin, 1958.

Smith, Thomas C. *The Agrarian Origins of Modern Japan*. Stanford, CA: Stanford University Press, 1959.

Vlastos, Stephen. *Peasant Protests and Uprisings in Tokugawa Japan*. Berkeley, CA: University of California Press, 1986.

Walthall, Anne, ed. and trans. *Peasant Uprisings in Japan: A Critical Anthology of Peasnt Histories*. Chicago: University of Chicago Press, 1991.

——. *Social Protest and Popular Culture in Eighteenth Century Japan*. Tucson AZ: University of Arizona Press, 1968.

On *general and topical intellectual studies*:

Bellah, Robert N. *Tokugawa Religion: The Values of Pre-Industrial Japan*. Glencoe, IL: Free Press, 1957.

Dore, Ronald P. *Education in Tokugawa Japan*. Berkeley, CA University of California Press, 1965.

Earl, David M. *Emperor and Nation in Japan: Political Thinkers of the Tokugawa Period*. Seattle: University of Washington Press, 1964.

Keene, Donald. *The Japanese Discovery of Europe, 1720–1830*. Stanford, CA: Stanford University Press, 1969.

Maruyama, Masao. *Studies in the intellectual History of Tokugawa Japan, trans.* Mikiso Hane. Tokyo: Tokyo University Press, 1974.

Najita, Tetsuo, ed. *Tokugawa Political Writings*. New York: Cambridge University Press, 1998.

Nakai, Kate Wildman. *Shogunal Politics: Arai Hakuseki and the Premises of Tokugawa Rule*. Cambridge, MA: Harvard University Press, 1988.

Ooms, Herman. *Tokugawa Ideology, Early Constructs, 1570–1680*. Princeton, NJ: Princeton University Press, 1985.

Wakabayashi, Bob Tadashi. *Anti-Foreignism and Western Learning in Early-Modern Japan*. Cambridge, MA: Harvard University Press, 1992.

On the *code of the warriors* there is the 18th century text for the samurai, a compilation of Yamamoto, Tsunetomo's *Hagakure: The Book of the Samurai*. trans. William S. Wilson. Tokyo: Kodansha, 1978.

On *literary and cultural* subjects see:

Ando, Tsuruo. *Performing Arts of Japan: Bunraku, the Puppet Theatre*. New York: Walker/Weatherhill, 1970.

Blyth, Reginald H. *Haiku*, 4 vols. Tokyo: Hokuseido Press, 1950–1952.

Bowers, Faubion. *Japanese Theatre*. New York: Hill & Wang, 1959.

Chikamatsu, Monzaemon. *The Major Plays of Chikamatsu*, trans. Donald Keene. New York: Columbia University Press, 1961.

Ermst, Earle. *The Kabuki Theatre*. New York: Oxford Univesity Press, 1956.

Henderson, Harold G. *An Introduction to Haiku*. Garden City, NY: Doubleday, 1958.

Hibbert, Howard. *The Floating World in Japanese Fiction*. New York: Grove, 1960.

Hillier, J. *Masters of the Colour Print*. London: Phaidon, 1954.

Ihara, Saikaku. *Five Women Who Loved Love*, trans. William T. de Bary. Rutland, VT: Tuttle, 1956.

——. *The Life of an Amorous Woman and Other Writings*, trans. Ivan Morris. Norfolk, CN: Laughlin, 1963.

Michener, James. *The Floating World: The Story of Japanese Prints*. New York: Random House, 1954.

GENERAL HISTORIES OF MODERN JAPAN

Beckmann, George M. *The Modernization of China and Japan*, New York: Harper & Row, 1962.

Borton, Hugh. *Japan's Modern Century*. New York: Ronald, 1970.

Duus, Peter, ed. *The Cambridge History of Japan*, vol. 6. *The Twentieth Century* New York. Cambridge University Press, 1989.

Hane, Mikiso. *Modern Japan: A Historical Survey*. Boulder, CO: Westview Press, 1992.

Jansen, Marius B., ed. *Cambridge History of Japan*, vol. 5. *The Nineteenth Century*. New York: Cambridge University Press, 1989.

Storry, Richard. *A History of Modern Japan*. Baltimore: Penguin, 1965.

Modern Japan: cultural, social, and political topics

Anderson, Joseph L. and Richie, Donald. *The Japanese Film: Art and Industry*. Princeton, NJ: Princeton University Press, 1982.

Barshay, Andrew E. *State and Intellectual in Imperial Japan*. Berkeley, CA: University of California Press, 1988.

Bartholomew, James R. *The Formation of Science in Japan: Building a Research Tradtion*. New Haven: Yale University Press, 1989.

Beckmann, George M. and Genji, Okubo. *The Japanese Communist Party, 1945*. Stanford, CA: Stanford University Press, 1969.

Brown, Delmer M. *Nationalism in Japan*. Berkeley, CA: University of California Press, 1955.

Brownlee, John S. *Japanese Historians and the National Myths 1600–1945: The Age of the Gods and Emperor Jimmu*. Vancouver: UBC Press, 1998.

Craig, Albert M. *Japan, A Comparative View*. Princeton, NJ: Princeton University Press, 1979.

DeVos, George and Wagatsuma, Hiroshi. *Japan's Invisible Race: Caste in Culture and Personality*. Berkeley, CA: University of California Press, 1966.

Doi, Takeo. *Amae: The Anatomy of Dependence*. Tokyo: Kodansha, 1974.

Dore, Ronald P., ed. *Aspects of Social Change in Modern Japan*. Princeton, NJ: Princeton University Press, 1967.

Edgerton, Robert B. *Warriors of the Rising Sun: A History of Japanese Military*. New York. Norton, 1997

Fukutake, Tadashi. *Japanese Social Structure: Its Evolution in the Modern Century*. Tokyo: University of Tokyo Press, 1982.

Garon, Sheldon. *The State and Labor in Modern Japan*. Berkeley, CA: University of California Press, 1987.

Gordon, Andrew. *Labor and Imperial Democracy in Prewar Japan*. Berkeley, CA: University of California Press, 1991.

Hane, Mikiso, *Peasants, Rebels and Outcastes*. New York: Pantheon, 1982.

Hardacre, Helen. *Shinto and the State, 1869–1988*. Princeton, NJ: Princeton University Press, 1989.

Iriye, Akira. *The Chinese and Japanese*. Princeton, NJ: Princeton University Press, 1980.

Ishida, Takeshi. *Japanese Society*. New York: Random House, 1971.

Jansen, Marius B., ed. *Changing Japanese Attitudes Toward Modernization*. Princeton, NJ: Princeton University Press, 1965.

Kaigo, Tokiomi. *Japanese Education, Its Past and Present.* Tokyo: Kokusai Bunka Shinkokai, 1968.

Kaplan, David and Dubro, Alex. *Yakuza.* New York: MacMillan, 1986. A study of the Japanese "Mafia."

Kasza, Gregory J. *The State and the Mass Media in Japan, 1918–1945.* Berkeley, CA: University of California Press, 1988.

Kayano, Shigeru. *Our Land Was a Forest: an Ainu Memoir,* trans. Kyoko Selden and Lili Selden. Boulder, CO: Westview Press, 1994.

Lebra, Takie Sugiyama. *Japanese Patterns of Behavior.* Honolulu: University Press of Hawaii, 1976.

Maraini, Fosco. *Meeting with Japan.* New York: Viking, 1959.

Mitchell, Richard M. *Censorship in Imperial Japan.* Princeton, NJ: Princeton University Press, 1983.

——. *The Korean Minority in Japan.* Berkeley CA: University of California Press, 1967.

Nakane, Chie. *Japanese Society.* Berkeley, CA: University of California Press, 1970.

Neary, Ian. *Political Protest and Social Control in Pre-war Japan: The Origins of Buraku Liberation.* Atlantic Highlands, NJ: Humanities Press, 1989. On the "outcaste" fight for equality and freedom.

Ohnuki-Tierney, Emiko. *Illness and Culture in Contemporary Japan: An Anthropological View.* Cambridge: Cambridge University Press, 1984.

Reischauer, Edwin O. *The Japanese.* Cambridge, MA: Harvard University Press, 1977.

Richie, Donald. *Japanese Movies.* Tokyo: Japan Travel Bureau, 1961.

Saga, Junichi. *Confessions of a Yakuza.* Tokyo: Kodansha, 1991.

Scalapino, Robert A. *Democracy and the Party Movement in Prewar Japan.* Berkeley, CA: University of California Press, 1953.

——. *The Japanese Communist Movement, 1920–1966.* Berkeley, CA: University of California Press, 1967.

Scheiner, Irwin. *Modern Japan: An Interpretive Anthology.* New York: Macmillan, 1974.

Schwantes, Robert. *Japanese and Americans: A Century of Cultural Relations.* New York: Harper & Row, 1955.

Seidensticker, Edward. *Low City, High City: Tokyo, 1867–1923.* New York: Knopf, 1983.

Smethurst, Richard A. *A Social Basis for Prewar Japanese Militarism.* Berkeley, CA: University of California Press, 1974.

Tsurumi, Patricia. *Japanese Colonial Education in Taiwan, 1895–1945.* Cambridge, MA: Harvard University Press, 1977.

Ward, R. E., ed. *Political Development in Modern Japan.* Princeton, NJ: Princeton University Press, 1968.

Waswo, Ann. *The Japanese Landlord.* Berkeley, CA: University of California Press, 1977.

Weiner, Michael. *The Origins of the Korean Community in Japan, 1910–1923,* Atlantic Highlands, NJ: Humanities Press, 1989.

International Relations

Beasley, W. G. *Japanese Imperialism, 1894–1945.* New York: Oxford University Press, 1987.

Duus, Peter, Myers, Ramon H. and Peattie, Mark R., eds. *The Japanese Informal Empire in China, 1895–1937.* Princeton, NJ: Princeton University Press, 1989.

Ikle, Frank. *German-Japanese Relations, 1936–1940.* New York: Bookman, 1956.

Iriye, Akira. *Across the Pacific: An Inner History of American-East Asian Relations.* New York: Harcourt Brace, 1967.

Jansen, Marius. *Japan and China: From War to Peace, 1894–1972.* Chicago: Rand McNally, 1975.

Myers, Ramon H. and Peattie, Mark R. *The Japanese Colonial Empire, 1895–1945.* Princeton, NJ: Princeton University Press, 1984.

Neumann, William L. *America Encounters Japan: From Perry to MacArthur.* Baltimore: Johns Hopkins University Press, 1963.

Nish, Ian, ed. *Anglo-Japanese Alienation, 1919–1952.* Cambridge: Cambridge University Press, 1982.

——. *Japanese Foreign Policy, 1869–1942.* London: Routledge & Kegan Paul, 1977.

Economic Developments

Halliday, Jon. *A Political History of Japanese Capitalism.* New York: Pantheon, 1975.

Hirschmeier, Johannes and Yui, Tsunehiko. *The Development of Japanese Business, 1600–1973.* Cambridge, MA: Harvard University Press, 1975.

Lockwood, William W., ed. *The State and Economic Enterprise in Japan.* Princeton, NJ. Princeton University Press, 1965.

Marsh, Robert and Mannari, Hiroshi. *Modernization and the Japanese Factory.* Princeton, NJ: Princeton University Press, 1976.

Marshall, Byron. *Capitalism and Nationalism in Prewar Japan; The Ideology of the Business Elite, 1868–1941.* Stanford, CA: Stanford University Press, 1967.

Ohkawa, Kazushi and Rosovsky, Henry. *Japanese Economic Growth.* Stanford, CA: Stanford University Press, 1973.

Patrick, Hugh, ed. *Japanese Industrialization and its Social Consequences.* Berkeley, CA: University of California Press, 1976.

Smith, Thomas C. *Native Sources of Japanese Industrialization, 1750–1920.* Berkeley, CA: University of California Press, 1988.

Taira, Koji. *Economic Development and the Labor Market in Japan.* New York: Columbia University Press, 1970.

Literature

Danly, Robert Lyons. *In the Shade of Spring Leaves: The Life and Writings of Higuchi Ichiyo.* New Haven, CN: Yale University Press, 1981.

Hibbett, Howard, ed. *Contemporary Japanese Literature.* New York: Knopf, 1977.

Keene, Donald. *Dawn to the West: Japanese Literature of the Modern Era,* 2 vols. New York: Holt, 1984.

Lyons, Phyllis. *The Saga of Dazai Osamu.* Stanford, CA: Stanford University Press, 1985. A critical Study of the author's autobiographical writings.

McClellan, Edwin. *Two Japanese Novelists: Soseki and Toson.* Berkeley, CA: University of California Press, 1969.

Miyoshi, Masao. *Accomplices of Silence: The Modern Japanese Novel.* Berkeley, CA: University of California Press, 1974.

Nakamura, Mitsuo. *Modern Japanese Fiction, 1868–1926.* Tokyo: Kokusai Bunka Shinkokai, 1968.

Ryan, Marleigh C. *Japan's First Modern Novel: Ukigumo of Futabatei Shimei.* New York: Columbia University Press, 1967.

Seidensticker, Edward G. *Kafu the Scribbler.* Stanford, CA: Stanford University Press, 1965.

Ueda, Makoto. *Modern Japanese Writers and the Nature of Literature.* Stanford. CA: Stanford University Press, 1976.

The Condition of Women

Bernstein, Gail. *Haruko's World: A Japanese Farm Woman and Her Community.* Stanford, CA: Stanford University Press, 1983.

——, ed. *Recreating Japanese Women, 1600–1945.* Berkeley, CA: University of California Press, 1990.

Brinton, Mary C. *Women and the Economic Miracle: Gender and Work in Postwar Japan.* Berkeley, CA: University of California Press, 1993.

Condon, Jane. *Japanese Women in the Eighties: Half a Step Behind.* New York: Dodd Mead, 1985.

Cook, Alice and Hayashi, Hiroko. *Women in Japan: Discrimination, Resistance and Reform.* Ithaca, NY: Cornell University Press, 1980.

Ericson, Joan E. *Be a Woman: Hayashi Fumiko and Modern Japanese Women's Literature.* Honolulu: University of Hawaii Press, 1997.

Hane, Mikiso, ed. and trans. *Reflections on the Way to the Gallows.* Berkeley, CA: University of California Press, 1988.

Hopper, Helen M. *A New Woman of Japan: A Political Biography of Kato Shidzue.* Boulder, CO: Westview Press, 1997.

Imamura, Anne E., ed. *Re-Imaging Japanese Women.* Berkeley, CA: University of California Press, 1995.

Ishimoto, Shidzue. *Facing Two Ways: The Story of My Life.* New York: Farrar & Rinehart, 1935.

Iwao, Sumiko. *The Japanese Woman: Traditional Image and Changing Reality.* New York: Free Press, 1992.

Kaneko, Fumiko. *The Prison Memoirs of a Japanese Woman,* trans. Jean Inglis. Armonk, NY: M. E. Sharpe, 1991.

Lebra, Joyce, *et al.* eds. *Women in Changing Japan.* Stanford, CA. Stanford University Press, 1976.

Lebra, Takie Sugiyama. *Japanese Women: Constraint and Fulfillment.* Honolulu: University Press of Hawaii, 1984.

Mackie,Vera C. *Fighting Women: A History of Feminism in Modern Japan.* NY: Columbia University Press, 1997.

Morley, John David. *Pictures from the Water Trade.* New York: Harper and Row, 1985.

Mulhern, Chieko Irie, ed. *Heroic Women with Grace: Legendary Women in Japan.* Armonk, NY: M. E. Sharpe, 1991.

Pharr, Susan. *Political Women in Japan.* Berkeley, CA: University of California Press, 1981.

Robins-Mowry, Dorothy. *The Hidden Sun: Women of Modern Japan.* Boulder, CO: Westview Press, 1983.

Rose, Barbara. *Tsuda Umeko and Women's Education in Japan.* New Haven, CN: Yale University Press, 1992.

Sievers, Sharon. *Flowers in Salt: The Beginnings of Feminine Consciousness in Modern Japan.* Stanford, CA: Stanford University Press, 1983.

Trager, James. *Letters from Sachiko: A Japanese Women's View of Life in the Land of Economic Miracle.* New York: Atheneum, 1982.

Tsurumi, Patricia E. *Factory Girls, Women in the Thread Mills of Meiji Japan.* Princeton, NJ: Princeton University Press, 1990.

Yamazaki, Tomoko. *Sandakan Brothel No. 8: An Episode of Lower-class Japanese Women,* trans. Karen Colligan-Taylor. Armonk, NY: M. E. Sharpe 1999.

——. *The Story of Yamada Waka, From Prostitute to Feminist Pioneer.* Tokyo: Kodansha International, 1985.

Women's Division of Soka Gakkai, ed. *Women Against War.* Tokyo: Kodansha International, 1986.

The Meiji Period

POLITICAL DEVELOPMENTS

Akita, George. *Foundations of Constitutional Government in Modern Japan, 1868–1900.* Cambridge, MA: Harvard University Press, 1967

Beasley, W. G. *The Meiji Restoration.* Stanford, CA: Stanford University Press, 1972.

Ike, Nobutaka. *The Beginnings of Political Democracy in Japan.* Baltimore, Johns Hopkins University Press, 1950.

Norman, E. H. *Japan's Emergence as a Modern State.* New York: Institute of Pacific Relations, 1940.

Scheiner, Irwin. *Christian Converts and Social Protest in Meiji Japan.* Berkeley, CA: University of California Press, 1970.

FOREIGN RELATIONS

Conroy, Francis Hilary. *The Japanese Seizure of Korea, 1868–1910.* Philadelphia: University of Pennsylvania Press, 1960.

Okamoto, Shumpei. *The Japanese Oligarchy and the Russo-Japanese War.* New York: Columbia University Press, 1971.

Walder, David. *The Short Victorious War: The Russo-Japanese Conflict, 1904–1905*. New York: Harper & Row, 1973.

Warner, Dennis and Warner, Peggy. *The Tide of Sunrise: The Russo-Japanese War.* New York: Charterhouse, 1974.

White, John Albert. *The Diplomacy of the Russo-Japanese War.* Princeton, NJ: Princeton University Press, 1964.

ECONOMIC DEVELOPMENTS IN THIS PERIOD

Hirschmeier, Johannes. *Origins of Entrepreneurship in Meiji Japan.* Cambridge, MA: Harvard University Press, 1964.

Nakamura, James I. *Agricultural Production and the Economic Development of Japan, 1873–1922.* Princeton, NJ: Princeton University Press, 1966.

Smith, Thomas C. *Political Change and Industrial Development in Japan: Government Enterprise, 1868–1880.* Stanford, CA: Stanford University Press, 1955.

INTELLECTUAL AND CULTURAL AFFAIRS

Blacker, Carmen. *The Japanese Enlightenment: A Study of the Writings of Fukuzawa Yukichi.* New York: Cambridge University Press, 1964.

Chisolm, Lawrence W. *Fenollosa: The Far East and American Culture.* New Haven, CN: Yale University Press, 1963.

Gluck, Carol. *Japan's Modern Myths: Ideology in the Late Meiji Period.* Princeton, NJ: Princeton University Press, 1985.

Irokawa, Daikichi. *The Culture of the Meiji Period*, trans. and ed. Marius B. Jansen. Princeton, NJ: Princeton University Press, 1985.

Kaikoku Hyakunen Kinen Bunka, ed. *Japanese Culture in the Meiji Era,* 10 vols. Tokyo: Obunsha, 1955–1958.

Nitobe, Inazo, *et al. Western Influences in Modern Japan.* Chicago: University of Chicago Press, 1931.

Pittau, Joseph. *Political Thought in Early Meiji Japan, 1868–1889.* Cambridge, MA: Harvard University Press, 1967.

Rubin, Jay. *Injurious to Public Health: Writers and the Meiji State.* Seattle: University of Washington Press, 1984.

MEMOIRS, BIOGRAPHIES AND STUDIES OF INTELLECTUAL AND POLITICAL PERSONALITIES

Baelz, Erwin O. E. Von. *Awakening Japan: The Diary of a German Doctor*, trans. Eden and Cedar Paul. New York: Viking, 1932.

Fukuzawa, Yukichi. *Autobiography.* trans. Eiichi Kiyooka. New York: Columbia University Press, 1966.

Hackett, Roger F. *Yamagata Aritomo in the Rise of Modern Japan, 1838–1922.* Cambridge, MA: Harvard University Press, 1971.

Hall, Ivan Parker. *Mori Arinori.* Cambridge, Mass.: Harvard University Press, 1973.

Huffman, James. *Politics of the Japanese Press: The Life of Fukuchi Gen'ichiro.* Honolulu: University Press of Hawaii, 1980.

Iwata, Masakazu. *Okubo Toshimichi, the Bismarck of Japan*. Berkeley, CA: University of California Press, 1964.

Kido, Takayoshi. *The Diary of Kido Takayoshi*, 2 vols. trans. Sidney Brown and Akiko Hirota. Tokyo: University of Tokyo Press, 1983–1986.

Kublin, Hyman. *An Asian Revolutionary: The Life of Katayma Sen*. Princeton, NJ: Princeton University Press, 1964.

Notehelfer, Fred. *Kotoku Shusui: Portrait of a Japanese Radical*. Cambridge: Cambridge University Press, 1971.

Pierson, John D. *Tokutomi Soho, 1863–1957: A Journalist for Modern Japan*. Princeton, NJ: Princeton University Press, 1980. Tokutomi emerged as an early Meiji liberal but became a staunch nationalist.

The Taisho Period

SOCIO-POLITICAL DEVELOPMENTS OF THIS PERIOD

Duus, Peter. *Party Rivalry and Political Change in Taisho Japan*. Cambridge, MA: Harvard University Press, 1968.

Large, Stephen S. *Organized Workers and Socialist Politics in Interwar Japan*. New York: Cambridge University Press, 1981.

Najita, Tetsuo. *Hara Kei in the Politics of Compromise, 1905–1915*. Cambridge, MA: Harvard University Press, 1967.

Silberman, Bernard S. and Harootunian, H. D., eds. *Japan in Crisis: Essays in Taisho Democracy*. Princeton, NJ: Princeton University Press, 1974.

ACTIVISTS AND LIBERAL THINKERS

Arima, Tatsuo. *The Failure of Freedom: A Portrait of Modern Japanese Intellectuals*. Cambridge, MA: Harvard University Press, 1969.

Bernstein, Gail. *Japanese Marxist: A Portrait of Kawakami Hajime*. Cambridge, MA: Harvard University Press, 1978.

Miller, Frank O. *Minobe Tatsukichi, Interpreter of Constitutionalism in Japan*. Berkeley, CA: University of California Press, 1965.

Stanley, Thomas. *Osugi Sakae, Anarchist in Taisho Japan*. Cambridge, MA: Harvard University Press, 1982.

Totten, George O. *The Social Democratic Movement in Prewar Japan*. New Haven, CN: Yale University Press, 1966.

LEADING PHILOSOPHICAL THINKERS OF MODERN JAPAN

Nishida, Kitaro. *A Study of Good*. trans. V. H. Viglielmo. Tokyo: Japanese Government Printing Bureau, 1960.

FOREIGN RELATIONS

Jansen, Marius B. *The Japanese and Sun Yat-sen*. Cambridge, MA: Harvard University Press, 1954.

Morley, James W. *The Japanese Thrust into Siberia, 1918*. New York: Columbia University Press, 1957.

The Road to War

PREWAR POLITICAL MOVEMENTS

Barnhart, Michael A. *Japan Prepares for Total War: The Search for Economic Security, 1919–1941*. Ithaca, NY: Cornell University Press, 1987.

Berger, Gordon M. *Parties Out of Power in Japan, 1931–1941*. Princeton, NJ: Princeton University Press, 1977.

Fletcher, William Miles. *The Search for a New Order: Intellectuals and Fascism in Prewar Japan*. Chapel Hill, NC: North Carolina University Press, 1982.

Irokawa, Daikichi. *The Age of Hirohito: In Search of Modern Japan*, trans. Mikiso Hane and John K. Urda. New York: Free Press, 1995.

Large, Stephen S. *Emperor Hirohito and Showa Japan: A Political Biography*. London: Routlege, 1992.

Maruyama, Masao. *Thought and Behaviour in Modern Japanese Politics*, ed. Ivan Morris. London: Oxford University Press, 1963.

Mitchell, Richard H. *Thought Control in Prewar Japan*. Ithaca, NY: Cornell University Press, 1976.

Morris, Ivan. *Nationalism and the Right Wing in Japan*. London: Oxford University Press, 1960.

Nakamura, Masanori. *The Japanese Monarchy, 1931–1991: Ambassador Grew and the Making of the "Symbol Emperor System,"* trans. Herbert P. Bix, *et al*. Armonk, NY: M.E. Sharpe, 1997.

Shillony, Ben-Ami. *Revolt in Japan: The Young Officers and the February 26, 1936 Incident*. Princeton, NJ: Princeton University Press, 1973.

Storry, Richard. *The Double Patriots: A Study of Japanese Nationalism*. Boston: Houghton Mifflin, 1957.

Titus, David Anson. *Palace and Politics in Prewar Japan*. New York: Columbia University Press, 1974.

Wilson, George M. *Radical Nationalist in Japan: Kita Ikki, 1883–1937*. Cambridge, MA.: Harvard University Press, 1969.

CONFLICT WITH CHINA AND THE SOVIET UNION

Borg, Dorothy. *The United States and the Far Eastern Crisis of 1933–38*. Cambridge, MA: Harvard University Press, 1964.

Boyle, John Hunter. *China and Japan at War*. Stanford, CA: Stanford University Press, 1972.

Chang, Iris. *The Rape of Nanking*. NY: Basic Books, 1997.

Coox, Alvin D. *Nomonhan, Japan Against Russia, 1939*. Stanford, CA: Stanford University Press, 1985.

Crowley, James B. *Japan's Quest for Autonomy: National Security and Foreign Policy, 1930–1938*. Princeton, NJ: Princeton University Press, 1966.

Dorn, Frank. *The Sino-Japanese War, 1937–41*. New York: Macmillan, 1974.

Honda, Katsuichi. *The Nanjing Massacre: A Japanese Journalist Confronts Japan's National Shame*, trans. Karen Sandness. Armonk, NY: M. E. Sharpe, 1999.

Lee, Bradford A. *Britain and the Sino-Japanese War, 1937–1939*. Stanford, CA: Stanford University Press, 1973.

Li, Lincoln. *Japanese Army in North China: July, 1937–December, 1941*. London: Oxford University Press, 1975.

Morley, James, ed. *China Quagmire*. New York: Columbia University Press, 1983.

Ogata, Sadako N. *Defiance in Manchuria: The Making of Japanese Foreign Policy, 1931–1932*. Berkeley, CA: University of California Press, 1964.

Thorne, Christopher G. *The Limits of Foreign Policy: The West, the League and Far Eastern Crisis of 1931–1933*. New York: Putnam, 1972.

Wilson, Dick. *When Tigers Fight: The Story of the Sino-Japanese War, 1937–1945*. New York: Viking Press, 1982.

Yoshihashi, Takehiko. *Conspiracy in Manchuria: The Rise of the Japanese Military*. New Haven, CN: Yale University Press, 1963.

DIPLOMATIC NEGOTIATIONS AND FOREIGN POLICY DECISION-MAKING PRIOR TO THE OUTBREAK OF THE WAR WITH THE UNITED STATES

Butow, Rober J. *Tojo and the Coming of the War*. Stanford, CA: Stanford University Press, 1961.

Feis, Herbert. *The Road to Pearl Harbor*. Princeton, NJ: Princeton University Press, 1950.

Grew, Joseph C. L. *Ten Years in Japan*. New York: Simon & Schuster, 1944.

Ike, Nobutaka, ed. *Japan's Decision for War: Records of the 1941 Policy Conferences*. Stanford, CA: Stanford University Press, 1967.

Iriye, Akira. *The Origins of the Second World War in Asia and the Pacific*. London: Longman, 1987.

Lu, David J. *From the Marco Polo Bridge to Pearl Harbor: Japan's Entry into Second World War*. Washington, D.C.: Public Affairs, 1961.

Maxon, Yale C. *Control of Japanese Foreign Policy*. Berkeley, CA: University of California Press, 1957.

Meskill, Johanna. *Hitler and Japan: The Hollow Alliance*. New York: Atherton Press, 1966.

Morley, James, ed. *Japan's Road to the Pacific War: The Final Confrontation: Japan's Negotiations with the United States, 1941*. New York: Columbia University Press, 1994.

Pelz, Stephen E. *Race to Pearl Harbor*. Cambridge, MA: Harvard University Press, 1974.

Schroeder, Paul W. *The Axis Alliance and Japanese American Relations, 1941*. Ithaca, NY: Cornell University Press, 1958.

Stephen, John J. *Hawaii Under the Rising Sun: Japan's Plan for Conquest After Pearl Harbor*. Honolulu: University Press of Hawaii, 1983.

Wetzler, Peter. *Hirohito and War: Imperial Tradition and Military Decision-Making in Prewar Japan*. Honolulu: University of Hawaii Press, 1998.

The war

Borg, Dorothy and Okamoto, Shumpei, eds. *Pearl Harbor as History.* New York: Columbia University Press, 1973.

Butow, Robert J. C. *Japan's Decision to Surrender.* Stanford, CA: Stanford University Press, 1954.

Costello, John. *The Pacific War.* New York: Rawson Wade, 1981.

Dower, John W. *War Without Mercy: Race and Power in the Pacific War.* New York: Pantheon, 1986.

Ienaga, Saburo. *The Pacific War: Second World War and the Japanese, 1931–1945*, trans. Frank Baldwin. New York: Pantheon, 1978.

Lebra, Joyce. *Japanese Trained Armies in Southeast Asia.* New York: Columbia University Press, 1977.

Lewin, Ronald. *The American Magic: Codes, Ciphers and the Defeat of Japan.* New York: Farrar, Strauss & Giroux, 1982.

Morison, Samuel Eliot. *History of the United States Naval Operations in Second World War,* 15 vols. Boston: Little, Brown, 1947–1962.

Prange, Gordon W. *At Dawn We Slept.* New York: McGraw-Hill, 1981.

——. *Miracle at Midway.* New York: McGraw-Hill, 1982.

Spector, John H. *Eagle Against the Sun.* New York: Free Press, 1985.

Tanaka, Yuki. *Hidden Horrors: Japanese War Crimes in World War II.* Boulder, CO: Westview Press, 1996.

Williams, Peter and Wallace, David. *Unit 731: Japan's Secret Biological Warfare in Second World War.* New York: Free Press, 1989.

Wohlstetter, Roberta. *Pearl Harbor: Warning and Decision.* Stanford, CA: Stanford University Press, 1962.

THE ATOMIC BOMBING OF HIROSHIMA AND NAGASAKI

Feis, Herbert. *Japan Subdued: The Atomic Bomb and the End of the War in the Pacific.* Princeton, NJ: Princeton University Press, 1961.

Hachiya, Michihiko. *Hiroshima Diary,* trans. and ed. Warner Wells. Chapel Hill, NC: University of North Carolina Press, 1955.

Hersey, John. *Hiroshima.* New York: Knopf, 1946.

Lifton, Robert Jay. *Death in Life: Survivors of Hiroshima.* New York: Random House, 1967.

Minear, Richard H., trans. and ed. *Hiroshima, Three Witnesses.* Princeton, NJ: Princeton University Press, 1990.

Nagai, Takashi. *The Bells of Nagasaki,* trans. William Johnston. Tokyo: Kodansha, 1974.

Postwar: The Occupation Years

THE WAR CRIMES TRIAL

Brackman Arnold. *The Other Nuremberg: The Untold Story of the Tokyo War Crimes Trials.* New York: Morrow, 1987.

Hosoya, Chihiro, *et al.* eds. *The Tokyo War Crimes Trial*. Tokyo: Kodansha International, 1986.

Minear, Richard. *Victor's Justice: The Tokyo War Crimes Trial*. Princeton, NJ: Princeton University Press, 1971.

Record of Proceedings of the International Military Tribunal for the Far East (microfilm). Washington, D.C.: Library of Congress.

The Tokyo Major Crimes Trial: The Record of the International Military Tribunal for the Far East, ed. R. John Pritchard. Lewiston, NY: Edwin Mellen Press, 1999.

OCCUPATION POLICIES AND REFORMS

Brines, Russell. *MacArthur's Japan*. Philadelphia: Lippincott, 1948.

Cohen, Theodore. *Remaking Japan*. New York: Free Press, 1987.

Dore, Ronald P. *Land Reform in Japan*. London: Oxford University Press, 1959.

Dower, John. *Embracing Defeat: Japan in the Wake of Second World War*. New York: Norton, 1999.

Fearey, Robert A. *The Occupation of Japan: Second Phase, 1948–50*. New York: Macmillan, 1950.

Finn, Richard B. *Winners in Peace: MacArthur, Yoshida and Postwar Japan*. Berkeley, CA: University of California Press, 1992.

Hadley, Eleanor H. *Antitrust in Japan*. Princeton, NJ: Princeton University Press, 1970.

Harries, Meirion and Harries, Susie. *Sheathing the Sword: The Demilitarization of Japan*. London: Hamish Hamilton, 1987.

Inoue, Kyoko. *MacArthur's Japanese Constitution*. Chicago: University of Chicago Press, 1991.

Kawai, Kazuo. *Japan's American Interlude*. Chicago: University of Chicago Press, 1960.

Martin, Edwin M. *The Allied Occupation of Japan*. New York: Pacific Relations, 1948.

Nishi, Toshio. *Unconditional Democracy: Education and Politics in Occupied Japan, 1945 1952*. Stanford, CA: Hoover Institution Press, 1982.

Schaller, Michael. *The American Occupation of Japan*. London: Oxford University Press, 1985.

Supreme Commander for the Allied Powers: Government Section. *Political Reorientation of Japan, Sept. 1945 to Sept. 1948: Report*, 2 vols. Westport, CT: Greenwood, 1968.

General developments from the postwar years to the present

GENERAL ACCOUNTS

Bell, Ronald. *The Japan Experience*. New York: Weatherhill, 1973.

Buckley, Roger. *Japan of Today*. Cambridge: Cambridge University Press, 1990.

Dale, Peter N. *The Myth of Japanese Uniqueness*. New York: St. Martin's Press, 1986.

Field, Norma. *In the Realm of the Dying Emperor.* New York: Pantheon, 1991.

Gordon, Andrew, ed. *Postwar Japan as History.* Berkeley, CA: University of California Press, 1992.

Hane, Mikiso. *Eastern Phoenix: Japan Since 1945.* Boulder, CO: Westview Press, 1996.

Koschmann, J. Victor. *Revolution and Subjectivity in Postwar Japan.* Chicago: University of Chicago Press, 1996.

Levine, Hillel. *In Search of Sugihara: The Elusive Japanese Diplomat Who Risked His Life to Rescue 10,000 Jews From the Holocaust.* New York: Free Press, 1997.

Taylor, Jared. *Shadows of the Rising Sun.* New York: Quill, 1983.

Weiner, Michael, ed. *Japan's Minorites: The Illusion of Homogeneity.* NY: Routlege, 1997.

THE POLITICAL SCENE

Campbell, John C. *How Policies Change: The Japanese Government and the Aging Society.* Princeton, NJ: Princeton University Press, 1992.

Curtis, Gerald L. *The Japanese Way of Politics.* New York: Columbia University Press, 1988.

Koh, B. C. *Japan's Administrative Elite.* Berkeley, CA: University of California Press, 1989.

Pharr, Susan J. *Losing Face: Status Politics in Japan.* Berkeley, CA: University of California Press, 1990.

Scalapino, Robert A. and Junnosuke Masumi. *Parties and Politics in Contemporary Japan.* Berkeley, CA: University of California Press, 1962.

Schlesinger, Jacob M. *Shadow Shoguns: The Rise and Fall of Japan's Postwar Political Machine.* New York: Simon & Schuster, 1997.

Yoshida, Shigeru. *The Yoshida Memoirs*, trans. Kenichi Yoshida. Boston: Houghton Mifflin, 1962.

ECONOMIC DEVELOPMENTS

Clark, Rodney. *The Japanese Company.* New Haven, CT: Yale University Press, 1979.

Cohen, Jerome B. *Japan's Economy in War and Reconstruction.* Minneapolis: University of Minnesota Press, 1949.

Dore, Ronald. *British Factory–Japanese Factory.* Berkeley, CA: University of California Press, 1973.

Fallows, James. *Looking at the Sun: The Rise of the New East Asian Economic System and Political System.* New York: Pantheon, 1994.

Johnson, Chalmers. *MITI and the Japanese Miracle: The Growth of Industrial Policy, 1925–1975.* Stanford, CA: Stanford University Press, 1985.

Morishima, Michio. *Why Has Japan "Succeeded"? Western Technology and the Japanese Ethos.* London: Cambridge University Press, 1982.

Vogel, Ezra. *Japan as Number One.* Cambridge, MA: Harvard University Press, 1979.

Yamamura, Kozo. *Economic Policy in Postwar Japan*. Berkeley, CA: University of California Press, 1967.

SOCIAL DEVELOPMENTS AND CONDITIONS

Cole, Robert C. *Japanese Blue Collar*. Berkeley, CA: University of California Press, 1971.

DeVos, George and Witherall, William. *Japan's Minorities: Burakumin, Koreans, Ainus, and Okinawans*. Claremont, NY: Minority Rights Group, 1983.

Fowler, Edward. *San'ya Blues: Laboring Life and Contemporary Tokyo*. Itacha, NY: Cornell University Press, 1996.

Lee, Changsoo and DeVos, George. *Koreans in Japan: Ethnic Conflict and Accommodation*. Berkeley, CA: University of California Press, 1982.

Plath, David, ed. *Work and Life Course in Japan*. Albany, NY: State University of New York Press, 1983.

Sumii, Sue. *The River with No Bridge*. trans. Susan Wilkinson. Rutland, VT: Charles E. Tuttle, 1990. A novel on Burakumin discrimination.

Tsurumi, Kazuko. *Social Change and the Individual: Japan Before and After Defeat in Second World War*. Princeton, NJ: Princeton University Press, 1970.

Tsurumi, Patricia, ed. *The Other Japan: Postwar Realities*. Armonk, NY: M. E. Sharpe, 1988.

Upham, Frank K. *Law and Social Change in Postwar Japan*. Cambridge, MA: Harvard University Press, 1987.

CULTURAL AND INTELLECTUAL AFFAIRS

Christopher, Robert C. *The Japanese Mind: The Goliath Explained*. New York: Linden Press, 1983.

Cummings, William A. *Education and Equality in Japan*. Princeton, NJ: Princeton University Press, 1980.

Duke, Benjamin C. *The Japanese Schools: Lessons for Industrial America*. New York: Praeger, 1986.

Curon, Sheldon. *Molding the Japanese Mind: The State in Everyday Life*. Princeton, NJ: Princeton University Press, 1997.

Havens, Thomas R. H. *Artists and Patrons in Postwar Japan: Dance, Music, Theatre and the Visual Arts, 1955–1980*. Princeton, NJ: Princeton University Press, 1982.

Koschmann, J. Victor. *Revolution and Subjectivity in Postwar Japan*. Chicago: University of Chicago Press, 1996.

Nathan, John. *Mishima, a Biography*. New York: Little, Brown, 1974.

Richie, Donald. *The Films of Akira Kurosawa*. Berkeley, CA: University of California Press, 1984.

Tsurumi, Shunsuke. *A Cultural History of Postwar Japan, 1945–1980*. New York: Columbia University Press, 1994.

White, Merry. *The Japanese Educational Challenge*. New York: Free Press, 1986.

Index